20th Century Los Angeles

20th CENTURY LOS ANGELES

POWER, PROMOTION, AND SOCIAL CONFLICT

Edited by

NORMAN M. KLEIN
and
MARTIN J. SCHIESL

REGINA BOOKS
Claremont, California

Library of Congress Cataloging in Publication Data

```
20th Los Angeles : power, promotion, and social
    conflict / edited by Norman M. Klein and Martin
    J. Schiesl.
    240 p.      23 cm.
    ISBN 0-941690-38-5 : $26.95. -- ISBN 0-941690-
      36-9 (pbk.) : $12.95
    1. Minorities--California--Los Angeles--Social
Conditions.  2. Los Angeles (Calif.)--Social
Conditions.  3. Los Angeles (Calif.)--Politics
and government.  I. Klein, Norman M., 1945-   .
II. Schiesl, Martin J., 1940-     .
F869.L89T84 1990                        90-8131
305.8'00979494--dc20                        CIP
```

Regina Books
P.O. Box 280
Claremont, Ca. 91711

Manufactured in the United States of America.

Contents

To Inez, Benjy, and the spirit of Carey McWilliams

and

To Sharon, Laura, my Mother and late Father

PREFACE

All great cities have erased communities and hidden great crimes. Los Angeles is no exception. Only the way it forgets is exceptional. From the thirties on, much of the center metropolitan area, from South Central L.A. to Burbank, from East Los Angeles to Hollywood, was utterly refashioned, even demolished, then "forgotten." Many Angelinos will announce, some proudly, that they have not visited much of this area for up to twenty years. It has become the lost sanctum of the city, the other Los Angeles.

A new financial district was built at its center. Phantom poverty developed in surrounding areas. Despite a new symphony hall and museum, the economic and cultural life of the city emigrated elsewhere. Civic leaders sponsored its demise, and at the same time, tried to salvage and rebuild. The ambivalence and cross-purposes make for a drama that is both tragic and a bit comical: a mix of racism, classism, long-term mistakes and short-term profit. Good intentions went sour. Cruel intentions were camouflaged. In short, to alter a phrase from a Preston Sturges movie (*The Great McGinty*), L.A. is like any other city, only more so.

This is a selected series of essays which concentrates on features of this hidden Los Angeles: minority politics and institutions whose role has tended to be hidden, such as police, promotion, planning, and organized crime. A few essential questions will repeat as models for further discussion. For example, on the street level, how have ethnic minorities "adjusted" to a culture dominated by white values and institutions? How did the "erasure" of the older districts take place, over the course of this century, and what has it left for the city to tackle today? The sum of these adds up to a selective history only, pointing toward what should be done next, to help turn Los Angeles away from policies of neglect toward a public life that engages its contradictions directly. Very few answers will be proposed here, if any—only a critical perspective on the contradictions themselves.

Los Angeles is entering a new epoch, and is being forced to reexamine its priorities, even the fantasies it promotes. This can only be accomplished on a firm footing, with a carefully documented, humanistic base of information, filled by more than broad statistics or glossy media hyperbole.

The need for a revised image of the city has motivated all the essays here, each written specifically for this project. Six of the essays evolved directly out of a 1986 public lecture series entitled "Beneath the Myths: A Social History of Los Angeles." In those lectures, specialists presented historical information they felt the city needed to confront, in its political life, in its culture, even in its films. This book tries to enrich that survey. We are convinced that L.A. should not be seen simply as "the greatest exception," but rather as a national model for studying urban life in the coming century.

The big earthquake has already hit Los Angeles. The city has been reshuffled by new waves of immigration and by a new world economy. Consumerist fantasies will not camouflage how power itself operates—in business, politics, and communities. Problems that were "erased" decades ago have reemerged, reminding us that L.A. cannot be the great exception, nor does it benefit by trying to be.

Though all the essays deal with parallel issues, we have essentially divided the book into two sections. One concentrates on the first half of the century, emphasizing promotion and ethnicity. The other concentrates on Los Angeles since World War Two, analyzing how power has been organized and exercised by public and private groups as well as communities.

As noted above, the idea for this book grew out of a series of lectures entitled "Beneath the Myths: A Social History of Los Angeles" sponsored by Beyond Baroque (Venice, California), with funding from the California Council for the Humanities. Once the essays were in place by the fall of 1989, the Edmund G. "Pat" Brown Institute for Public Affairs at California State University,

Los Angeles, thoughtfully provided financial support to help see them into print. Our publisher Richard Dean Burns shepherded the essays through the various stages of preparation. Finally, we thank our families for understanding that a book like this demands a great deal of time and work that is not always anticipated, particularly the long editorial meetings and numerous telephone calls.

                                            Norman M. Klein
                                            Martin J. Schiesl

This is a view of Bunker Hill (1968) showing Angels Flight located along Third Street between Hill and Olive. Soon after, all of the remaining buildings were torn down and the hill was leveled. Courtesy of William Reagh.

Chapter 1

THE SUNSHINE STRATEGY: BUYING AND SELLING THE FANTASY OF LOS ANGELES

Norman M. Klein

In 1899, the secretary of the Los Angeles Chamber of Commerce wrote:[1]

> The prosperity of Los Angeles is founded on the immutable forces of nature, combined with the inevitable needs of mankind; and it will remain, as the sea and the clouds and the mountains remain, and will increase as the nation and the race increases.

This is classic L.A. boosterist language, like a cross between the Apostles, and a salesman's handbook, as if a deal had been cut with God about how to promote real estate. Like many adventurous businessmen of the day, the market managers for Los Angeles claimed to be selling something even grander than leather-tooled editions of the Good Book. They were selling the City on the Hill as prime real estate, including the hill itself, which was located near the new train station immediately downtown, near full city lots for sale, along newly paved streets, with a view of good farmland for sale in the valleys surrounding. It was the new Jerusalem, first come first served, at the semi-arid, most westerly—and newly civilized—corner of the great frontier.

However inflated the language, the strategy was simple enough. Through a consortium of local businessmen and large railroad interests, a small city would be merchandised into a metropolis and a financial disaster would be turned around.

In 1888, following the collapse of a feverish real estate boom, L.A. was losing about a thousand people a month, from a high of about 65,000.[2] By 1890, a third of the newcomers were gone.

Land values had declined severely, by over $14 million. And yet, something substantial remained. There were still about 50,000 people left in the city. From 1883 to 1888, the population had multiplied by 400 per cent. Unfortunately, the business infrastructure had not changed enough to provide jobs for that many people. The economy of L.A. was too primitive for a city of fifty thousand.

To reverse the trend, the new chamber of commerce turned toward the only industry that promised immediate returns—tourism mixed with real estate speculation. Other doors were tried in the 1890s, attempts to invite industry into L.A., or to enlarge the citrus market (major advertising for both after 1897). But even as late as 1900, tourism still accounted for over a quarter of all business revenues, more than all manufacturing combined, and second only to agriculture.

To keep tourism healthy, as the foundation for economic growth, leading businessmen in Los Angeles personally financed a war chest for large promotional campaigns that went nationwide. Exhibitions about exotic and fertile Los Angeles were featured in Chicago, in Iowa, at state fairs and world's fairs. Hundreds of brochures reached millions of people,[3] attracting the desired Protestant newcomers from small towns in the midwest, also attracting movie producers with capital from "back East," and cheap labor from all corners of America. The brochures promised a sunny, "green-acre" city free of urban stress, and class warfare—in short, a farm town without unions, and without dark industrial tenements to interfere in the conduct of business.

* * * * * * * * *

By 1900, boosterism in Los Angeles had developed virtually into a public-service corporation, centered around three industries: tourism, real estate, and transportation. As those industries changed, the promotional rhetoric shifted considerably. The shifts were most evident during the late 1930s and the Second World War, when much of the background to the freeway city (or multi-tropolis) was set up. These various shifts are emphasized in following sections:

The Myth of the Climate (1880s-1930s) provides a background to real-estate policies, and to the L.A. streetcar.

The Myth of A Freeway Metropolis (1936-1949) reveals the impact of decentralization.

The Myths of Downtown Renewal (1936-1949) focuses on Bunker Hill and Chinatown.

And finally, as conclusion, *L.A. Myths for the Eighties and Afterward* examines the preparing of downtown for the Pacific Byzantium.

For each myth, I have isolated highlights: the popular misconceptions fostered by mass promotion from one era to the next. That allows me to examine the myths more thoroughly, combining social history with reception aesthetics. Streetcars vanish, freeways surface, downtown gets plowed under, in urban planning, in crime fiction and in the film *Chinatown*. We see what was imagined, why it was imagined, and what actually took place.

MYTH OF THE CLIMATE (1880S TO 1930S)

Lucky Baldwin was one of many entrepreneurs who arrived in L.A. during the boom of the 1880s. He came with a considerable fortune to invest, bought the land that later became the townships of Baldwin Hills and Santa Anita, juggled bank investments with horse-breeding, lived with an opulent disregard for Victorian conventions, and got himself into various financial and moral scrapes (was shot by a young woman who claimed he forced his attentions on her.) Often, he stretched his real estate investments to the edge of bankruptcy, but died a very wealthy man in 1909. His biographer, a specialist in books about gilded-age plutocrats, wrote:[4]

> In real-estate promotion, Lucky Baldwin unquestionably was ahead of his time; and equally without question he knew his stuff. In reply to one prospect who protested that $200 an acre for some unimproved ground was too much, he answered indignantly: "Hell! We're giving away the land. We're selling the climate.

Sales pitches about "the climate" repeat more often than any other in early brochures about Los Angeles. The boosterism continues in articles into the forties and fifties, and is well remembered in novels, films, critical essays, into the present. As Aldous Huxley writes in 1939, the sunshine in Los Angeles worked on tourists like a spotlight, "as though on purpose to show the new arrival all the sights."[5]

The fantasy seems as light as the air itself, deceptively innocent. It is hardly a secret that the climate in Southern California is very moderate, a liberation from winter coats. Of course, the campaign far exceeded that patent observation. First, brochures from the 1890s repeated the claims made famous in travel books on Southern California written during the 1870s and 1880s, particularly by an Eastern journalist named Charles Nordhoff.[6] To Nordhoff, Los Angeles was a Protestant Eldorado in old Mexico, a magical lotus-land of sleepy adobes and Mediteranean, semi-arid grandeur, but a potential mother lode for someone with Yankee ingenuity.

Then, the brochures promised miracle cures. By removing oppressive humidity of all types (particularly industrial humidity), the air could cure tuberculosis, rheumatism, asthma, sleeplessness, even impotence. Indeed, the climate did clear the lungs for many (including Harry Chandler, who slept in an orange grove, and was cured). For a time, L.A. was called "the city for those with one lung." In the winters, as many as 20,000 tubercular and rheumatic patients would take the air, or the hot springs in the Los Angeles area, often within a mile of downtown itself.[7] Health foods and sanatoriums were already a major industry.

Late Victorians were obsessed about fresh air. What passed through an open window had to be invigorating, but not "emasculating." It had to be fresh enough to keep men "vim and fit." In the very popular medical handbook, *The Physical Life of Woman,* the well-known Boston physician, George Napheys advised that married couples should not sleep together without an open window, and even then, at least "twenty cubic feet of fresh air a minute are required for every healthy adult."[8] The air space had to be larger than 2,400 square feet, to replace old air once an hour. "Rebreathed air," Dr. Napheys warned, "is poisonous."

Late Victorians suffered from lung diseases much more often than we do. Dry air was considered one of the only cures. With Americans feeling invaded rather suddenly by urban expansion after 1870, by poor sanitation growing worse in expanding cities, by thickening traffic jams fetid with horse-driven carriages, by a plague of syphilis that seemed untreatable, medical texts of the day often described the body as a frail temple threatened by tormenting vapors. Germ theory was understood awkwardly, or not at all. To many, the air itself was a holistic science (like theories about body fluids in the seventeenth century, and medical cures by bleeding, practiced as late as the Civil War).

No wonder then that doctors' offices in Los Angeles often were built with porches on all sides, to ventilate the air for patients. What's more, it was air that made the soil curative as well. The air in Los Angeles was not only fresh, it was fragrant, very intense with the smells of what grew here. New arrivals to Los Angeles often mentioned the overpowering aroma of orchards, and vineyards, that the air smelled like wine. The rustic alternative to city life was not vague at all; it was very sensual, much the way suntans often were described as exotic journeys into the world of brown-skinned races, free from the restraints of Protestant sexual codes. And yet, in the case of L.A., the sensuality was improved by moral order. Not only was L.A. the faraway land of Ramona, of miscegenous romance, of missions and ranchos, of banditos like Vasquez; it also was wholesome farm country—and Protestant. One could enjoy the exotic freedom from civilization, and still remain civil and productive, while the desert air sanitized the body.

The promotion of L.A.'s climate had much to camouflage. Certain problems with climate were endemic to Los Angeles in the 1890's, and in fact, well-known to many travelers. Brochures as late as 1910 claimed that crops in Southern California could grow practically without water; and so, apparently, could towns. But the trench irrigation system (called zanja) barely provided enough water for a population of 33,000, much less 60,000, at the height of the boom. (Campaigns for improved water from the Los Angeles River were highest on the list of public works by 1900, and remained so for a generation.)

As of 1890, though, the water supply was filthy; it brought on spells of typhoid during the summer, or "fever season. During the rainy season, there were floods. The Los Angeles River would swell into the lowlands, and run directly down Alameda Street, where the trains from Kansas City turned en route to the main depot. In winter, many houses in the downtown flatlands would fill up with as much as two feet of water.[9] Then, during the dry season, water was desperately scarce, of course, despite reservoirs and pumps for some of the nearby hills.

Perhaps, it was best for tourists to look up at the sky, and not down at the hazardous water systems. Despite the new aqueduct in 1913, the city continued to struggle for water. And despite the new sewers, in place by the twenties, there were still floods and mudslides. In the early decades of boosterism, the future had to be promised, even invented.

By 1913, much of what had been promised was finally in place, though—a larger job market, particularly in agriculture, but also in light industry, and oil, and finally in the film business. Shipping grew tremendously after the dredging of San Pedro Harbour (re-opened in 1913), and soon after, with the opening of the Panama Canal. The promise of a greenbelt city seemed to survive as well. From 1912 until the mid-fifties, Los Angeles was the richest farm county in the nation.[10]

This is all standard information, of course. By the twenties, Los Angeles had become an economic giant, in shipping, petroleum, agriculture, cinema. By the mid-forties, it had become an industrial giant, particularly in aeronautics. By the eighties, it became the banking center of the Pacific world, or as one frequently quoted article in *The Atlantic Monthly* explained: "The Eastern capital of the Pacific."[11]

Today, the lotus-land for Caucasians has become "the new Ellis Island" for the largest influx of non-white immigration in the world, far exceeding the numbers arriving in New York. Many of the old boosterist images become running jokes in conversation, about the toxins of the week, or plans to convert the cement banks of the trickling L.A. River into a freeway alternate. Certainly, the air is no longer alluring, not since the shocks of wartime pollution brought the problem to public attention in 1943.[12] News on the climate looks ominous, with public warnings about earthquakes, greenhouse effects, inversion layers, and offshore oil spills. But the selling of climate initiated the fantasy of Los Angeles, and continued to dominate promotion into the twenties.

In 1921, to expand summer tourism, the All-Year Club was established as a private company, through the leadership of the *Los Angeles Times*. With county bonds, as well as private donations, it raised a one million dollar budget for the first three years, and became the dominant promotional machine for the rest of the decade.[13] During one four-month period, it published more than 90 million separate advertisements, 55 million in local newspapers, and 35 million in national magazines.[14] With slogans like "sleep under a blanket every night all summer in Southern California," the promotion worked so well that by 1928, the number of tourists in summer equaled those visiting in the winter, then exceeded winter tourism by the forties. "But," wrote Carey McWilliams (1943), "like most campaigns of the sort, the All-Year Club has been too successful.[15]

Its seductive advertisements were partly responsible for the great influx of impoverished Okies and Arkies in the thirties. Since 1929 its advertisements carry the caption "Warning! Come to California for a glorious vacation. Advise anyone not to come seeking employment."

During the Depression, the marketing of the climate seemed to backfire. Promotion about weather was cut back, particularly during the war years, when rationing made tourism impractical anyway, even unpatriotic. Also, the sunshine, lotus-land image was hardly appropriate for selling the new industrial Los Angeles so evident during the Second World War. When the Chamber of Commerce was interviewed by *Life Magazine* in 1943, a shift was apparent. In the modified puff piece based heavily on the interview, the reporter clearly was taking a slant very much in line with the new aggressive strategy of business leaders in Los Angeles. The sub-heading, provided by editors in New York, read: "The city that started with nothing but sunshine now expects to become the biggest in the world."[16] There was blight evident downtown, a large Mexican presence throughout the city, and many new factories; together, these added a new dimension to the selling of Los Angeles: a city of airplanes, shipping, oil and steel. Through the guidance of the interviews by the chamber of commerce, the article is peppered with references to L.A. aggressively promoting heavy industry, particularly Douglas Aircraft, to make L.A. "the aviation capital of the world." The president of Lockheed was quoted as saying: "In any logical scheme the aviation industry should be back in the manufacturing center of the country and not out in a beautiful resort like this." The city had outgrown its farm-town image.

Streetcars and the Myth of Climate: The Balloon Route

Public transportation in Los Angeles has been held hostage to real estate promotion virtually from the beginning. A vast interurban and streetcar system was built from the 1880s on, and it was promoted as the largest, and most efficient in the world, approximately 1,200 miles of track altogether. However, the leaven that kept the system growing was not public need, but land speculation. Most of the profits for Henry Huntington's Pacific Electric empire came from real estate, not the fare box. And Huntington was not the only player. Land syndicates would invest in new streetcar franchises, buy up real estate near the proposed stations, then after completion of the line, sell off quickly for considerable profit.

The opening of Hollywood in 1903 is a ripe example. Hollywood already had a streetcar by 1900, running along Prospect Avenue, now called Hollywood Boulevard. But only 500 people lived in the small town. Sites were linked mostly to tourism, through the Tally-Ho tours, like the Stritchley Ostrich Farm, in what is now Griffith Park, inns up at the Cahuenga Pass, or the rose garden at the Glen Holly Hotel. Sheep ranching, pea farming and lemon orchards intermixed with the occasional home (at first, wealthy homes, for lthe most part). There was also enough scrub and dirt road, lined with pepper trees, to give Hollywood the appearance of dry frontier hillside. From 1911 on, the view around the Blondeau Tavern at Sunset and Gower was used for cowboy one-reelers; in 1913, a barn at Selma and Gower for the cowboy feature, *The Squaw Man*.[17]

By 1903, this underpopulated township came directly in the path of development. That year, Sunset Boulevard was opened west, past the Edendale area (Echo Park); Sunset was the first predecessor of freeway boulevard in Los Angeles, and a signal of what was about to begin. Hollywood was formally incorporated as a city. At the Hollywood Hotel, the only location in the area that cabbies at the Alexandria downtown seemed to know, three real estate agents established residence, waiting for a land rush into the Ocean View Tract, at the western end of town, north of Hollywood Boulevard between LaBrea and Cahuenga.

The premier builder of streetcars, General Moses Sherman formed a land syndicate with realtor/contractor Hobart J. Whitley, and *Los Angeles Times* publisher, Harry Chandler. An inter-urban line to Hollywood opened in 1903, with considerable fanfare. A brass band played for the first riders, at the downtown station at Hill and Fourth. Lemonade was dispensed. Then, along the way, riders were invited to meet local celebrities. At Cahuenga Boulevard, they visited the home of French painter Paul de Longpre, who specialized in Impressionist landscapes mixed with the sunshine of Los Angeles; visitors also could study his collection of rare hanging rugs. At the Outpost, the oldest building in Hollywood, General Otis, co-founder of the *Times*, originator of the Chamber of Commerce, leader of the anti-union movement, gave a lecture on the future of the area. Meanwhile, getting down to business, at the Ocean View Tract itself, "promoters piled bricks and lumber on alternative lots, which they marked *SOLD*."[18] Mounds of earth were added strategically, as if houses were about to blossom like sunflowers.

At that time, the showpiece of the streetcar system was the Balloon Route, so-called because it made a balloon-shaped circuit from downtown to the beach towns, then back again. (Its first stop was in Hollywood, probably because the Balloon Route was developed by the same man who had started the Tally-Ho Route through old Cahuenga.) In the teens, when the streetcar network reached its maximum efficiency, Balloon Route brochures were quite fancy, with three-color photo-lithos under vellum paper, the sunshine of a watercolor for free. They were pitched at the Sunday workman and his family, riding in imperial splendor to the ocean, where inexpensive property was listed for sale (land along the beach was cheaper than downtown, at that time). Venice was described as "the Coney Island of the West." Redondo Beach was "the happy medium for the masses and attractions." Huntington Beach was "the rendez-vous for the little families."[19]

By the twenties, however, the use of streetcars for weekend leisure diminished. With the quick speculative fortunes already made, the lines at their maximum, both the Pacific Electric (Red Cars) and the Los Angeles Railway (Yellow Cars) began to show losses. They asked the city to buy them out, or to allow a penny fare hike, and fund improvements through city bonds.[20] As a privately held trust, the transit system had lost its promotional usefulness, even for its owners. Now it needed public revenues to stay efficient. The city's answer was to back off, but keep promising. As a result, little more than commission reports on mass transit were funded for the next fifty years.

The history of how these streetcars finally were destroyed has been rehashed constantly (even in film parodies like *Who Framed Roger Rabbit*). In brief, the trolley system was eclipsed by the automobile. From the twenties on, routes endangered by auto traffic were allowed to go fallow. Attempts to expand the system, add subways, push for elevated lines were blocked, stalled, or deemed too costly—and not in the spirit of the sunshine expansion of Los Angeles. In the sixties, finally, the truncated remains of the system were torn up. The interest groups who lobbied to destroy it after World War II included the auto industries, railroads, urban planning commissions, suburban chambers of commerce, and quite frankly, the majority of the voters in Los Angeles, whom it was believed, would never support a city bond needed to sustain the traction companies. There is also evidence that streetcars were linked in the public mind to corrupt, grasping railroads, the octopi from San Francisco or back East.[21] During the first decade of the twentieth century, when L.A. leaders were fighting San Francisco railway empires, the Southern Pacific pressured to haul freight along streetcar routes. Streetcar companies were accused of milking city money to get land at broker's rates. Help the traction companies? The resentment ran very deep. Consider this anecdote: In 1906, oil patriarch, Edward Doheny appeared in court to fight a $15 speeding ticket given to his chauffeur. This was the sixth ticket issued to a Doheny driver, and each time, the millionaire Doheny, with a touch of the "shanty" Irish, would refuse to pay without first complaining to the judge.

"Street car companies are constant violators of the speed laws," Doheny told Judge Austin. "Why don't you arrest them and hale them into these courts?"

Judge Austin agreed: "That is ground well taken, Mr. Doheny. I suggest that you have warrants issued in a few cases and cause arrests yourself."

"I'll do that, your honor." Doheny replied, and paid the fine.[22]

Streetcars were run by the rich, above the law. Even plutocrats who were above the law felt so. Vestiges of this progressivist resentment remained even in the thirties, after the street cars became hostage to bank loans, and hardly a threat to the great leviathan of Los Angeles.

The car, on the other hand, was the great liberator, for cruising in the open air, at forty miles an hour, along wider roads. The car came heir to the sunshine strategy, and the Balloon Route took on a grimmer aspect. By the late thirties, noted often in virtually every newspaper, the streetcars, without unguarded rights of way, ran much more slowly than before. They were described increasingly as symbols of urban blight, too primitive for the new image of Los Angeles.

What indeed this new image looked like becomes the next focus in this essay. The next stage of the sunshine strategy, beginning with the late thirties, centered around the automobile, but also involved fantasies about the causes of urban blight, about the end of rustic innocence, about how to replace it with suburban innocence; and finally with no innocence at all. It is a Balloon Route of another sort, from downtown west, and back downtown again, over a period of fifty years.

THE MYTH OF A FREEWAY METROPOLIS (1936-1949)

In 1937, just as the Depression seemed to be worsening again, plans for building the first freeways were released to the public. Schemes about what were called "elevated and crossingless motorways" had been in the news before, as early as 1906,[23] seriously in the mid-twenties, and occasionally afterward. But now the campaign began in earnest, after a new traffic survey, followed by long articles in the *Los Angeles Times*, brochures from the Auto Club, meetings of think tanks and speeches in the City Council. The first freeway, the Arroyo Seco, was funded, as part of an elaborate scenario for a new city, even including photo-sketches of an orderly cityscape that bore no resemblance to what actually stood at the time. Then, during the war years, the rest of the babylonian fantasy was laid out on paper, and the expenses calculated.

Ed Ainsworth, writing for the *Times* in 1937, stated the problem very succinctly: Los Angeles was "ideally situated...for this first great experiment in loosening the strangling noose of traffic." The plan would rehabilitate business, and become "a national model upon which to mold the city of the years to come," clearly a city dedicated to auto-mobility.[24] Roads left over from "the dim days of the pedestrian, the horseman and the horsedrawn vehicle" would be modernized.

It took longer to cross ten blocks downtown by car (14 minutes) than by horse and buggy fifty years earlier. The traffic problem caused quite a furor, so awesome that it became a metaphor for a much deeper anxiety about the future of Los Angeles. The city seemed to be spiralling backwards.

Planning documents from the war years repeat very much the same message—an utter contradiction of the sunshine image of the city. Neighborhoods cannot "just grow, like topsy." Business and housing standards were being damaged. Stores and filling stations came too close to residential housing. Office buildings went up where they were not needed. Vacancy rates increased—and crime. The natural, or unplanned city was beginning to look more like Chicago than a rustic arcadia.

Like nature gone awry, the language describing these slums used bizarre medical metaphors: Los Angeles was afflicted by urban diseases, like a herd of livestock attacked by mosquitoes or an orchard threatened by the Japanese beetle. Planner Mel Scott writes (1942, in a report widely circulated throughout the forties, then expanded into a book in 1949): Traffic circulation is "afflicted by traffic fever," with "sick boulevards," and "high-speed arteries...ruined by straggling roadside businesses."[25] Even more unfortunately, Los Angeles was "blighted," as shown on a map where twenty square miles of urban blight were darkened, like an x-ray of spots on the lung. (Actually, blight is more a botanical than a mammalian disease—spots on leaves. In planning jargon, blight was defined as the first step toward slum, or terminal decay.)

Despite the rude oversimplifications, many of these models were designed to address the problems of poorer, struggling neighborhoods; and deeply influenced plans for public housing in the forties. But consider what the model suggests: buildings are the host victims, and therefore alive; poor residents are only part of the corpus, seemingly further down the chain. The unique dynamics of specific working-class communities often were ignored, primarily because the basic problem was first of all, the body of the city (tax base), and second, the blood system (roads).

Social planning for communities (except to plan leisure for families) was subsumed far below these, often described as part of the tissue that was diseased. To paraphrase the old Dadaist joke, L.A. needed an operation:

> In our dreams the Los Angeles metropolitan community of the future has safe, well-planned streets on which traffic flows smoothly, through convenient, self-contained neighborhoods, numerous regional parks, connected by beautiful parkways, miles of publicly- owned beaches, and prosperous industries....Enchanted by this vision, we sometimes forget that if it is to become more than just a vision, we actually must replace much of the community that exists today. We must create many things still in the imagination. Block after block of buildings must be cleared to make way for freeways. Outworn, dilapidated nighborhoods must be razed, hundreds of new dwellings contructed. Disfiguring roadside stands and signs must come down, so that motorists may enjoy the beauty of the countryside and drive undisturbed by the commercial activities at the side of the road....[26]

To promote this 1940s dream, planning campaigns took on the spirit of wartime propaganda, particularly aerial bombings: "Outworn, dilapidated buildings must be razed." Urban decay was compared to cities after blitzkrieg: "Blight had gotten in its deadly work on sections of London long before the blitz came." Finally, and even more tellingly, urban decay suggested the coming of another depression, which many felt was still just around the corner, forestalled only by the wartime prosperity:[27]

> Our cities have decayed so badly that many of them are bankrupt or soon may be. This process is terribly wasteful. It destroys property values. It breeds slums.

In wording reminiscent of recruitment ads, public vigilance was demanded. "Planning, like democracy, needs more than experts." It needs support on the home front, because "cities have stopped growing during the war."

A widely distributed article from *The Architectural Forum* asks: "How can we fix decay?" And answers: "The way a dentist does— by cleaning out the infected area and guarding it against further trouble."[28]

What a telling metaphor: poorer neighborhoods as tooth decay. Communities were not described as a delicate balance of institutions, damaged by high unemployment, declining commercial streets, growing absentee landlordism, or the loss of political, religious, and cultural centers. Instead, communities were massive urban cavities to scoop out, in order to restore a healthy tax base to the city, and end the looming threat of a new depression after the war. Real estate prices were indeed slipping in the old metropolitan centers. In 1938, a prestigious committee of ten agents for downtown office buildings complained to county supervisors that vacancy rates were alarmingly high, that businesses were leaving for the suburbs.[29] The downtown area in Los Angeles clearly had suffered a considerable loss of trade since the late twenties, losing out to the Miracle Mile along Wilshire, to chain stores, to neighborhood movies, and to suburban shopping areas, where there were no parking problems.[30]

The image that came with rapid decentralization played havoc with myths about the rustic city. Farm city became casual consumer city, in the 1941 *Time* magazine description of midwestern housewives dressed in pajamas while "shopping in one of the decentralized business centers."[31]

Out in the suburbs (often identified as areas west of La Brea), parking restrictons were unnecessary, traffic jams unknown, utterly the reverse of downtown. And yet, since the teens, population growth had been slowing in the already dense downtown area. The downtown share of citywide shopping had dropped by as much as fifty per cent from 1929 to 1935. However, the decline was not seen as irretrievable. The stores downtown were still mobbed at Christmas season. Major streets downtown were packed with traffic every rush hour—too much traffic.

The war had accelerated decentralization. Over fourteen million people were expected to have changed localities by the end of the war. Also, eleven million more had gone into the military. As another planning specialist, Catherine Bauer explained in 1943:[32]

> All in all, one-quarter to one-sixth of our population are in a state of flux, physically and psychologically. If you ask them where they expect to be five years from now, they shrug their shoulders. When the soldiers stream down the gang-planks to meet their wives and fiancees, the central question for some twenty to thirty million people will be: Where do we go from here?

Then Bauer explained how this "state of flux" was changing cities. "Five or six million people have moved from open country to metropolitan districts since 1940," much faster than earlier. The number of farmers had declined, meaning that "urbanization is still roughly equivalent to economic progress." But what sort of urbanization? While the industrial labor force kept growing, it was not necessarily moving into the old metropolitan centers:

> During the war, twenty billion dollars of streamlined modern war plants have been built, almost doubling the value of industrial plants in the country....Where are they? Not in old city centers nor yet in isolated small towns, but for the most part on the outskirts of metropolitan areas.[33]

War-time industrialization and decentralization were crippling cities. The concern for these two problems transformed the image of Los Angeles very markedly, with the period after 1936 as the dividing line. From the 1890s on, the number who came from farm areas continued to decline in L.A., until by the forties, they became almost insignificant.[34] Then, with the Depression, rural tourists, who had been rich and desirable in the 1890's, when farm prices had zoomed, now became associated with the dispossessed that Steinbeck would describe in *Grapes of Wrath*. From 1936 on, police at the state borders sent back thousands who were headed for L.A. from the Dust Bowl, the beginning of a rude shift in image and policy, as declining services failed to keep up with the continual in-migration. This policy was undertaken with active support from the L.A. Chamber of Commerce. In 1936, for example, the Chamber was invited to send a speaker to the small town of Blythe, about three miles form the state line. Eight LAPD officers were stationed at every highway entrance to the state. After the visitor's lecture, the Chamber at Blythe agreed to send a letter supporing the border checks to the Los Angeles police chief.[35]

Clearly, the L.A. farm-city image had begun to backfire, into a problem. Promotional imagery, for a time, was tilted away from descriptions of L.A. as a sunshine cornucopia toward L.A. as a home for those with industrial skills. Migration from the Dust Bowl was discouraged, even though that area of the country had once been considered crucial for tourism. During the war competition to attract government defense money was fierce. L.A. became the center for military industries serving the war in the Pacific conflict, and many of these remained afterward, as part of the huge postwar defense industry here.

By the late thirties, and increasingly in the forties, the market image of the city was very much divided. There were two opposites that needed to be blended: first, the sunshine city (1885-1929); second, the Depression, war-time, industrial city (1929-1945). Somehow, these two economic strategies would have to be organized into a bivalve organism that was easy to advertise—a new urban model for planning and investment. Stated another way: how were profits made through decentralization going to coordinate with profits needed to save downtown? Suburban real estate was a plum, no doubt, or would be, after the war. But most of the investment capital, and investment leaders, were still centered in downtown, along with the financial life blood of the city itself.

Catherine Bauer offered the following solution:[36]

> It's too late, if indeed it ever was possible, to think of 'saving' the old city centers in their congested nineteenth century form. A regional organism is striving for birth, with centers and sub-centers and open areas permanantly differentiated for varied functions, much more complex and refined than the amoeba-like nineteenth century city and hence requiring more discipline and conscious purpose.

What these biological similes amount to is a plan for orbit cities, to be designed from scratch or enlarged around the knots where freeways would meet. The freeways would radiate from downtown, liberating the center from traffic congestion, while allowing for experiments in ideal city life without the baggage left over from old neighborhoods, with their shabby houses, and what Bauer called "the dreary inefficiency of present cities," meaning the roads, the blight and the irrational architecture.[37] In terms of this essay, one image—decentralized suburbs—would be made to coexist with another—a revived downtown center. (The term Bauer used, by the way, was "decentrist.")[38]

For lack of a better term, I have decided to call this imaginary model a *multi-tropolis*, essentially an industrial blueprint laid over a rapidly decentralizing city. It resembles other versions of the City Efficient or even Corbusier's Radiant City, but does not encourage the pockets of high density that such plans allowed. The key was, of course, the freeway, and the uneven attempts to salvage downtown; to integrate business outside of downtown; to isolate bedroom community life from heavy industry—in short, to isolate each problem from the other as much as possible, and keep the traffic flowing at all costs.

The gestation for this plan took over thirty years, with considerable shifts from year to year. In brief, leaders, promoters and residents were uncertain about how a sunshine farm city could be mixed with more factories and more industrial transportation. In early L.A. planning (1908 on), the rustic myth still seemed capable of absorbing more industry. Industrial districts could be integrated into the landscaped city. The focus was still tourism, to bury the factories beneath the picturesque, to please the eye of the tourist. Broad "Parisian" boulevards were to be added, along with agricultural parks, for "pleasure drives," by coach more than automobile, and radiating out of downtown along wide, luxuriant streets.

In the twenties, with a flourish of new master plans (and the formation of the Regional Planning Commission), the germ of the multi-tropolis was first suggested. As historian David Clark explains, in 1925, as a way to save taxpayers the cost of new subways or elevated lines, the City Club proposed "a harmonious developed community of local centers and garden cities."[39]

An orbit-city model was refined further in the late thirties, in the spirit of government reform during the New Deal. This considerably more industrial model also arrived after massive political scandals in the city, during the reform coalition that came into power with the election of Fletcher Bowron as mayor in 1938. (Similarly, after 1908, the City Beautiful arrived with the Progressivist coalition that destroyed the ward politics dominated by San Francisco interests.)

Waves of urban planning (and the imaginary cities it blueprints) often arrive immediately after political scandals. New plans promise a future free of old forms of corruption. In L.A., these promises generally meant weakening community politics, keeping the wardheels and bag men away from city hall, but also stifling grass roots community groups who were obstacles to real estate investment.

The master plans for multi-tropolis itself (where to build freeways, what to tear down, etc.) came during the Second World War. They were anxious plans, coming out of the scars of the Great Depression, and the pressures of the war-time economy. Housing shortages were severe. Whites were frightened by the rapidly growing black population. Powerful interests pushed for isolating low income housing in areas like Watts. Many were afraid that the sudden growth of heavy industry would end after the war, that public works programs would be needed to handle unemployment.

Plans like these existed elsewhere as well, but one must never underestimate "the L.A. penchant for large-scale planning."[40] In Los Angeles, from theme parks to city plans, utopian models tend to be taken very literally. In 1941, the imaginary multi-tropolis was put on display, at a public exhibition sponsored by the Regional Planning Commission. Scale models showed a geometric wave of entirely new buildings, replacing virtually everything standing downtown. *Time* magazine called it a "Lewis Mumford dreamworld", and added: "If the city planners could burn Los Angeles down they would rebuild it differently."[41]

One should never underestimate the L.A. penchant for apocalypse either. Planning reports described blight as more virulent here than elsewhere (it certainly was not, of course). Architect Richard Neutra asked: "Was this metropolis a paradise, or did there exist here a type of blight which fitted none of the classical descriptions?"[42]

Within a few years after the war, priorities had shifted again. Even more population increases had filtered back toward downtown, increasing the occupancy rate. The Depression had not returned. A new housing boom was underway, with promotional campaigns to build modernist suburban communities and shopping centers. By 1949, downtown shopping already was being written off (and during the fifties, after an anti-communist smear campaign, public housing downtown as well). From then on, downtown would be seen primarily as an executive and investment center. Decentralization had won, and another sunshine fantasy with it— the much expanded multi-tropolis. By the late fifties, with Valley farmland under rapid conversion into housing subdivision, L.A. became a Balloon Route again—by car now, along cement freeways under a Mediterranean sky, ploughing endlessly past orbit cities.

There is no space here to detail the entire process that put this multi-tropolis into place. The first projects began right before the Second World War: Union Station; Arroyo Seco Freeway. At that point, ironic as this may seem today, much of the strategy was still designed to strengthen the downtown center, by reducing traffic congestion. After the war, the downtown focus became increasingly less important, as the fever of developing the San Fernando Valley overtook downtown planning. Much of the money for revitalizing the city was poured into the freeway system, while decentralization finally reached the point of no return for downtown businesses. Thus, the downtown side of the plan was abdicated for a decade or more. Energy went into finding ways to drive through downtown rapidly, and little more.

By the late sixties, two-thirds of the metropolitan center was devoted to the automobile (garages, roads, filling stations, etc.),[43] an anecdote that spoke directly to the problem—the full-scale evacuation of downtown, far beyond what the forties planners had imagined. In the mid-sixties, to reverse this trend, a "growth coalition," in connection with the Community Redevelopment Agency for the downtown area, created a massive financial district downtown. The Growth Coalition/CRA also made awkward stabs at reversing the general distrust of downtown as a residential alternative, but with extremely limited results. Perhaps that is all the housing that the very narrow infra-structure downtown could bear (limited electric capacity; aging gas and water pipes; limited police, fire protection), at least without getting in the way of high-rise banks, hotels, and insurance companies. The services for a substantial number of permanent residents downtown certainly would have cost the taxpayers more than the city leaders felt was feasible. And there was clearly no land rush of home buyers heading back to the old center city anyway (not until the late eighties). For the most part, except for sponsorship of a few condominums away from the financial district, housing in the downtown area has been systematically ignored, or simply knocked down.

The multi-tropolis began under the assumption that the general downtown area was unlivable, and collapsing (this was not entirely true at all; many of the neighborhoods were quite stable until the sixties). But a barricaded look developed, nonetheless, in the new downtown, like a white settlement among the aborigines. Despite a campaign planned in the late eighties to encourage museums and ethnic plazas in the northern end of downtown, the great concrete stockades still dominate, and may never be humanized. Cement pedways resemble a modernist version of the castle town (not unlike sketches of imaginary cities by the Italian Futurist Saint-Elia in 1913—purely a coincidence, but a revealing one).[44]

The multi-tropolis, like many variations of "modernist" planning after the Second World War, also was built upon a profound anxiety about guarding against crime. Cars moved along guarded freeways. Civic buildings needed security against too many winding alleys or hidden public places. The so-called "International School" found its widely accepted mission after World War II, during moments of high urban decay, when cities seemed to need a quarantine. As a result, crime-proof plazas became rather popular, probably not always for the reasons architects envisioned. These plazas removed street-level shopping, made the path up steps very visible, into heavily lit, flat areas, and made unplanned congregations of people far less likely (as we know from the complaints by critic Jane Jacobs, and others, during the fifties).

By the mid-seventies, after the first decade of the Growth Coalition, this passion for safety became essential to the way downtown was promoted (on TV, in posters). From a safe height, one saw the glass curtain maze, an overhead helicopter shot of a vertical Oz that was virtually unpopulated at night. From the helicopter, the chalk-white hives of condominiums resembled feudal walls for the great freeway cloverleaf, which became a sculptural medallion in the middle of downtown.

Since the shocks of the Watts Riot (1965), the multi-tropolis has been designed even more passionately toward security.[45] The rich districts are being walled off more coherently against the poor. During the eighties, with considerable investments in real estate between Hancock Park and Fairfax, a wall of safety emerged along the Wilshire Corridor—continuing into the nineties, with plans for a "West Bank," beyond the Harbor Freeway to extend this barrier between north and south all the way to downtown. The boundary will follow the arc of the Metro Rail, and along the Wilshire Corridor, with a life line extended down Figueroa, and the expanded Convention Center, into South Park, and ultimately, if plans continue, toward the University of Southern California.

In the late sixties, when the multi-tropolis seemed at its point of highest efficiency, L.A. was praised worldwide as a city that functioned extremely well. In possibly the most famous homage to multi-tropolis, art historian Reyner Banham in 1973 described the freeway system as a unique ecology (he compared it to a man-made climate, superior to nature), an "autopia."[46]

By contrast, Banham added a tiny "note on downtown, because that is all downtown Los Angeles deserves."[47] He saw no viable architecture in the downtown area. A few office towers added near the Civic Center only revealed how hopeless the situation had become. Old pedestrian sites like Pershing Square and the pueblo area were corroded, proof that the residents of L.A. no longer cared. Downtown was "a badly planned and badly run suburban shopping centre for those who cannot afford cars to get to the 'real' suburbs." In the first illustration of the book, to show how badly planned the old downtown was, he included a photo of Echo Park Avenue, near the neon parking display of the Pioneer Market. The nest of store signs looked discombobulated, beyond hope. Even today, that part of Sunset Boulevard is, indeed, quite a jumble. However, the community around it is one of the most stable in the city, and rather unique in its mixture of classes and ethnicities. In Banham's eyes, except for an overhead photo of the freeway cloverleaf, downtown did not qualify as a modernist, architectural superspace.

The multi-tropolis had achieved its goal, to fashion L.A. into a national model for the modernist city: efficient, sensually liberating, strangely free of an urban center, like a cognate of abstraction in art, a Rothko painting where the center floats in an existential absence. The French critic Roland Barthes compared downtown Los Angeles to Tokyo, two urban giants evacuated at their center, as a strange liberation from classical codes of urban experience.[48] But in fact, downtown was not a blank cipher at all, far from it. It was more the scene of the crime, a crisis to ignore, the un-touristed non-image. One might say it was the tree that was designed to fall without anyone watching in the forest. It was a blank because the hotels had turned into flop houses, and they had been removed from the promotion of the city altogether, except in fantasy, as part of a nether world that one found in L.A. literature and film; and also in urban planning documents, as the downtown of no hope, a precursor of the "bladerunner" city. It became the polyglot nightmare in people's imagination, as famous in its way as the Sunkist orange.

THE MYTHS OF DOWNTOWN RENEWAL (1936-1949)

Two districts downtown have vanished into myth, like corpses for a case that never went to trial. The first myth relates to Bunker Hill, and Forties Noir: "Old Town, Lost Town, Shabby Town, Crook Town." This passage, frequently quoted in descriptions of downtown L.A., comes from Raymond Chandler's novel *The High Window* (1942).[49] It lays out a romance of urban blight that matches very closely what urban planners during the Second World War saw as beyond redemption. The passage describes the Bunker Hill area downtown: "Once, very long ago, it was the choice residential district of the city, and there are still standing a few of the jigsaw Gothic mansions....They are all rooming houses now....The wide sweeping staircases are dark with time and with cheap varnish laid on over generations of dirt."[50]

Chandler's version of Bunker Hill is peopled with the hopeless and the criminal: "Landladies bicker with shifty tenants." Old men wearing cracked shoes have "faces like lost battles." It is an old neighborhood, with evil lurking beneath the quaintness, "little candy stores where you can buy even nastier things than their candy." At "ratty hotels...nobody signs the register except people named Smith and Jones....The night clerk is half watchdog and half pander...

"Out of the apartment houses come women who should be young but have faces like stale beer." Among the derelict types are "men with pulled-down hats and quick eyes;...fly cops with granite faces;...cokies and coke peddlars; people who look like nothing in particular and know it."

Chandler's description of the Florence Apartments, at the northern end of Bunker Hill, is suitably gothic: "dark brick in front, three stories, the lower windows at sidewalk level and masked by rusted screens and dingy net curtains." At the entrance door, only "enough of the names" could be read. Out toward the alley, instead of sunshine fantasy, there were "four tall battered garbage pails in a line, with a dance of flies in the sunlit air above them."[51]

Chandler had lived in Bunker Hill himself, for a short time, in 1913, before his career as an oil executive had transformed his finances, also before he was fired (in 1933). Afterward, he plunged into a new career writing detective fiction, living in cheaper districts west of the old metropolitan center and also in the Pacific Palisades.[52] After 1946, with income from screenwriting, and a growing disenchantment with Los Angeles—in his words, "that old whore"[53]—he moved to La Jolla. It is unlikely that Chandler had any direct connection with Bunker Hill after 1913, or even downtown very much, only of its reputation.

Bunker Hill had become the emblem of urban blight in Los Angeles, the primary target for redevelopment downtown from the late twenties on. A steep hill, rising from Fourth Street to Temple, from Hill Street west, past Figueroa, it represented 200 acres of impasse. The hill stifled traffic. It offered little opportunity for commercial development. It seemed suitable only for residential housing. By the late twenties, that housing also looked run down. Its median year of construction was 1895.[54] Ninety-eight per cent of the homes had been built before 1920. Bunker Hill was the oldest cityscape in Los Angeles, with more showboat Victorians than anywhere else in Southern California, but virtually all of them were being converted into rooming houses. After 1930, nothing new was built up there. Between 1930 and 1940, the population on the hill increased by 19% to a density above 63 per acre, rivaling eastern cities. As of 1940, over 75% of the residents had less than eight years of schooling. Most were immigrants, predominately from Mexico, but also from Italy, Canada, Russia, Germany and England. Even more damaging, however, Bunker Hill housed a very large number of elderly retired people. This became the crux of the debate, where to relocate the aged, who claimed that the community was intact, and quite charming still, isolated above downtown. By 1957, the Department of Building and Safety identified 60% of the buildings as hazardous, meaning worse than simply sub-standard. Police reports indicated high crime, also considerable trade in narcotics, particularly just north of the old funicular cable car, Angel's Flight.

In the novel *Ask the Dust* (1939), John Fante remembered Bunker Hill as it had looked ten years earlier:[55]

> I went up to my room, up the dusty stairs of Bunker Hill, past the soot-covered frame buildings along that dark street, sand and oil and grease choking the futile palm trees standing like dying prisoners, chained to a little plot of ground with black pavement hiding their feet. Dust and old buildings and old people sitting at windows, old people tottering out of doors, old people moving painfully along the dark street.

In another novel of the Depression, *Fast One* (1932), by Paul Cain (the first major hard-boiled crime novel set in L.A.), Bunker Hill is the first neighborhood the criminal outsider visits, a world of molls, gangster dialogue, and professional crooks. Scheming losers live there. In Paul Cain's description of buildings downtown, mixed use and blight take on the gothic spirit of Dickensian byways: "Ansel's turned out to be a dark, three-story business block set flush with the sidewalk. There were big For Rent signs in the plate-glass windows and there was a dark stairway at one side."[56]

However glamorous the crime novel, or well-intentioned its "realism," the myth of Bunker Hill virtually always was presented through the eyes of the tourist, in this case, the beleaguered, disillusioned tourist, not unlike Nathaniel West's vision of how fantasies were destroyed in Depression Los Angeles:[57]

> Once [tourists get] there, they discover that sunshine isn't enough. They get tired of oranges, even of avocado pears and passion fruit. Nothing happens....The sun is a joke. Oranges can't titillate their jaded palates. Nothing can ever be violent enough to make taut their slack minds and bodies. They have slaved and saved for nothing.

Fante called these battered tourists "the uprooted ones, the empty sad folks, the old and the young folks, the folks from back home....[Retirees] came here by train and by autombile...with just enough money to live until their last days....And when they got here they found that other and greater thieves had already taken possession, that even the sun belonged to others."[58] But, Fante adds, these disgruntled locust people were still better off than the poor in flop houses downtown, who could not afford a fancy polo shirt and sunglasses.

These examples above are among the most famous literary descriptions of the downtown myth. The reader has probably encountered them before, or variations. Dozens of crime films from the forties and fifties worked off this myth and its cognates. By the forties, the image of failing to make a go in Hollywood, with its various scandals and "boulevards of broken dreams" became synonymous with the Depression fantasies of urban blight, and with gangster fiction. By the sixties, crime novelists like Jim Thompson set the downtown myth along the Sunset Strip, another swanky area gone downhill, now a vice district (tacitly permitted by the police), with massage parlors, nudie bars, and a chance for new arrivals to watch live sex acts for the price of a five dollar drink.[59]

In brief, as a structuralist paradigm based on dozens of examples, the downtown fable works this way: The outsider arrives (or lives insecurely) in Los Angeles, to find a world peopled by other outsiders. Among the rich, if he rises that far, mostly to mop up their crimes, he finds a perverse ruling class. They are debauched, new rich; they send out false messages about success, schemes that cheat the hopeless multitudes who want a shot at celebrity, or life in the sunshine.

Downtown becomes a ruined abbey in a Victorian guide book. Finally, the abbey is torn down. Meanwhile, the downtown manse is peopled by hundreds of thousands, who serve the story mostly as "local color." They are ornamental, to enhance the glamour of the journey. The gothic crime novel may comment with compassion about "local color," but never quite enters the spirit of social relationships. It suggests that local color has no community, only transcient souls beyond redemption. Better for the honest man to move on.

In that sense, the very popular dark side of L.A. tourism, using images of urban blight, has also sold real estate. The "noir image" has glamorized, quite unintentionally, the need to destroy downtown communities. That is the ironic genius of imaginary cities, either of the sunshine variety or the shady: they always wind up selling products, in a culture so well adapted to promotion—and I speak not only of Los Angeles, of course.

The downtown myth also stands in for the segregated nature of the city—indeed, any tourist town tends to be segregated carefully, through commercial zoning, housing covenants, careful promotion, and the way police patrols operate from one area to the next. Cities for tourists often have twin images, one for families, one for the underground weekend. L.A. was famous for its underground world, including red light districts set up by the city itself during the boom of the 1880s. But these shady services had to be isolated carefully from the real estate promoted to white, prosperous tourists. The raunchy businesses were best left in, or near, non-white areas. That tended to be north and east of downtown, away from residential real-estate expansion.

As the city kept expanding, the myth of an underground downtown came to be associated also with crooked vice cops, gambling tenderloins, exotic pleasures for sale, and finally, with Mexican and Chinese neighborhoods, located downtown in particular (other areas as well, of course, like East Hollywood). In the publicity sanctioned by the city leaders, the underground image was neither denied nor repressed, so much as walled off. The

Balloon Route Tour of old Chinatown (ca. 1912) promised a family guide who also knew about the opium trade.

This dark or noir mystique of the city was intensified during the thirties—or revived—during the scandals of the Shaw administration. By then, the downtown myth had become linked with police campaigns against vagrancy, with professional crime, drug use, with losers living on the edge of oblivion downtown. It also had its high bourgeois correlary: detectives like Chandler's Marlowe meet decadent rich women slumming with gangsters on gambling ships, or doing drugs in seedy back alleys (*Farewell My Lovely* is the obvious example). One might call these fantasy stories urban primitivism, like the classic image of young English women getting a tan among brown-skinned races, then committing crimes unimaginable in the Protestant normalcy of the Anglo-Saxon family.

By the mid-sixties, Bunker Hill had been stripped entirely of houses. Through the Community Redevelopment Agency, the city decided to level the hill, but keep the tunnels, which still remain, as monuments to urban erasure. A few of the old Victorian houses from Bunker Hill were moved to a site along the Pasadena Freeway, a fitting place; the building of that freeway had initiated the planning that made residential life in the old downtown practically extinct.

In the eighties, attempts to reassemble a community life downtown continue, along with stop-gap measures to control the problems of homelessness. But communities are like necklaces. When the clasp is removed, the necklace is as good as lost. It will take many years for a balance to be restored, if ever.

Also in the 1980s, another Bunker Hill was torn down, at least 850 units, with thousands more to follow, in an old area that is being called Center City West (west of the Harbor Freeway downtown). Clearly, some efforts are being made to avoid another Bunker Hill syndrome. The architect's plans for this new imaginary downtown adjunct are glamorous, calling for a mixed use, pedestrian-oriented community, with rich and poor reasonably close together, with high-rise hotels, medium-sized office buildings, apartments and even possibly small parks, with a small trolley over the Harbor Freeway. It is a fantasy community, as early plans for

Bunker Hill were, but beneath the elegant prospects, there is also the death of a community, and the struggle to split up the financial pie (between developers, council people, the school board, Cal-Trans and slumlords). Twenty thousand people had once lived in this general area, now growing bald, and so erratically, that wildcat oil wells have opened in some of the empty lots where houses used to be. It is another version of the scorched-earth policy of the multi-tropolis. Struggles to force developers to add low income housing may actually work this time, but where and how, and for which political war chest, is not certain yet. Eminent domain is not being used as freely, even to build a school that is badly needed there. And the commmunity itself is desperately chaotic in its response. Tenants are understandably exasperated, even form alliances with slum landlords, to stay in low income apartments, while the same landlords cut deals with developers, to sell out, now that a full city lot there can go for as high as $500,000. The sadness, the good intentions, the brokering for power and profit continue.

The second downtown myth is equally elaborate, about the imaginary Chinatown (1883-1973). According to legend, there was once a Chinese underground city beneath downtown Los Angeles—a nest of catacombs where inscrutable sins were committed. Presumably, it was located underneath the Garnier Building, south of the old Plaza, but the basement there was used mostly for storage, from bins of rice to live chickens, for the restaurants above. The myth of a Chinese underground came primarily out of white civic policies, for tourism. From 1887 to 1909, the streets assigned for legalized prostitution were situated officially on the streets of Chinatown, very much above ground, without any approval from residents there. The same was true for the opium trade (where dealers who signed the "poison book" for the police could operate, free from arrest). It was felt that Chinese were used to opium and whores, so the seedier aspects of tourism could be isolated there, away from the other areas of downtown. Meanwhile, the cribs for whores and the dens for drugs were run, and frequented, mostly by whites. As a result, white gangs, and addicts, would mug Chinese regularly on the street. In 1887, the center of Chinatown was burnt down, probably by arson, while the Fire Department nearby refused to answer the call.[60] Chinese businesses complained constantly, but had little recourse. For generations, particularly following the Alien Exclusion Act (1883), Chinese were not permitted to give testimony in court.

By the 1930s, the image of a vice-ridden downtown had been linked clearly with Chinatown, particularly in reports by the vice cops who worked in the Chinese district. Chinatown also was identified with the Mexican barrio nearby, known as the Sonora or "Dogtown"; and with the old vaudeville district on Main Street, that John Fante remembered as "neon tubes and a light fog (at midnight), honky tonks and all night picture houses...secondhand stores and Filipino dance hall, cocktails 15¢, continuous entertainment."[61] With Chinatown at its heart, this was indeed a blighted place, still popular for tourists, but also the home to a very stable Chinese community that had been there for over fifty years. The novelist and critic Louis Adamic described the Mexican part of the Plaza in 1928:[62]

> [Even] as it is, the Plaza district is the most interesting part of Los Angeles. It consists, for the most part, of cheap wooden tenements occupied by Mexicans and Chinks[Chinese], of various camouflaged bawdy houses, dance halls, forlorn-looking bootleg dives, hop joints, movie shows, tamale stands, peep shows, shooting galleries, and stores selling rosaries and holy pictures. Main Street North, the principal thoroughfare of the district is a moron stream, muddy, filthy, unpleasant to the nose...an awful stew of human life....
>
> But just as I write this, the doom of the Plaza is sounding. A few millionaire realtors had got together with the railroads running into Los Angeles and cooked up a scheme to build a Union Station on the Plaza, which would give a tremendous boost to the land values in that vicinity.

Adamic goes on to describe the Mexican church of Our Lady at the Plaza. He watches an old toothless woman praying there, then a few blocks away, visits a cheap dance hall with a "crowd of young Mexicans, frail-bodied, foppish, decadent-looking boys and girls, the sweat of their bodies mingling with the scents of cheap perfumes and talc; their deep-sunk black eyes aglow with a desperate passion for joy; humming American ragtime."

Just as Adamic was writing this, over $1.4 million of state funds and much private donation was about to be designated to redesign the plaza area into a pueblo for tourists.[63] To clean up the area, Chinese were evacuated from the Plaza. In the thirties, the eastern end of Chinatown was torn down, to make way, at last for the Union Station, while the site of the old cribs was allowed to burn down (for fear of contamination by bubonic plague; a new central post office was built there a few years later). Still, in the forties, around the Union Station, picturesque blight dominated, with some of old Chinatown left, much of Main Street, the Sonora, and farther northwest, up hills, along dirt roads, part of Chavez Ravine looked to some like a failing chicken farm.[64]

By 1949, all that was slated to go, as *Los Angeles Times* columnist Lee Shippey explained:[65]

> The one hundred million dollar grant for slum clearance which the city has secured from the federal government should turn Chavez Ravine and other breeding places for delinquency and disease into pleasant, sanitary and well-serviced areas for low-income families. (Finally, of course, Chavez Ravine was turned over to the Dodgers for a baseball stadium)....The thirty-five million dollar additions to the freeway system are resulting in the clearing away of ugliness which used to face the union Station, and whatever new structures arise there will give persons arriving by train a wholly new first glimpse of the city.

Within fifteen years, every eyesore visible from the train station would be gone entirely. Of course, by then, the Union station itself had begun to look blighted, victim to freeway expansion, and the decline of rail travel. Still, the dream persisted into the eighties.

Today, the L.A. subway will radiate from the Union Station, overlooking a new Chinatown, essentially where the old Sonora used to be, beside the great freeway cloverleaf, where the old Chinatown used to be, in what has come to be called Downtown North. Southwest of there, on the precise spot where the exorcism of ethnicity had begun, directly over part of the cloverleaf, quixotic plans are underway to add a massive, glass, city complex, in honor of multi-cultural Los Angeles. A small Chinese museum will also be added south of the Plaza, as well as offices behind Union Station, and a de-hispanicized theater district on Broadway north of Third Street, all part of what is called Downtown North, a crescent of multi-ethnic tourism, from Little Tokyo to Olvera Street. Downtown "blight" now is being aestheticized. Even Angel's Flight will be restored, as an elevated funicular up an invisible hill, near the Museum of Contemporary Art.

In 1973, the legend of the underground downtown resurfaced in the film *Chinatown*, based on Robert Towne's extraordinary screenplay. This movie, more than any other ever made, has fixed in the public mind what the downtown myth looked like, updated the old film-noir images of Los Angeles, provided an allegory about land speculation and corruption here, and added a hot desert light to the myth of L.A. on film.

Towne explains that he learned about Chinatown from a retired Hungarian vice cop who claimed, "that police were better off in Chinatown doing nothing, because you could never tell what went on there."[66]   Thus, Chinatown—and the downtown myth—are deepened into a metaphor for the ambiguity of modern life, "of the futility of good intentions." It is a powerful reminder of the glamour to all of us in the downtown myth, of its links to buried secrets, about the contradictions between promotion and urban policies here in Los Angeles. We believe the romance, and need the romance. But we must realize that the myths, whether of tinsel town, of the sunny village, or of the downtown babylon, never represented the city accurately. They always ignored systematically the life of communities in the city, as if the small stores, fragile rituals, mix of classes together in a neighborhood could not exist in our imagination when we thought of Los Angeles. Indeed, these imaginary cities reveal the futility of our good intentions.

L.A. MYTHS FOR THE EIGHTIES AND AFTERWARD

Greater Los Angeles is about to become the new Pacific Byzantium, with only a minority of whites, and a population exceeding Greater New York. Statistics on crime grow worse. The underclass grows steadily larger. New museums, art endowments, freeway sculpture, murals programs, cultural Olympics add window-dressing to the new image in the making. The Pacific Byzantium becomes a brokerage center for huge investments from Japan, Taiwan, the EEC. It is also becoming as primitive as many Pacific Rim cities, with new sweatshops, depleted medical services and a two-tier, segregated society increasingly more similar to many Pacific cities. L.A. serves as the Grand Tour for many Japanese, who want to be seasoned for a few years in the mysteries of cosmopolitan Western life. It has also become a vital intermediary for the Chinese Democratic movement in exile. A new internationalist fantasy is emerging around Los Angeles. As always, this fantasy will be translated into another series of master plans, involving transportation, investment, and promotion.

There are already fantasy maps of "pedestrian-friendly" "urban villages" planned for downtown, in place of the "bunker mentality."[67] In debates over where to place a freeway bypass, one consultant for Center City West said: "I will not have this plan go down in history as having destroyed five neighborhoods in Los Angeles."

But we must not take these hopeful plans about the new Los Angeles strictly at face value—nor the headlines about new programs for South Central L.A., or the war against drugs (another downtown myth camouflaging the destruction of a community, i.e. *Colors*). Metro Rail remains, at this early stage, essentially a cement contractor's idea of progress, not a solution to the problems of mass transit. Cost over-runs have been devastating. Timetables are years behind. More political sabotage is coming. Most importantly, who in charge understands how few people may actually ride such a tiny system? Earlier plans for mass transit, from the twenties on, always advocated at least three to five hundred miles of track, for the system to reach enough people to function well. Now, the optimistic plans call for 150 miles, to be built within twenty years. And even those are posited, some say, on the city buying all the Southern Pacific rights-of-way that were put up for sale in July 1989, and must be purchased intact by January 1990. At this pace, a minimally adequate light rail may not be in place until about 2040.

The Community Redevelopment Agency is losing its independence, an indication that the multi-tropolis is no longer a working strategy—but also that City Council wants more control over planning, and resources than it had earlier. Mayor Tom Bradley is shrouded in scandal, as his administration rapidly diminishes. What else diminishes with him? The wheel is turning, though I suspect, not as much as one might imagine. L.A. has promised a lot before, but its image, as always, is guided by the power of real estate firms, the transportation industry, and tourist planning to lure outside investors. The images promise, but policies dictate. Then, as the needs of these three key industries shift, new images emerge, to camouflage new policies—as ever, about a completely new city, redesigned from wall to wall. Certain humanistic intentions are mixed into these policies, but the larger interests tend to dominate. L.A. becomes a disposable city, planned whole and devoured whole. There is profit when the new city is built, and profit when it is demolished. That is why there are so many ruins left over from old plans acted on, then destroyed.

For example: The crime film *Criss-Cross* (1949) opens just west of the old downtown. A streetcar rolls out from the subway tunnel on First and Glendale (now a ruin across from the First Street bridge). Burt Lancaster gets off, and walks up a steep hill, along a hatchwork of wooden steps, into his old neighborhood. That entire hill has since been emptied of houses, and is about to become part of Center City West. The subway below (1925), that rose into Glendale Boulevard, was abandoned in the sixties.[68] But in the eighties, the builders of the new Pacific Stock Exchange were allowed to send a foundation into the space where the subway had run. In a sense, the fiction of this film is practially the only evidence of the fact. For Los Angeles, often fiction is virtually the only fact left, for events only a few decades back.

L.A. is the most photographed and least remembered city in the world. But despite its seemingly short memory, much of what planners had hoped to avoid—or erase—has come to pass anyway. The social pathology of the city cannot be ignored, particularly its extraordinary disregard for the fabric of community life, in pursuit of both a new Babylon and a new Jerusalem.

NOTES

1 Charles D. Willard, *A History of the Chamber of Commerce of Los Angeles, California, 1888-1900* (Los Angeles: Kingsley-Barnes & Neuner, 1899), 12. Among the many sources on the boom, the most thorough is: Glenn S. Dumke, "Boom of the Eighties in Southern California," (Los Angeles: UCLA dissertation, 1942), chs. 4 & 5 in particular.

2 Willard, p. 47.

3 These highly ephemeral brochures can be found in libraries and private collections throughout the city. The L.A. Museum of Natural History and UCLA Special Collections have an enormous number of them.

4   C.B. Glasscock, *Lucky Baldwin, The Story of An Unconventional Success* (Indianapolis: Bobbs-Merrill, 1933), 222.

5   Aldous Huxley, *After Many A Summer Dies The Swan* (New York: Harper & Row/Perennial, 1965, orig. 1939), 5.

6   Nordhoff was published by Harpers, the most powerful press of the day (1870s), Willard, p. 30. Also, frequently cited in Carey McWilliams' classic study: *Southern California: An Island on the Land* (Santa Barbara: Peregrine Smith, 1973, orig. 1946). Nordhoff started out as a reader for Fletcher Harper and remained extremely influential in editorial policy, as well as a popular writer on politics and travel (also father of Charles Nordhoff who co-wrote the Bounty trilogy), Eugene Exman, *The House of Harper, 150 Years of Publishing* (New York: Harper & Row), 77, 99, 132.

7   John E. Baur, *The Health Seekers of Southern California, 1870-1900* (San Marino, 1959), 16ff.

8   George H. Napheys, *The Physical Life of Woman* (Toronto, n.d.[orig. 1890s], many eds.), p. 75.

9   Some details were taken from talks with William Mason (in 1986 & 1989), the very informative curator of history at the Museum of Natural History in Los Angeles.

10   William R. Bigger, "Flood Control in Metropolitan Los Angeles" (Los Angeles: UCLA dissertation, 1954).

11   Charles Lockwood and Christopher B. Leinberger, "Los Angeles Comes of Age," *The Atlantic Monthly* (Jan. 1988): 31-62.

12   Marvin Brienes, "Smog Comes to Los Angeles," *Southern California Journal* (Winter 1976): 515-532.

13   Laurance L. Hill, *La Reina: Los Angeles in Three Centuries*, 4th. ed. (Los Angeles: Security-First Bank, 1931), 169-171.

14   Morrow Mayo, *Los Angeles* (New York: Knopf, 1933), 319.

15   McWilliams, *Southern California: An Island on the Land*, p. 137.

16   Roger Butterfield, "Los Angeles is the Damndest Place," *Life Magazine* (22 Nov. 1943): 102ff.

17   Joseph P. Beaton, "A Hollywood Case Study of District Issues" (Los Angeles: UCLA dissertation, 1981), 117. See also Bruce Torrence, *Hollywood: The First Hundred Years* (Hollywood: Hollywood Chamber of Commerce, and Fisk Enterprises, 1979), 34-38.

18   William Fulton, "'Those Were Her Best Days:' The Streetcar and the Development of Hollywood Before 1910," *Southern California Journal* (Fall 1984): 242-252.

19   *Miniatures of the Sunny Southland* (Los Angeles: Pacific Electric brochure, ca. 1907).

20   Robert C. Post, "The Fair Fare Fight: An Episode in Los Angeles History," *Southern California Journal* (Sept. 1970): 275-297.

21   An autophilic summary of many of the key documents on this matter: Scott L. Bottles, *Los Angeles and the Automobile: The Making of the Modern City* (Berkeley: University of California Press, 1987), chs. 2, 4, 5, 6. Summaries that defend the streetcars, while reviewing the old animosity toward the traction companies include: *The Metropolitan Transit Authority (MTA) Newsletter*,

particularly numbers 1-19 (1959-63); preliminary reports by the Assembly Fact-Finding Committee on Highways, Streets and Bridges (1949), by Assembly-Interim Committee on Public Utilities and Corporations, (1950); various records of public hearings in 1963; news stories in 1938, on the debt problems of the traction companies.

22 *Los Angeles News*, 31 July 1906.

23 Among various news items on subway and elevated plans: *L.A. Railways*, 27 Jan. 1907—suggesting elevated trams along L.A. Street north from 6th (essentially the same route as the subway that will be completed in the 1990s). As early as 1904, plans for subways in L.A. were presented to civic leaders.

24 Ed Ainsworth, *Out of the Noose* (Los Angeles: Automobile Club of Southern California, 1937), opening page. Reprinted from the *Los Angeles Times*, 12-18 June 1937.

25 Mel Scott, *Cities Are For People: The Los Angeles Region Plans for Living* (Los Angeles, Pacific Southwest Academy, 1942), 71, 73. This study accompanied a show (1941) sponsored by the Regional Planning Commission, and by architects from the L.A. branch of Telesis. The later edition of the study (1949), revised and expanded is entitled *Metropolitan Los Angeles: One Community* (Los Angeles: The Haynes Foundation). Consider what seven years had wrought. The earlier version (1942) has much more material (with photos) on urban blight, to reinforce the plans for a new city in the exhibition of 1941. The rewritten edition (1949) has considerably more on the outreach of freeways, much less on the threat of blight.

26 Scott, *Metropolitan Los Angeles*, p. 98.

27 *Planning Is With You* (New York: *Architectural Forum*, 1943). Reprinted and apparently given to various planning organizations in Los Angeles.

28 Ibid.

29 John Anson Ford, *Thirty Explosive Years in Los Angeles County* (San Marino, CA: Huntington Library, 1961), 108-109.

30 Summary in Lester D. Estrin, "The Miracle Mile: An Example of Decentralization in Los Angeles," (Los Angeles: UCLA dissertation, 1955), 2-17. An important source is Martin J. Schiesl, "City Planning and the Federal Government in World War II: The Los Angeles Experience," *California History* 59 (Summer, 1980): 126-143.

31 David Gebhard and Harriet Van Breton, *L.A. in the Thirties, 1931-1941* (Santa Barbara, CA: Peregrine Smith, 1975), 34. This study accompanied an exhibition of the same title, in Santa Barbara (1975).

32 Catherine Bauer, "Cities in Flux: A Challenge to the Postwar Planners," *American Studies* (Winter 1943-44): 70. The Statement for the Greater Los Angeles Citizens Committee is in the Haynes Foundation Papers, Box 240, in Special Collections at UCLA. Bauer, housing activist, former book editor, lived in Los Angeles. She was a close friend of Lewis Mumford, see Donald L. Miller, *Lewis Mumford, A Life* (New York: Weidenfeld & Nicolson, 1989), 288ff., 312ff.

33 Bauer, p. 72.

34 Gregory H. Singleton, "Religion in the City of Angels: American Protestant Culture and Urbanization in Los Angeles, 1850-1930" (Los Angeles: UCLA dissertation, 1976), 224.

35   "Letter to the Editor," *Nation* (Mar. 4, 1936): 295.

36   Bauer, p. 78.

37   Bauer, p. 82.

38   Bauer coined the term "decentrist," defined in Charles Abrams *Language of Cities* as follows (New York: Viking, 1971): 82—"A group of urban theorists who believe in thinning out the dense cities and dispersing businesses and people to smaller places." Other decentrists were Lewis Mumford, Clarence Stein, and Henry Wright. An earlier source is Ebenezer Howard, *Garden Cities of Tommorrow.* Thus, there is a clear link between the garden city and what I call the multi-tropolis, at least as imaginary solutions to urban problems. The core dilemma for decentrists was urban density (Abrams, p. 85), as in the phrase from Sir Raymond Unwin: "nothing gained by overcrowding." Mumford used the term "poly-nucleation:" satellite cities around a central city.

39   David L. Clark, *Los Angeles, A City Apart* (Woodland Hills, CA: Windsor, sponsored by L.A. Historical Society, 1981), 79.

40   Pat Adler, *The Bunker Hill Story* (Glendale, CA: La Siesta Press, 1963), 5.

41   Gebhard and Van Breton, p. 35. In the early forties, sketches of this imaginary downtown were widely disseminated, to builders and civic organization alike. For example: *Plans for Downtown Los Angeles' Four Pressing Needs,* appeared in *Southwest Builder and Contractor,* Jan. 7, 1944; then was reprinted as a promotional brochure. Sketches show virtally all of downtown north from Pershing Square gone and replaced, particularly Bunker Hill, already drawn as leveled, located west of an imaginary cloverleaf. (These plans borrowed considerably from the spirit of the 1939 New York World's Fair: the "Futurama" display of a freeway-centered city)

42   Gebhard and Van Breton, p. 34.

43   Victor Gruen, *The Heart of Our Cities, The Urban Crisis: Diagnosis and Cure* (New York: Simon & Schuster, 1967), 79. This fact is offered as proof of the following: "The city core of Los Angeles is not only small but void of true urban life as well." Also, this same fact (2/3 of downtown devoted to cars) is used in Banham's study, which appeared a few years later (see footnote 41). Urban life was described without reference to communities, or neighborhood institutions (i.e. community shopping, mixed use, ratio by class, race and home ownership, community centers, balance of streets to buildings, sites crucial to integrated experience within a community, power vis-a-vis city authorities). Again, communities were defined by the experience inside an automobile— essentially as a tourist driving through.

44   For example: Reyner Banham, *Theory and Design in the First Machine Age* (New York: Praeger, 1967), 116-119, and chapter beginning with 127. The second edition was completed shortly before Banham beginning his study of Los Angeles.

45   Mike Davis, "Chinatown, Part Two? The 'Internationalization' of Downtown Los Angeles," *New Left Review* 164 (1987): 65-90.

46   Reyner Banham, *Los Angeles: The Architecture of Four Ecologies* (New York: Penguin Books, 1976, orig. 1971), Ch. 11 ("Ecology IV: Autopia), pp. 215ff. Autopia was the last "ecology" presented, essentially the crowning achievement of the city. The book opens with quotes by literary tourists of the sixties on Los Angeles. The only quote from L.A. itself is "Burn, Baby, burn," from the 1965 Watts rioters.

47 Banham, *Los Angeles*, p. 201.

48 Roland Barthes, *Empire of Signs*, tr. by R. Howard (New York: Hill & Wang, 1982), 30. "Quadrangular, reticulated cities[Los Angeles, for instance] are said to produce a profound uneasiness; they offend our synesthetic sentiment of the City, which requires that any urban place have a center to go to, return to, return from, a complete site to dream of and in relation to which to advance or retreat; in a word, to invent oneself." He goes on to debunk those urbo-centric assumptions, even lists various institutions linked in the popular imagination to downtown areas, and the myth of downtowns representing a "social truth."

49 Raymond Chandler, *The High Window* (New York: Vintage, 1976, orig. 1942), 53. This description was cannibalized from the opening to Ch. 3 in his thirties novella, *The King in Yellow*:

> Court Street was old town, wop town, crook town, arty town. It lays across the top of Bunker Hill and you could find anything there from down-at-the-heels ex-Greenwich-villagers to crooks on the lam, from ladies of anybody's evening to County Relief clients brawling with haggard landladies in grand old houses with scrolled porches....

The earlier version makes less reference to urban blight, and more to transcient street life, closer perhaps to Chandler's mood during his years of professional transience; or as part of the "beleaguered neighborhood" fantasies of gangster films, 1930-1939, clearly different than the grimmer fantasies about urban blight during the forties (i.e. Film Noir). The location remains the same, for the most part; only the fantasy changes.

50 Chandler, p. 33.

51 Chandler, p. 54.

52 While there are many fine books and articles on Chandler, Philip Durham's biography has a useful chapter on L.A., entitled "The City," *Down These Mean Streets A Man Must Go, Raymond Chandler's Knight* (Chapel Hill: University of North Carolina Press, 1963), 48-60. In the thirties and forties, Chandler rode a lot through Wilshire and Sunset Boulevards, and L.A. west of Hollywood. His description of why he got to hate L.A. has a curious ring: "[Before] Los Angeles was just a big dry sunny place with ugly homes and no style, but good-hearted and peaceful." (p. 51); but after (quoting from Durham's text) "pansy decorators, Lesbian dress designers, riffraf of a 'big hardboiled city with no more personality than a paper cup—' a city without the 'individual bony structure' a real city must have. What Chandler meant precisely by "individual bony structure" is certainly interesting to imagine. Durham also goes on to document examples of Chandler's extraordinary influence on the image of L.A. as realist, and then to explain that Chandler was hardly trying to be a "realist" (this is frequently mentioned, even by Chandler himself, in various letters).

53 Durham, p. 60.

54 Adler, pp. 29-31.

55 John Fante, *Ask the Dust* (Santa Barbara, CA: Black Sparrow Press, 1984, orig. 1939), 55. Fante revisited the same settings, with a much gentler eye toward the dynamic of the downtown community, more nostalgic obviously (with very little reference to blight at all, ironically enough), in the novel *Dreams From Bunker Hill* (Santa Rosa, CA: Black Sparrow Press, 1988, orig. 1982).

56 Paul Cain, *Fast One* (Berkeley, CA: Black Lizard, 1987, orig. 1932), 62. Cain's real name was George Sims (also wrote for movies as Eric Rurik), 1902-1966.

57   Nathaniel West, *The Day of the Locust* (New York: New Directions, 1962, orig. 1939), 177. West's vision of mass violence coming out of the broken promises made by consumer promotion was shared, ironically enough, by Max Horkheimer and Theodor Adorno, whose book *Dialectic of Enlightenment* (1944) had an introduction signed Los Angeles 1947. A relevant line: "The culture industry perpetually cheats its consumers of what it perpetually promises." (p.139).

58   Fante, p. 45.

59   Jim Thompson, "Sunrise at Midnight" (ca. 1963), *Fire-Works: The Lost Writings*, ed. Polito and McCauley (New York: The Mysterious Press, 1988), 145. The Strip is also featured in Thompson's novel *The Grifters* (Berkeley, CA: Creative Arts/Black Lizard, 1985; orig. 1963), 92, 107.

60   Special Collections, El Pueblo Museum (L.A.).

61   Fante, p. 22.

62   Louis Adamic,*The Truth About Los Angeles* (Girard, Kansas: Haldeman-Julius, 1927), pp. 10-11. Adamic is a much neglected literary figure. For more material on his attitudes toward L.A., see Carey McWilliams, *Louis Adamic and Shadow America* (Los Angeles: Arthur Whipple, 1935), 79ff. An article dealing with Adamic will appear in a book being completed by Mike Davis.

63   Ford, p. 103.

64   I believe the photo entitled "Inconvenience," in Scott's *Cities Are for People* (1942), p.55, is of Chavez Ravine, though it looks a bit like rural West Virginia, near downtown L.A.; also in photo by Max Yavno (p.64; see fn. 65).

65   Lee Shippey, *The Los Angeles Book* (Boston: Houghton-Mifflin, 1950), 105. The photos in this book, by Max Yavno are remarkable, and unique, among the most clearly "community-centered" of any photographic record from the late forties.

66   Conversations with Robert Towne, 1985-1986.

67   From two articles opening on the front page of the *Los Angeles Downtown News*, 31 July 1989: "Developers' Beefs, An Open Dialogue About Progress," by Sue Laris; and "A Close Look at the City West Plan," by Marc Porter Zasada, p. 16. Also, another article quoting the term "urban village," from planning hearings: Diane Bailey, "Central City West Plan Unveiled," *Los Angeles Independent*, 2 Aug. 1989, p. 1. Also, December 1989 maps of the Center City North plan were released, indicating more room for Chinatown to grow, more pedways for luncheon traffic, and more deals to come. Apparently, too much "bulldozing" has made the view deary around Union Station, just where the MetroRail will complete its Blue Line. This may discourage subway travelers, as they emerge from the station below. Therefore, on the map, a pedestrian-friendly habitat of 15,000 is drawn, just east of MetroRail, where nothing but industrial yards stands right now. Probably something resembling the plan will be built. Only time will tell whether it ends up as yet another cement fortress (this time, with a Pacific, or a Mexican theme). Stephen Wolf, "ABird's-eye View of City North Plan," *Downtown News*, 11 Dec. 1989, p. 1.

Chapter 2

THE MEXICAN IMMIGRANT FAMILY: ECONOMIC AND CULTURAL SURVIVAL IN LOS ANGELES, 1900-1945

Gloria E. Miranda

The Mexican Revolution of 1910 and the Cristero Rebellion of the 1920s greatly stimulated the growth of the Mexican population in the United States. Over one million inhabitants fled the political and social upheaval that raged in their homeland during the first decades of this century. These refugees entered the United States seeking jobs and a temporary place to relocate their families until the civil strife in Mexico subsided. The geographical proximity and the historic and cultural affinity of the southwestern United States attracted most of the migrating Mexicans as they settled in urban and rural communities throughout the region.

Los Angeles was among the most popular destinations. The city's location offered more diverse employment opportunities and a familiar cultural setting in which Mexican immigrants could rear their families. Southern California also represented both a fertile agricultural region and an expanding urban and industrial center in pre-World War II times. The rapidly growing agribusiness necessitated the recruitment of a local work force willing to labor in the fields. The passage of anti-Asian legislation at the turn of the century paved the way for Mexican campesinos (rural workers) during the World War I to become the principal labor force in Southern California agriculture.[1]

Proximity to the border also enhanced the appeal of Los Angeles as a resettlement site for displaced Mexicans.[2] The Mexican who migrated north during this period generally brought his family with him. In some cases, single and married men journeyed to the United States without their relatives but women rarely traveled by themselves to this country.[3] Mexican migrants who arrived in Los Angeles at the turn of the century discovered that the former Mexican cultural dominance had been substantially altered by the large numbers of non-Mexicans who had settled in Southern California during the 1870s, 1880s and 1890s.

In 1890, the once numerous native-born Spanish speaking community comprised a mere ten percent of the region's total population. At the initiation of statehood forty years before, the new Mexican Americans had represented over ninety percent of Los Angeles' inhabitants. One of the reasons for this shift in population was the expansion of the railroads into the southland which resulted in the transplanting of Easterners and Midwesterners along with new European immigrants to the City of the Angels.

The majority of Mexican Americans no longer lived in a manner resembling the pre-American social setting. Only a minority of professional and middle class families, who considered themselves Spanish, had succeeded in gaining acceptance into the dominant Caucasian mainstream. At the beginning of the twentieth century most brown Americans could be found living in segregated downtown Los Angeles barrios such as Sonoratown and the adjacent Plaza district. These isolated enclaves later became the home of many new Mexican immigrants. This occurred for several reasons. First, the barrios represented already established communities with the city's only Mexican cultural core. Second, the downtown area offered immigrants affordable housing. And third, the homes in this sector were but a short distance from the work place for most residents.

The immigrants and their native-born counterparts in Los Angeles who shared life in these local barrios during pre-World War II times also experienced racial discrimination, cultural contempt, inferior education and economic impoverishment because of their heritage. The general pattern of anti-Mexicanism in Los Angeles was intense but it never fully succeeded in breaking up the cohesiveness of the two groups. By the onset of World War II, the local brown community was still resilient, in spite of anti-Mexican propaganda by nativists and Social Darwinists who campaigned in the 1920s to restrict the flow of immigrants from Mexico to the United States and who supported a national deportation campaign during the Great Depression. The half-hearted efforts of local religious organizations and the public schools at Americanizing the Mexican succeeded only in alienating most of the second generation Mexican American youth from their heritage while failing to incorporate the immigrants into the Caucasian mainstream.[4] The role of family life in sustaining the cultural integrity of Mexicans, which prevailed in pre-World War II times in Los Angeles, was instrumental in the group's ability to survive the general and hostile anti-Mexicanism of the era.

Most studies of family life among native-born Mexican Americans and Mexican immigrants have focused on the migrant sector. The Mexican American has only received slight attention from scholars who characteristically lumped the two groups together. To some extent the two had similar life experiences in Los Angeles before the Second World War since they shared the same residences. Demographic realignment, which assisted in the assimilation of Mexican into the Caucasian American mainstream, would not become evident until after 1945. Consequently, the cultural dimension of family life for both groups through World War II retained a more compatible quality than one perceives today. The barrio was home for both groups.

Their common experiences noticeably intensified in the 1910s with the increase of immigrants into downtown Los Angeles. Subsequently, the city's original Sonoratown and Plaza district barrios became overcrowded. As the influx continued over the next decade, the Plaza district's numbers swelled to 50,000 residents— some forty percent of the city's total Mexican and Mexican American population.[5] This overcrowding stimulated the first of several exoduses as the newcomers were forced to relocate. Soon, many began moving eastward across the Los Angeles river, while others followed the railroad tracks southward toward Watts and adjacent communities. Some families even moved into the eastern San Fernando Valley. For many Mexicans, the new barrios they established generally signaled the first opportunity they had to live in an urban setting because the majority of them came from rural sections of Mexico.[6] Their unsophisticated appearance stemmed from the hardships of life in their homeland. Mainly impoverished and illiterate upon arrival in Los Angeles, they lacked the social refinements considered essential to sophisticated city dwellers. Tragically the immigrant's lowly class status created social tensions between themselves and Mexican Americans.

To the native-born the immigrant did not appear sophisticated enough to be accepted as a social equal. To emphasize their case, some Mexican Americans began characterizing these immigrants as *cholos* (low class), *chuntaros* (stupid), *zurumatos* (dumb), or in other equally demeaning terms. In self-defense, the Mexicans considered their United States-born counterparts aliens to their own heritage, and labelled them *pochos* (faded Mexicans).[7] How extensive this practice of name calling became in Los Angeles never has been fully examined, but similar friction prevailed in other pre-World War II southwestern communities.

Despite these socioeconomic class conflicts, the two groups typically intermingled freely in the barrios. As still traditional ethnics, their cultural clannishness enhanced barrio life and afforded both the opportunity more often to celebrate their common ties and heritage than to engage in verbal abuse. Both spoke Spanish as their primary language and identified with their Mexican Catholic faith and customs. Immigrants and the native-born unanimously upheld the importance and integrity of family life. Furthermore, in the 1920s and 1930s intermarriage between the two groups took place at a greater rate than with non-Mexicans.[8] These statistics emphasize the extent of cultural solidarity that barrio life gave to its residents regardless of birthplace. Marital bonds strengthened and unified barrio communities in Los Angeles in spite of the poverty, squalor, and political isolation of these enclaves.

The economic improverishment of early twentieth century barrios did not escape the notice of local officials. Mexican families inhabiting the downtown plaza area in the first fifteen years of the century lived in overcrowded, slum conditions. The one and two-room shacks (called *jacales* in Spanish) were without adequate running water, heating or lighting. A number of Los Angeles' reform-minded citizens considered these residences to be the city's most disgraceful homes. The Progressives contended that the horrendous living standards of immigrant families were a blemish on the community's reputation.[9] The Los Angeles Housing Commission, founded in 1906 largely to solve this housing crisis, two years later surveyed the extent of the housing shortage. The commission's official report revealed that the Plaza district was indeed an eyesore.

> Here we found filth and squalor on every hand. Miserably constructed houses, made of scrap sheet iron, old bagging and sections of dry goods boxes, were huddled together without any attempt at proper construction or order....The more Mexicans to the lot, the more money for the owner.[10]

The commission also noted that generally most of the sector's families had four or more members living with them in the congested shacks.

The city hesitated for a few years before deciding to condemn and finally demolish these slums. However, in arriving at this decision the housing commissioners were guided less by humanitarian factors than by the business sector's demand for more city land upon which to build commercial buildings since the growing business district was adjacent to the barrio.

Consequently, the displaced residents were dispersed in different directions, but a significant number of them moved east of the Plaza across the Los Angeles River lured there by employment opportunities and inexpensive housing. This relocation resulted in the creation of one of the largest brown communities of Los Angeles. By the end of the 1920s the community of Belvedere numbered in excess of 30,000 residents. Reverend Robert McLean, a Protestant proselytizer working among Mexican immigrants in this era, marvelled at the rapid development of Belvedere:

> Just outside the city limits a real estate company secured possession of some rolling acres which had formerly been used as pasture land for a dairy. This was divided into fifty-foot lots, and sold out to the Mexicans on small payments. There were no sewers, no sidewalks, no playgrounds; and the only restriction as to the number of houses which could be built upon a single lot was the size of the lot. In a few short months a miraculous change took place. Mexicans bought property, lost it through the failure to make payments, and then bought again. They built their houses out of second-hand lumber—"*jacales*" they call them—and in some cases roofed them over with tin cut from Standard oil cans. Two, four, five, and sometimes six little shacks were built on a single lot.

It seemed as if all Mexico were moving to Belvedere. A public school which was opened with a few hundred in less than five years. Everywhere there were the usual evidences of overcrowding and inadequate housing, for the families were not only large, but were augmented by the aunts and uncles and cousins coming from Mexico who, with ready hospitality were entertained until they could build for themselves.[11]

Other Southern California barrios experienced similar phases of growth and development much as Belvedere.

The growth of these pocket settlements, like Chavez Ravine, resembled Belvedere in character. According to Carey McWilliams, another observant local analyst of the pre-war era, in Chavez Ravine which was located in the hills between Elysian Park and North Broadway, "shacks cling precariously to the hillsides and are bunched in clusters in the bottom of the ravine." McWilliams noted that the city generally neglected this area and offered the ravine's residents little or no municipal services.

At various points in the ravine, one can still see large boards on which are tacked the rural mail-boxes of the residents—as though they were living, not in the heart of a great city, but in some small rural village in the Southwest. Goats, staked out on picket lines, can be seen on the hillsides; and most of the homes have chicken pens and fences. The streets are unpaved; really trails packed hard by years of travel. Garbage is usually collected from a central point, when it is collected, and the service is not equal to that which can be obtained in Anglo districts bordering the ravine. The houses are old shacks, unpainted and weatherbeaten.[12]

Yet in spite of the isolated and neglected condition of these barrios, newly arrived immigrants in the 1920s marvelled about city life. For this reason, they bestowed the nickname of *Maravilla* (wonderful) on the cow pasture of Belvedere.[13] This influx to alluring Los Angeles tripled the size of the eastside settlements and gained for the city by 1930 the title of "Mexican capital of the United States."[14]

In the evolving social and cultural milieu of these barrios, immigrants succumbed to the tragic consequences of their impoverishment. Illness and disease plagued them incessantly since they resided in areas with as inadequate facilities as those in the older downtown slums. In due time, Los Angeles county health officials became alarmed by the extremely high incidence of communicable disease prevalent among the Mexicans. Respiratory ailments like pneumonia and tuberculosis, influenza and even meningitis swept through the barrios. In the middle of 1920s the local health department reported that one-sixth of all tuberculosis related cases and one-fourth of all such deaths in Los Angeles occurred in the brown community. The children were the most vulnerable. Statistics on infant mortality revealed that two to eight times more Mexican and Mexican American babies died than Caucasian newborn.[15]

Noticebly alarmed, health officials in 1921 launched a campaign to reduce infant mortality rates throughout the county. Within less than ten years, infant fatalities declined by one-half in Southern California, but the rate in the Mexican community still remained one-third higher. At a loss to explain the disparity, local health authorities concluded that the inferior genetic makeup of Mexicans was to blame.[16] The socioeconomic conditions of barrio life for families trapped in the vicious cycle of miserable poverty eluded the officials in their assessments.

Predictably, family sizes suffered because of the high infant mortality rate. Between 1918 and 1927 the average number of children for Mexican and Mexican American couples was 4.3 in Los Angeles. Many families actually had more than four children, but a significant number averaged less than three offsprings. Thus, the impact of infant death on family size is startling since in the 1920s the City's brown populace experienced the highest birthrate of any group.[17]

Male heads of families who sought employment to support their wives and children discovered that widespread job discrimination meant either low status and low paying jobs insufficient to feed their families, or unemployment. Those who found work labored mainly in agriculture, on local railroad lines and in manufacturing plants. In many instances, job opportunities in the urban sector became scarce, forcing the "Mexicans" to leave the city in search of seasonal employment. Emory Bogardus, the distinguished sociologist who researched the status of Mexican immigrants in the 1920s, lamented the deplorable circumstances which uprooted already impoverished families.

30-YEAR CHANGE IN ETHNIC POPULATION

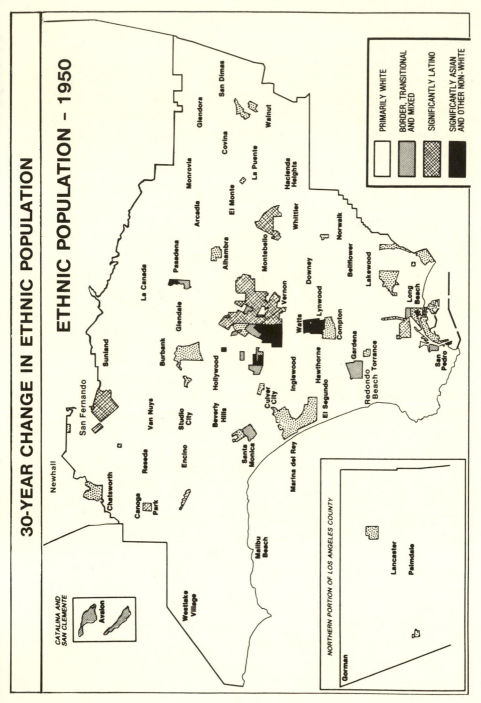

ETHNIC POPULATION – 1950

Legend:
- PRIMARILY WHITE
- BORDER, TRANSITIONAL AND MIXED
- SIGNIFICANTLY LATINO
- SIGNIFICANTLY ASIAN AND OTHER NON-WHITE

CATALINA AND SAN CLEMENTE

Avalon

NORTHERN PORTION OF LOS ANGELES COUNTY

Gorman

Lancaster

Palmdale

Newhall
San Fernando
Chatsworth
Canoga Park
Reseda
Van Nuys
Encino
Studio City
Sunland
Burbank
Glendale
La Canada
Pasadena
Hollywood
Beverly Hills
Santa Monica
Culver City
Marina del Rey
Malibu Beach
Westlake Village
Inglewood
El Segundo
Hawthorne
Redondo Beach
Torrance
Gardena
Vernon
Watts
Lynwood
Compton
Downey
Bellflower
Lakewood
Norwalk
Long Beach
San Pedro
Montebello
Whittier
Alhambra
El Monte
Arcadia
Monrovia
La Puente
Covina
Hacienda Heights
Glendora
San Dimas
Walnut

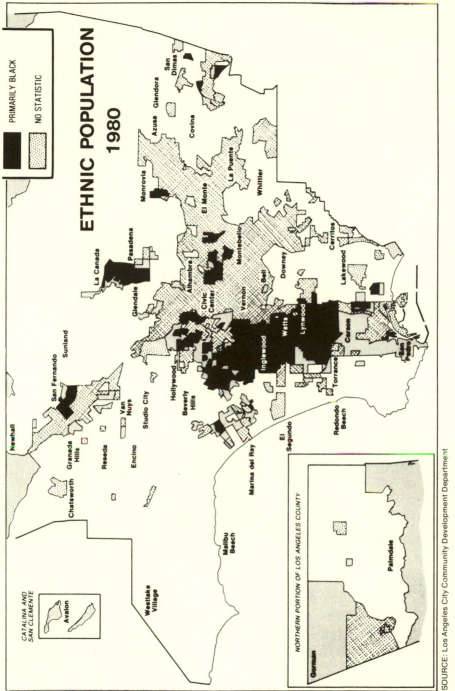

ETHNIC POPULATION 1980

PRIMARILY BLACK

NO STATISTIC

CATALINA AND SAN CLEMENTE

Avalon

NORTHERN PORTION OF LOS ANGELES COUNTY

Westlake Village

Malibu Beach

Marina del Rey

El Segundo

Redondo Beach

Chatsworth

Granada Hills

Reseda

Encino

Newhall

San Fernando

Sunland

Van Nuys

Studio City

Hollywood

Beverly Hills

Torrance

Carson

Lynwood

Inglewood

Watts

Civic Center

Vernon

Bell

Downey

Montebello

Alhambra

Glendale

La Canada

Pasadena

Monrovia

El Monte

La Puente

Whittier

Covina

Azusa

Glendora

San Dimas

Cerritos

Lakewood

Gorman

Palmdale

SOURCE: Los Angeles City Community Development Department

In 1950 the majority of Los Angelenos were white, with Latinos and blacks the only sizable minorities; by 1980, the minorities were approaching the majority.

The Mexican has been a victim of the seasonal labor situation. In order to make a living he has piled his family into "the old Ford" and almost become a transient in seeking out the widely separated seasonal labor fields.[18]

Bogardus also decried the consequence of seasonal employment which aggravated housing patterns. "Migratory labor conditions beget deplorable housing accommodations, and the Mexican and his family have suffered," he observed.[19] Statistics reveal the depth of socioeconomic dispair of families: only six percent of male wage earners were classified as professionals or as skilled laborers.

Out of sheer necessity, Mexican women—mothers, daughters and other relatives—joined the labor force. The women found employment in service related jobs and in manufacturing. In the 1930s the city's garment industry relied extensively on these females.[20] Others found work in the food processing sector which employed "more Mexican women that did any other local industry, including the apparel firms." In Los Angeles County, "88.8 percent of Mexican food processing workers were women."[21] They generally suffered the same job discrimination as Mexican males endured and frequently were "assigned the least skilled and most routine tasks, such as packing lemons or washing peaches."[22]

Confined to low status employment and equally low wages, most Mexican and Mexican American families could not improve their standard of living. In the 1930s Bogardus surmised that even if the Mexican immigrant became a citizen, improved his skills and salary and sought to enhance his life in Los Angeles, he would be rebuffed. According to Bogardus, when the immigrant selected a home in a better neighborhood, the "neighbors...opposed...him" and "threaten him if he moves in."[23]

Struggling to survive, the immigrant family's adjustment to life in the United States also was hampered by the rise of a nationwide neo-nativist and anti-Mexican campaign—a campaign that increased in momentum after World War I. The reactionary posture of racial supremacists toward Mexicans gave local impetus to the notion that the United States had a serious "Mexican problem." Staunch nativists depicted the issue in simple economic terms—immigrants took jobs from citizens. However, the real issue was more profound. Social Darwinists considered the Mexicans racially and culturally inferior to Caucasians and thus unassimilable. One social commentator who considered all Mexicans to be peons described them as "among the most unassimilable of all immigrants." The nativist's greatest fear was articulated in racial terms as the xenophobics underscored their aversion to miscegenation or racial fusion. "Ultimately his descendants will be our descendants, and 'gringo' and 'greaser' will be one," argued one nativist.[24] Others feared that uncontrolled immigration from Mexico would ultimately lead to a general disintegration of the more superior "American way of life." Even Reverend Robert McLean, who worked among the Mexican people, theorized that they posed a major challenge to the W.A.S.P.—White, Anglo-Saxon, Protestant—ethos because their culture was based on an Indian racial, and Roman Catholic, value system. McLean cautioned that the Mexican way of life, as imported by immigrant families, had the potential to destroy the country's culture. He explained the crisis in the following colorful manner:

> Fifty and one hundred years ago Uncle Sam accomplished some remarkable digestive feats. Gastronomically he was a marvel. He was not particularly choosy! Dark meat from the borders of the Mediterranean, or light meat from the Baltic, equally suited him, for promptly he was able to assimilate both, turning them into bone of his bone, and flesh of his flesh—But this *chili con carne*! Always it seems to give Uncle Samuel the heartburn; and the older he gets, the less he seems to be able to assimilate. Indeed, it is a question whether *chili* is not a condiment to be taken in small quantities rather than a regular article of diet. And upon this conviction ought to stand all the law and prophets so far as the Mexican immigrant is concerned.[25]

In other words, the assimilation of the distinctive Mexican would not resolve the "Mexican problem."

Yet other southland nativists in the twenties claimed, almost hysterically, that Mexicans were "diseased of body, subnormal intellectually and moral morons of the most hopeless type."[26] Conversely, few sympathetic assessments of Mexican cultural traits appeared in print. Reverend Vernon McCombs, a contemporary of McLean's, took exception to the popular commentary. McCombs praised the spiritual depth of Mexican character when he remarked that they were "self-forgetful and generous beyond all measure—or even common cause. They share their last crust [of bread] with each other. Sacrifices of life itself are not uncommon."[27]

Unfortunately, the content of their character mattered very little to critics who were more concerned with the burden immigrants placed on the local economy.

Widespread discrimination increased in these years and impeded the immigrant's struggle for dignified treatment. Extensive segregation practices in many southland areas resurfaced as recreational facilities, business establishments, schools and even churches were guilty of anti-Mexicanism.[28] Ironically, Protestant groups who eagerly sought converts failed to convince Mexicans that American Christianity was color blind. Protestant churches in greater Los Angeles reportedly engaged in segregation by denying their brown membership the right to worship alongside Caucasian co-religionists.[29] Discriminatory treatment created serious barriers for immigrants seeking to adjust to life in the United States.

For the family, the greatest challenge concerned their cultural survival. In general, the Mexican immigrants perceived Caucasian Americans as members of a society with a pronounced secular, materialistic and individualized values. In turn, Caucasians generally viewed Mexican culture in an equally narrow light. The earliest sociological and anthropological studies on Mexican family life depicted it as monolithic and patriarchal. To the avid nativist, the Mexican family's sole function centered on "excessive breeding." During the peak years of the restrictionist crusade to halt the free flow of Mexican immigration, supporters of closing the border vehemently argued that Mexicans, because of their prolific fecundity would eventually outnumber the nation's white population if immigration continued unchecked by legislation.[30]

The nativist's emotionally charged impressions of Mexican culture heightened the already volatile climate. They failed, however, to realistically assess the actual nature of the immigrant's lowly condition. In the first place, many Mexicans came from rural regions with deeply rooted cultural traditions and provincial attitudes. Second, these rural areas represented pre-industrial and staunchly patriarchal communities where the family lacked the more secular, material or individualized features found commonly in industrialized societies.

Ignoring these circumstances, nativists in the 1920s continued to clamor for restrictionist legislation. Disappointed when Congress failed to enact laws to stop Mexican immigration, they were delighted when the depression reopened the issue and appeared to offer a solution to the "Mexican problem." In 1931, a national repatriation campaign was launched by the federal government to deport Mexican nationals living in the United States without proper credentials. By decade's end, when the campaign had subsided, one-third of the officially listed Mexican population of the United States had been deported.

In Los Angeles during 1931 federal and local agencies quickly began conducting raids of public places and private residences. The government willingly sponsored the shipment south of many of the deportees. But other families, fearing they would never be allowed to remain in the area, left of their own volition. In the city's barrios, the Mexican Consulate and other community organizations offered assistance to those families whose sudden dislocation interrupted their efforts to join the American society. They provided both official and moral support for the repatriates in an effort to minimize the trauma of readjustment to life in Mexico.

Many of the repatriated Mexicans had been longtime residents of Southern California with children accustomed to life in the United States. Other children were born in this country and had never visited Mexico. In the course of repatriation, an unknown number of families experienced painful separations when youngsters remained in the care of relatives who escaped deportation. In other instances, the children accompanied their parents to a land they considered a foreign country.[31] According to the Mexican Consulate, who organized some of the U.S. government's sponsored repatriation efforts, "the majority of the men were quiet and pensive," while the women and children "cried on the journey south to the border." The experience of the repatriated families was indeed traumatic.[32] Even though the repatriation campaign diminished after the mid-1930s Mexican nationals and Mexican Americans understandably were bitter for a longtime afterwards because they had been singled out for deportation. Nonetheless, the remaining brown populace overcame the depression's trauma in large part due to the group's instincts for cultural survival.

Longtime immigrant residents in Los Angeles concluded that American family life, which included the belief that a greater degree of individuality, freedom and independence, was to be preferred. Customarily, Mexican culture placed greater value on family solidarity, good manners and respect for parents. Retention of these traits posed dilemmas for Mexican immigrant parents since many of their adolescent offsprings favored the more relaxed urban social environment of Los Angeles. Parents who responded by reasserting their parental authority soon found a clash of cultures within their families.

In the 1920s and 1930s Bogardus studied the culture conflict experienced by immigrant and native born families, and recorded numerous comments made by Mexican parents. He particularly noted that Mexican mothers agonized over the affects of the social freedoms on their daughters. One mother interviewed by the sociologist lamented that she could "never get used to it...the freedom which our women enjoy. She cannot understand how women can go unaccompanied on the street, or how they can go about to and from their homes and their work alone." The woman added:

> It is because they can run around so much and be so free, that our Mexican girls do not know how to act. So many girls run away and get married. This terrible freedom in this United States. The Mexican girls seeing American girls with freedom, they want it too, so they go where they like. They do not mind their parents; this terrible freedom. But what can Mexican mothers do? It is the custom, and we cannot change it, but it is bad. I do not have to worry because I have no daughters, but the poor *senoras* with many girls, they worry. I only had three sons; they are gone now, they have been dead many years.[33]

Parents limited their childrens' freedom through curfews in an attempt to protect them from discrimination, which as heads of households, they frequently experienced. Some parents believed that reinvigorating the custom of chaperoning young females seemed to be a reasonable way to handle the problems posed by urban living. Elena Torres de Acosta, an immigrant from Guadalajara, Jalisco, recalled that in the 1920s she never went out alone in Los Angeles. "I always went out with the lady [her landlord] or with her daughters."[34]

style—they felt their parents "old fashioned" and not "liberal" like "Americans". Consequently, joining the work force not only supplemented a family's income, but also afforded young women the opportunity to purchase tickets to local movie houses or other luxuries they never knew in Mexico, such as cosmetics and the latest in dress fashions. In extreme cases, employment served as a ticket out of their parent's home. Generational parent-daughter conflicts even prompted a few to declare that they would never marry a Mexican man. But judging from the statistics on racial intermarriage in Los Angeles during the 1920s and 1930s, these emotional threats never amounted to much. Many wed at a young age, but they married men with similar cultural ancestry. For most of them, disobedience or defiance was unthinkable since the family remained more important to them than individual desires.

But the fears of Mexican parents were not totally unfounded. In the course of his field work, Bogardus interviewed women who lamented that excessive independence in the United States led to the disintegration family life. One Mexican mother observed the process first hand.

> The thing that shocked me most about the United States was the lack of solidarity in the home. The American children do not have much regard for their parents. I was renting in an American home where there were four daughters from nine to sixteen years of age and every one of them was out until three o'clock at night. Their parents had no control over them. In Mexico I had to be in at eight o'clock with my father and mother. But here it is different. Of course it makes for individuality and independence. They learn to think for themselves, but experiences teach wonderful lessons, and they refuse to use or accept the lesson which the broader experiences of their parents have taught them. The freedom and independence in this country bring the children into conflict with their parents. They learn nicer ways, learn about the outside world, learn how to speak English, and then they become ashamed of their parents who brought them up here that they might have better advantages.[35]

The majority of Mexican parents held similar views of Anglo-American behavior and family life. Understandably, the majority of immigrants rejected these customs in favor of retaining their own.

Elisa Silva, another transplanted Angelino, put it succinctly: "Of the customs of this country I only like the ones about work. The others aren't anything compared to those of Mexico." Silva felt

Elisa Silva, another transplanted Angelino, put it succinctly: "Of the customs of this country I only like the ones about work. The others aren't anything compared to those of Mexico." Silva felt that people were kinder in Mexico than in the United States, and "less ambitious about money."[36] Another immigrant, Fernando Sanchez, supported this sentiment. "I follow my Mexican customs and I won't change them for anything in the world. I haven't let my sisters cut their hair or go around like the girls here with all kinds of boys and I have also accustomed my sons to respect me in every way."[37]

As attractive as the more liberal social mores and customs of the United States were to the adolescents, the solidarity of the family was never seriously jeopardized. Barrio life revolved around family oriented activities such as religious fiestas, patriotic Mexican celebrations or even community beauty contests. Parents encouraged children to participate in these events which included Cinco de Mayo, Mexican Independence (September 16th) and the feast of the Virgin of Guadalupe. The latter event received official sanction as an archdiocesan sponsored procession in 1928 when Bishop John Cantwell agreed to review the parade and officiate at the benediction service.[38]

In spite of the disapproval immigrants demonstrated towards the secular and individualized dimension of Anglo-American culture, they nonetheless gave wholehearted support to the principal of education. In the 1920s Mexican and Mexican American children accounted for 17.1 percent of the total elementary school enrollment in the city and 13.15 percent of the county total.[39] More than eighty percent of these youngsters attended segregated schools which were popularly called "Mexican schools." These schools scarcely provided the sons and daughters of immigrants the same educational opportunities that Caucasian youngsters received in the more affluent communities.

Educators rationalized that school segregation practices were essential for providing more effective learning assistance to Spanish speaking children who needed to master English. Other more outspoken officials even went so far as to suggest that segregation was crucial to the safety of the larger student body of the city because of the "Mexican temperament, the high percentage of

Genuine sympathy and motivation for educating immigrants on a fair and equal level was supported by only a small minority Caucasians. Social workers and clergymen generally backed an Americanization program of instruction as the means of integrating Mexican children into the dominant society. As a rule, however, Americanization schools concentrated on vocational training and English language instruction. In the chauvinistic and ethnocentric educational climate of the 1920s and 1930s, few educators supported a curriculum aimed at preparing these youngsters for a college education. Without a professional base upon which to build community leadership, second generation Mexican Americans had little hope for a better life in this society.[41] Educational sentiments of this type persisted into the 1940s. The Superintendent of Schools for Los Angeles County in 1943 charged that secondary school principals supported the practice which denied children of Mexican ancestry the opportunity to enter the tenth grade.[42]

The consequences of the decade old program of instruction which deemphasized and assailed the Mexican's heritage traumatized many children to the point that they left school before reaching the senior high level. In Los Angeles schools, punishment for speaking Spanish on school grounds, callous reidentification of children with Anglo sounding names, omission in class studies of positive Mexican role models and ignoring the historical contributions of Mexicans to North American history created considerable cultural conflict and disillusionment for brown children. Superintendent C. C. Trillingham's 1943 observations on the state of local education, as it related to the brown youngsters confirmed that these classroom practices seriously impeded any opportunity they might ever have for success and mobility in the mainstream society. Trillingham proposed a corrective solution. The superintendent's "good neighbor policy," as he called it, was a master plan to introduce a culturally pluralistic curriculum into Los Angeles classrooms. The "good neighbor" approach which included community involvement was a forerunner of today's city school district bilingual-bicultural programs.[43]

The well-intentioned superintendent was astute enough to conclude that a culturally sensitive educational policy would serve as a deterrent to culture conflict. For too long, Mexican American

The well-intentioned superintendent was astute enough to conclude that a culturally sensitive educational policy would serve as a deterrent to culture conflict. For too long, Mexican American children eager to master the skills necessary for success in American society had discovered that the secular, material and individualized focus of the American way of life depreciated their culture by demeaning their heritage of service and devotion to family, community and religious convictions.

During these years, many teachers were insensitive to the culturally pluralistic needs of immigrant youth. These educators had failed to strike a meaningful balance when evaluating the two contrasting cultural systems. For most adolescents, leaving school prematurely was the only way to avoid the unsettling affects of alienation that psychologically and culturally demoralized other non-whites. The majority "dropped out" of school before permanent emotional anguish undermined their sense of self-worth. By World War II, most brown kids had come to accept the futility of seeking a high school education in the hostile and indifferent environment of the Los Angeles educational system.[44]

For a minority of the adolescents, lowered self-esteem, distorted self-images and generalized insecurity produced a major crisis of identity. While the alienated second generation adolescent lost touch with his heritage, he also realized that Caucasian society rejected him because he was "Mexican." In response to their dilemma, these adolescents created their own distinctive but nonetheless subcultural lifestyle. Their deviation from the general cultural values of their parents peaked by World War II when they became known locally as Pachucos.

Their mannerisms, tough demeanor, flashy zoot suits and peculiar argot (called *calo*) easily distinguished them in the barrios where they continued to live. In their search for new role models to emulate, these Pachucos and their female admirers adopted the fictional villans of the cinema like Humphrey Bogart, James Cagney and the "Dead-End Kids" as surrogate examples of defiance. And as they linked up with other disoriented adolescents, the Pachucos organized the first major gangs in the emerging new bicultural Chicano experience which fully matured after World War II.[45]

Most families, however, were not burdened with marginal behavior and antics among their children so they did not share in the personal bewilderment of the few parents whose offspring had become alienated from their roots. Statistically, only a small percentange of Mexican American youth joined these neighborhood gangs in Los Angeles.[46] Yet concerned experts believed that this minority segment in the barrios could be assisted—in containing the confusing and demoralizing affects of cultural alienation— through social service assistance to the parents of gang affiliated youngsters. Bogardus, for one, believed that minimizing cultural conflict aided successful assimilation of first generation United States born children.

> Too many of these parent are at a loss to know how to help their children to make adjustments as bicultural human beings. The trained welfare worker is needed to carry into the homes of Mexican-American children a scientific knowledge of parent-child relations, especially where two cultures are in contrast and in conflict. Social workers need a training, which most do not have, whereby they can interpret the immigrant parents' culture to the children, and also the parents' problems in our country to the children. The youth also need greatly the skillful assistance of the social worker who is trained in the social psychology of leadership and who thereby can help immigrant children to see and to assume their responsibilities in helping their parents to become culturally assimilated. Thousands of homes need the social worker who is versed in the nature and methods of cultural assimilation.[47]

Unfortunately, few agencies cared enough to respond to Bogardus' challenge. Instead, the hostile resurgence of the earlier prewar "Mexican problem" flared anew in Los Angeles during the war, culminating in the race riots of June 1943. Locally, these outbursts were called the Pachuco or Zoot Suit Riots. In the later official assessment of the vigilantism by local servicemen on the brown community during the riots, few analysts understood the depths of frustration and resentment Mexican and Mexican American families felt at this injustice. After all, far more of their sons heroically served their country than drifted into a life of juvenile delinquency. Real progress in overcoming the traditional chauvinistic Caucasian image of the Mexican family structure had not yet been realized. But the successful outcome of World War II ameliorated some of the ill will as one era drew to a close and another more distinctive bicultural one was about to begin.

Many scholars consider World War II a watershed in the Chicano experience in the City of Angels. The creation of a new and permanent bicultural synthesis in the years after 1945 was to be directed by the sons and daughters of the immigrants.

The war had redirected the course of family life although its traditional cultural clannishness still influenced barrio residents. But no longer would the barrio remain as insular as it had in the years before World War II. In that prewar period, racial and ethnic pride, Spanish linguistic solidarity and community social involvement were hallmarks of the family's place in these enclaves. By war's end, greater social mobility and bilingual skill among children, together with fascination with Anglo-American food, fads, fashion and film heroes, governed the new interests of the young. Consequently, when immigrant children reached maturity, wed and started their own families, they succumbed more readily to the fast paced life of the technologicaly prosperous post war decades.

Social and economic mobility seemed for the first time within reach of many families. Returning World War II veterans who aspired to realize the "American dream" for their own children led the first significant exodus of Mexican Americans out of the Los Angeles barrios. Their parents, though, generally remained behind in the older enclaves, a testimony to the earlier struggle for cultural and socioeconomic survival in pre-World War II Los Angeles.

NOTES

1   Mark Reisler, *By the Sweat of Their Brow, Mexican Immigrant Labor in the United States, 1900-1940* (Westport, CT: Greenwood, 1976) 25.

2   Ricardo Romo, *East Los Angeles, History of a Barrio* (Austin: University of Texas Press, 1983), 59.

3   Ibid., p. 54.

4   For an effective study of the national climate of the 1920s and the rise of anti-Mexicanism, see Reisler, pp. 151-183.

5   Alberto Camarillo, *Chicanos in a Changing Society, From Mexican Pueblos to American Barrios in Santa Barbara and Southern California, 1848-1930* (Cambridge, MA.: Harvard University Press, 1979), 205.

6   Manuel Gamio, *Mexican Immigration to the United States, A Study of Human Migration and Adjustment* (New York: Dover, 1971), 13-23: Romo, pp. 33-40.

7   Gamio, p. 129; E.C. Orozco, *Republican Protestantism in Aztlan* (Glendale, CA: Petereins, 1980), 242.

8   Constantine Panunzio, "Intermarriage in Los Angeles, 1924-1933," *Journal of Sociology* 47 (March 1942): 692.

9   Romo, p. 9.

10 Camarillo, p. 203.

11 Robert McLean, *That Mexican! As He Really Is, North and South of the Rio Grande* (New York: Fleming H. Revell, 1928), 146-147.

12 Carey McWilliams, *North From Mexico: The Spanish-Speaking People of the United States* (New York: Greenwood, 1968), 224.

13 Ibid.

14 Antonio Rios-Bustamante and Pedro Castillo, *An Illustrated History of Mexican Los Angeles, 1781-1985* (Los Angeles: Chicano Studies Research Center, University of California, Los Angeles, 1986), 130. The county of Los Angeles identified 167,000 Mexican and Mexican American residents.

15 "Health, Relief, and Delinquency Conditions among the Mexicans of California," in Manuel P. Servin, ed. *An Awakened Minority: The Mexican Americans* 2nd ed. (Beverly Hills: Glencoe Press, 1974), 72.

16 Ibid., p. 73.

17 Ibid., p. 70.

18 Emory Bogardus, "Current Problems of Mexican Immigrants," *Sociology and Social Research* 25 (1940): 170.

19 Ibid.

20 Rosalinda M. Gonzalez, "Chicanas and Mexican Immigrant Families, 1920-1940: Women's Subordination and Family Exploitation," in Lois Scharf and Joan M. Jensen, eds., *Decades of Discontent: The Women's Movement, 1920-1940* (Westport, CT: Greenwood, 1983), 70.

21 Vicki L. Ruiz, *Cannery Women, Cannery Lives: Mexican Women, Unionization, and the California Food Processing Industry, 1930-1950* (Albuquerque: University of New Mexico Press, 1987), 14.

22 Ibid., p. 168.

23 Bogardus, p. 168.

24 Glenn E. Hoover, "Our Mexican Immigrants," *Foreign Affairs* (1929): 103-104.

25 McLean, pp. 162-163.

26 Reisler, p. 161.

27 Vernon McCombs, *From Over the Border, A Study of the Mexicans in the United States* (New York: Council of Women for Home Missions and Missionary Education Movement, 1925), 61.

28 Beatrice Griffith, *American Me* (Westport, CT: Greenwood, 1973), pp. 191-192; John D. Weaver, *Los Angeles: The Enormous Village, 1781-1981* (Santa Barbara; CA: Capra Press, 1980), 119.

29 Griffith, pp. 191-192.

30 Reisler, pp. 155, 157.

31 Abraham Hoffman, *Unwanted Mexican Americans in the Great Depression: Repartriation Pressure, 1929-1939* (Tucson: University of Arizona Press, 1974), 146.

32 Francisco Balderrama, *In Defense of La Raza: The Los Angeles Mexican Consulate and the Mexican Community, 1929 to 1936* (Tucson: University of Arizona Press, 1982), 28.

33 Emory S. Bogardus, *The Mexican Immigrant in the United States* (New York: Arno, 1970), 28.

34 Manuel Gamio, *The Life Story of the Mexican Immigrant: Autobiographical Documents* (New York: Dover, 1971), 239.

35 Bogardus, p. 29.

36 Gamio, p. 161.

37 Ibid., p. 68.

38 Balderrama, p. 77.

39 Ibid., p. 55.

40 Ibid., p. 56.

41 Edward McDonagh, "Status Levels of Mexicans," *Sociology and Social Research* 33 (1949): 343.

42 C.C. Trillingham and Marie M. Hughes, "A Good Neighbor Policy for Los Angeles County," *California Journal of Secondary Education* 18 (1943): 343.

43 Ibid., 343-346.

44 Emory S. Bogardus, "Gangs of Mexican American Youth," *Sociology and Social Research* 28 (1943): 61.

45 Bogardus, pp. 53-58, 61.

46 McDonagh, p. 451.

47 Bogardus, p. 65.

Chapter 3

ASIAN-PACIFIC ANGELINOS: MODEL MINORITIES AND INDISPENSABLE SCAPEGOATS

Donald Teruo Hata, Jr. and *Nadine Ishitani Hata*

Since the end of World War II, an increasingly broad range of Asian and Pacific immigrants has replicated, if not replaced, the older Chinese and Japanese American sections of the inner city. The complexity of the city's Asian and Pacific communities has been enriched by the influx of new immigrants. Inaccurately counted in the 1980 U.S. census but clearly discernible in the Los Angeles-Long Beach metropolitan area are a richly diverse representation of peoples from the three distinctive cultural regions of Asia: East Asia, dominated by the influence of Chinese culture; South Asia, with its cultural legacy from India; Southeast Asia, the confluence of both traditional Chinese and Indian culture; and the Pacific Basin.[1]

The old stereotypical definition of Asian Americans ("Orientals") as limited only to Chinese and Japanese no longer describes the rich diversity of subcultures inherent in these new and old Americans from across the Pacific. The terms "Asian" and "Asian American" and "Asian-Pacific American" have replaced "Orient" and "Oriental American" as geographically more objective and less laden with the latter's connotation of nineteenth century Western imperialism and colonial exploitation.

Fundamental changes in federal immigration policies after World War II had a dramatic impact on Asian and Pacific Americans. The federal exclusionary laws were relaxed for the Chinese in 1943 and for the Japanese by 1952. In California, the

State Supreme Court declared the state's alien laws unconstitutional and in violation of the due process and equal protection clauses of the Fourteenth Amendment (*Fuji* v. *State*, 1952). In 1943, China was a key U.S. ally in the midst of the vast war against totalitarianism; thus propaganda, if not humanitarian purposes, led to a token relaxation for the Chinese. In 1952 the Walter-McCarran Act, (Immigration and Nationality Act), relaxed the rigid restrictions of the 1924 National Origins Act. The 1952 law provided that all races were eligible for naturalization and citizenship. Quotas were still maintained and remained significantly discriminatory toward immigrants from Asia and the Pacific.

It was the Immigration and Nationality Act of 1965 which dramatically altered the faces of Asian America, and particularly Angelinos, by expanding all immigration quotas to an annual total of 20,000. Now, irrespective of race or national origin, immigration was placed on a first-come, first-served basis. Twenty years ago, trans-Pacific immigrants constituted a mere six percent of the annual total; today they are 40 percent annually. And in the process, Los Angeles has replaced Angel Island in San Francisco Bay as the Ellis Island of the West Coast. This extraordinary increase, in part, explains the growing anti-Asian backlash and subsequent re-emergence of "Yellow Peril" fears.

Recent population figures and predictions for California and Los Angeles are intriguing. The 1980 census counted 1.3 million Asian and Pacific Islanders in California, or about five percent of the state's total population. By 1985 the total statewide Asian and Pacific Islander population rose to 7.5 percent; by "the turn of the century, Californians of Asian ancestry are predicted to number more than three million, or nearly 11 percent of the total population, making them the state's second largest ethnic minority group behind the Hispanic population."[2] Moreover, others expect the state's total Asian population to double between the year 2000 and 2030, "to comprise nearly 16 percent of the state...more than a five-fold increase in population, a percentage unmatched by any ethnic group in California—including Hispanics."[3] The figures for Los Angeles are no less significant. In 1980, Asians comprised 4.9 percent of L.A.'s total population. Some experts anticipate the percentage to rise to 9.4 percent of the total population by the year 2000, and to 13.6 percent by 2030.[4]

Although the more recent arrivals, unlike the earlier residents of Chinatown and Little Tokyo, are largely dispersed throughout the Greater Los Angeles Basin, clearly identifiable enclaves have emerged in the form of Koreatown in the central city; Samoans and Pacific Islanders in Carson, Wilmington, San Pedro and Long Beach; Thais and Vietnamese in Hollywood; Cambodians in Lakewood and Long Beach; Chinese in Monterey Park, Palos Verdes and San Marino; Japanese in Venice, Sawtelle and West L.A., as well as Montebello, Monterey Park, Gardena and the South Bay; and growing concentrations of Asian Indians and Southeast Asians in the areas where L.A. and Orange counties converge (Cerritos, Westminster and Huntington Beach). Perhaps the smallest of these groups are the fifty Tibetan Americans who live from Santa Monica south to San Diego.[5]

The trans-Pacific newcomers have faced enormous challenges in learning a new language, securing jobs, promotions, adequate housing, and both basic and advanced education. But there is significant evidence that some of the new immigrants and their children are moving rapidly into the mainstream. Many new arrivals continue to play the traditional first generation immigrant game of bending over backwards to be seen and accepted as "two hundred per cent Americans." The overt acculturation and accommodationist survival strategy has, by some accounts, worked well. Asian and Pacific Americans are hailed as exemplary representatives of a "model minority" who "outwhite Whites"[6] as increasing numbers of trans-Pacific Angelinos take their places as elected and appointed public officials, civil servants, judges, television and entertainment personalities, student valedictorians, skilled artisans, and professionals.

While many admirers who marvel at the trans-Pacific immigrants' adoption of the Horatio Alger myth are well-intentioned, they are no less inaccurate than the overt anti-Asian bigots of L.A.'s distant past.

A parade taking place in Chinatown on Marchessault Street about 1900. Like so many photographs of this community, it shows the Celestial "Other" from a distant height, with the outline of the city beyond. Courtesy of the Seaver Center for Western History Research, Natural History Museum of Los Angeles County.

FIRST ARRIVALS: THE CHINESE

There were no Asian and Pacific peoples present among the eleven founding families of Los Angeles in 1781, although there could have been, had a twelfth family of Asians made the trek north from Mexico. Antonio Miranda Rodriguez, originally recruited as one of the Pobladores and described as "Chino" in the census of 1781, might have been the first native of the Philippines in Los Angeles had he not stayed behind to care for a sick daughter.[7]

Less than a century later, the small dusty pueblo took on an Asian dimension with the appearance of Los Angeles' first Chinatown in and adjacent to what is now El Pueblo State Historic Park.[8] One of the earliest public acknowledgments of their presence was on 22 October 1859, when the *Los Angeles Star* reported the arrival of the first Chinese woman.

Responding to the discovery of gold and railroad jobs in the north, large numbers of Chinese came to California in the 1850s. When the State Legislature convened in 1852, an estimated 25,000 Chinese comprised the largest single group of non-naturalized residents in the state. While thousands of Chinese played a major role in the construction of the trans-continental railroad, many others moved south to link Los Angeles by rail to other parts of the state and the nation. This dramatic improvement in transportation was a key factor in stimulating the subsequent development of intensive agriculture and manufacturing. Chinese workers also helped to build the great aqueduct which brought water to the parched basin. And as Chinese railroad and farm workers looked to Chinatown for refuge between seasonal employment, the segregated ethnic enclave attracted an expanding variety of small shops stocked with dry goods and produce, laundries, saloons and restaurants. By the early 1860s Chinese merchants had established themselves along the short block named Calle de Los Negros, later known as Negro or Nigger Alley, near the Garnier Building, along Los Angeles Street. By 1870 one-third of the local Chinese population was concentrated within walking distance of that site. Beginning with the arrival of Chinese during the Gold Rush, California's lawmakers and judges quickly established an anti-Chinese climate which encouraged nativists' demands: In 1854 the California State Supreme Court held that Chinese could not testify against Caucasians in the courts. The next year, an attempt was made to discourage sailing vessels from embarking Chinese by levying a $50 tax on a ship's master, owner or consignee who allowed on board any person "ineligible to become a citizen." In 1858 a law prohibited Chinese from landing "upon the Pacific Coast except when driven by stress of weather." The law warned that "any captain landing such a person was liable to a fine of $400 to $600 or to imprisonment."[9]

By the early 1870s, railroad construction declined. The completion of the trans-continental railroad in 1869 and a depressed labor market found Chinese in direct competition for scarce jobs. In July 1870, the first large scale "anti-Oriental" mass meeting in America took place in San Francisco. The unions accused the Chinese of taking scarce urban and rural jobs away from "native" Americans, and a converging coalition of racist, nativist and xenophobic demands resulted in legislative and mob harassment. A key figure in the statewide outcry was Denis Kearney, who was himself a recently arrived immigrant from Ireland. Instead of settling in the East, where the Irish were at the bottom of the pecking order, he came to California where a new social and economic hierarchy placed the Chinese and other Asians at the bottom.[10]

The Chinese in Los Angeles were not immune to the increasingly hostile atmosphere. In October 1871, for example, a mob invaded L.A.'s Chinatown, killed at least 16 Chinese, looted shops and burned homes, and demonstrated that the anti-Chinese movement was not limited to mere rhetoric.[11]

Politicians at the state and national level responded readily to California's leadership of the anti-Chinese mood. After 1870, the official status of Chinese and other Asian and Pacific peoples in America was that of "aliens ineligible to citizenship." This category was created by the government's exclusionary implementation of the naturalization clause in the Fourteenth Amendment to the U.S. Constitution. Citizenship via the naturalization process was open only to Whites and Africans because they were mentioned in the amendment.[12]

The early Chinese community in Los Angeles was, as elsewhere, overwhelmingly comprised of single males who had come from southern China to the West Coast as sojourners, "birds of passage," seeking jobs. Anti-miscegenation laws deprived them of the opportunity to marry and raise families, and other legislation severely restricted the entry of brides and families from China. Thus among the 2,000 Chinese in Los Angeles at the turn of the century, there were barely 60 families.[13]

During the 1880s, California's Chinese began to leave the northern mining regions in large numbers for the San Joaquin Valley and Los Angeles where opportunities in agriculture beckoned. Los Angeles County's population swelled from 1,169 in 1880 to 4,424 in 1890. In 1880, an astonishing 208 or 88.9 percent of the county's 234 truck gardeners were Chinese. Chinese tenant farmers in Southern California grew primarily vegetables.[14] During the winter of 1878-79, Chinese vegetable peddlers went out on strike for several weeks to protest new restrictive ordinances aimed at regulating their businesses.

Earlier in March 1860, fishermen in Los Angeles found themselves competing with a Chinese company. An estimated one-third of the county's abalone fishermen in the 1870s and 1880s were Chinese. Chinese fishing for shark off the Santa Catalina waters during these same decades had no competitors.[15]

Two-thirds of the 1500 workers on the 6,975 foot San Fernando Tunnel, the longest tunnel west of the Appalachians, were Chinese. Completed by July 1876, the tunnel linked Los Angeles to San Francisco by rail. Later that same decade, Chinese workers followed the Southern Pacific into Arizona, New Mexico, and Texas; in the 1880s, they helped build the California Southern Railway between National City, San Bernardino and Waterman. Later, many remained to operate restaurants, laundries, and other small business establishments.[16]

The early Chinese in Los Angeles, as elsewhere throughout the West, became convenient scapegoats for problems ranging from unemployment to outbreaks of epidemics. Their very success at surviving under adverse conditions and enduring intense and sustained hostility seemed to make them even more of a threat to organized labor and nativist-racist groups.

THE ANTI-CHINESE MOVEMENT

In 1882, Congress enacted the first of several federal laws which prohibited free immigration for 10 years—long enough to stop the flow of adult male sojourner-laborers. A decade later, the movement to renew the 1882 law saw "middle class" proponents discarding union charges that the "Chinese Coolie" or "Oriental" labor threatened Caucasian workers to emphasize the danger to White "racial purity" and "Western civilization."[17] After 1892, the earlier anti-Chinese accusations of unfair labor competition were overshadowed by charges that all "Orientals" were the vanguard of a "Yellow Peril," unsuitable for either future acculturation or racial assimilation.

By 1900, the number of Chinese living in California had dropped to 45,753 from an earlier high of 75,132 in 1880. Many of those who decided to remain in America now moved to such East Coast cities as New York. Moreover, the discriminatory legislation resulted in the Chinese population declining nationwide to 89,863 from 107,488 in 1890.[18]

With the permanent enactment of the federal Chinese Exclusion Law in 1904, the cruel cliché, "you don't have a Chinaman's chance," was at once tragic and true. Although they were largely cut off from the majority society and their ancestral homeland, the Chinese stubbornly stood their ground. Low wages notwithstanding, they managed to save money and established their own lending institutions. A variety of community associations were also organized for mutual support and survival, to arbitrate disputes between members, and to provide social services. The associations were organized around villages and districts, clans and families, benevolent services, businesses and professions, and secret societies.[19]

EARLY KOREANS, ASIAN INDIANS AND PACIFIC ISLANDERS

The labor vacuum caused by Chinese exclusion was partially filled by other Asian and Pacific emigrants, all of whom inherited the image of an unassimilable and unacculturable "Yellow Peril." Although Japanese immigrants were the most numerous and therefore the most visible group, small numbers of other Asian and Pacific peoples began to settle in the Los Angeles area by the turn of the century.

Aside from a few political exiles who came to the United States as early as 1885, there was little Korean emigration until 1903-1905—when some 7,000 laborers moved to Hawaii and another 1,000 arrived in Mexico. In spite of the miserable conditions reported from those areas, far fewer moved to the U.S. mainland. The 2,000 Koreans counted in the 1930 census were concentrated in California, with the majority of those drawn to the Los Angeles area by railroad and agricultural jobs. The first Korean graduate of the University of Southern California, a young man named Shin Heung-Wu, completed his studies in 1910,[20] just as a small Korean community began to form around the Korean United Presbyterian Church on Jefferson Boulevard near the USC campus and about two miles south of today's Koreatown. Pioneer Korean Angelinos included Leo C. Song, who was born in Kumsan in 1894 and arrived in America in 1916. Song first tried rice farming in Sacramento and later moved to L.A. where he established K & S Jobbers, a wholesale fruit and vegetable company which helped popularize the new hybrid nectarine.[21]

Imperial Japan's annexation of their homeland in 1910 created a particularly ironic situation for Los Angeles' Koreans. An active group of political exiles worked out of an office near the USC campus until 1945, organizing support and raising funds for the liberation of Korea from Japan. But Koreans were also the targets of American racists who could not distingish them from Japanese. In 1913 eleven Korean fruit pickers were attacked by "an angry crowd of several hundred white farm workers" in Hemet. "This incident, which was not isolated, was widely reported, ironically enough, only because the crowd of white workers had mistaken the Koreans for Japanese." Insult was added to injury when the Japanese Consul General in Los Angeles intervened on behalf of the Koreans—an offer rejected by the Southern California Korean National Association in a wire to the U.S. Secretary of State.[22] Following the Hemet incident, Los Angeles' Koreans went virtually unnoticed, isolated from other Asian immigrants due to distinctive differences in language, and mistaken for Japanese by anti-Asian exclusionists, until the Korean War (1950-1953) and the 1965 Immigration Act.

Of some 5,800 immigrants who arrived between 1900 and 1911 from the British colony of India, the majority were mainly Sikhs from the Punjab region of the Indian subcontinent, and overwhelmingly male (only 109 were women). Starting in railroad and lumber jobs, they quickly shifted to agriculture and established communities in the interior northern (Sacramento Valley) and southern (Imperial Valley) regions of California. Although Asian Indian women were extremely scarce, a high percentage (80 percent) of marriages took place—usually with women from Mexican and Mexican American migrant labor families.[23] Many Asian Indians supported nationalist movements[24] until 1947, when the subcontinent was dividied into two independent nations, India and Pakistan. Immigration to the U.S. after that date forms a second and distinctively different phase of Asian Indian immigration.

The presence of Pacific Islanders in early twentieth century Los Angeles reflected America's gathering of overseas territories after the Civil War. Justified by jingoists as her "Manifest Destiny," the United States employed cash (Alaska), gunboats (Samoa) and war (Spain, 1898) to make itself the master of an empire which included the Philippines, part of Samoa, Guam, Hawaii, and Alaska. American colonial policy toward the native inhabitants of her overseas possessions soon revealed an all too familiar pattern of ambivalence toward equal rights for people of color, for they were given neither the privileges nor the protections of citizens although they lived under the American flag.[25] Those who left the islands established small enclaves along the West Coast of the United States, including Long Beach, Wilmington and San Pedro. Like the Koreans, they would remain largely unnoticed until after World War II.

THE EARLY JAPANESE AND ASIAN EXCLUSION

The scarcity of cheap labor created by the exclusion of Chinese was largely filled by Japanese emigrants. The majority entered California through San Francisco with only a handful settling in

Los Angeles prior to the turn of the century. The unexpected Japanese victory in the Russo-Japanese War (1904-1905) caused the growing anti-Japanese movement in San Francisco to focus on them as a threat to national security. Labor unions were particularly enraged by the entry of Japanese workers into logging, mining, fishing, canneries, and railroad work. Organized labor regarded them as "scabs" like the Chinese before them. By 1905, delegates from more than 67 labor organizations met in San Francisco to form the Asiatic Exclusion League. They moved quickly in other areas as well. In 1906 the San Francisco School Board bowed to the League's pressure and banned all Japanese and Koreans from attending integrated schools. The devastating San Francisco earthquake of 1906 combined with the intense discrimination in the north led many Japanese emigrants to seek opportunities in Southern California.[26]

Between 1907-1908, six notes were exchanged between the United States and Japan. Under the terms of the so-called Gentlemen's Agreement, Japan "agreed not to issue passports valid for the continental United States" to unskilled and skilled laborers alike. While the agreement lessened tensions between the two powers, it dramatically altered the ratio of females to males in the Japanese American population because the executive agreement allowed passports to "be issued to the 'parents, wives and children of laborers already resident'" in the United States. The once overwhelmingly male population began to reach parity by 1924 due to the thousands of women who came as mail-order or "picture brides."[27]

In the meantime, Los Angeles emerged as the largest concentration of Japanese in the continental United States:

> By 1910 Los Angeles had become the metropolis of Japanese America, and it has remained so except for the years of the wartime evacuation. From a population of about 1,000 in 1900, Japanese in Los Angeles County numbered almost 9,000 in 1910, nearly 20,000 at the next census, and just over 35,000 in 1930.

By 1940, there were 36,866 Japanese in the county; of this number, two-thirds or 23,321 lived in Los Angeles city. In contrast, Seattle had 7,000 in 1940 and San Francisco had 5,000 Japanese Americans.[28] By 1910, as the concentration of shops and residences later known as Little Tokyo rose next to Chinatown, many farm laborers had saved sufficient funds to purchase or lease farming lands for vegetable, berry and flower crops in virtually every suburb around the inner city.[29] In addition to truck farmers from Palos Verdes Peninsula, Gardena, Bellflower, and throughout the San Gabriel and San Fernando valleys, other Japanese emigrants entered the wholesale produce and flower markets and thereby influenced the overall development of agricultural production and distribution in the region, while still others invested in small mom-and-pop entrepreneurships throughout the inner city. Until World War II, however, "agriculture was the foundation of much of the enterprise and prosperity " of the Japanese in Southern California.[30]

As in Little Tokyo where clusters of Japanese immigrants settled for reasons of "economic necessity, white hostility, and ethnic solidarity," other groups of Japanese Americans congregated in "the fishing villages of East San Pedro and Santa Monica, and the farming center of Moneta-Gardena." Typically, in East San Pedro the Japanese discovered a need which was not yet exploited. In 1901, a Japanese fisherman discovered abalone at White's Point in San Pedro. Dried, the abalone could be shipped to Japan, and several young Japanese fishermen moved a shed to White's Point and began to catch and dry abalone. Driven out by hostile neighbors, the entrepreneurs moved to Terminal Island where they soon began to add other species of fish to their catch. Their ability to bargain collectively with White businessmen, in this case cannery owners—an advantage shared by the labor contractors in Little Tokyo—the Japanese who had a clear head start were able to establish themselves as a significant force in the Los Angeles commercial fishing industry.[31]

Moreover, the State Legislature's efforts to pass an anti-alien fishing bill in 1923 were defeated because Japanese fishermen in Los Angeles were well-integrated into the industry and because of "their close relationship to the large American canneries." (In 1920, nativist James D. Phelan "had attacked the Los Angeles Japanese fleet on grounds of illegal registry as well as super-efficiency, maintaining that behind this convincing front the fleet hid its real functions: espionage and the smuggling of Japanese laborers.")[32]

Their economic successes, coupled with Imperial Japan's growing strength in Asia and the Pacific, combined to reinforce xenophobic fears that Japanese emigrants were a "Yellow Peril" to the state's economy and the nation's security. By 1913, the racist-nativist coalition engineered the enactment of the notorious California alien land laws, which banned the sale or lease of land to "aliens ineligible to citizenship." Similar laws were adopted by other Western states.

IMMIGRATION EXCLUSION & THE GREAT DEPRESSION

In 1924, as part of an intensive anti-immigration movement across the nation, Congress passed the National Origins Act which established, for the first time in the history of this nation of immigrants, permanent quotas on immigrants from outside northwestern Europe, and added a special provision for the total exclusion of Japanese. Until 1952, when the law was relaxed, Japanese immigration ceased.

The decade and a half following the 1924 federal immigration law until the eve of World War II saw Los Angeles' various Asian communities left to their own resources as the nation staggered through the Great Depression. Asian and Pacific Angelinos out of necessity established their own separate self-help organizations in the face of the Great Depression and the more "normal" forms of legal, economic and social discrimination experienced by all minorities in Los Angeles and the nation.[33]

Pilipinos (as "Filipinos" often prefer to be known) and Pacific Islanders were the only groups untouched by the 1924 federal immigration law's exclusion of Asians. While few Pacific Islanders settled in California until after World War II, large numbers of Pilipinos began to arrive in the 1920s. Prior to 1920, aside from students, most Pilipinos who migrated to the United States were domestic servants and unskilled workers—many of whom had moved to the West Coast after being first recruited to work on the Hawaiian sugar plantations. The exclusion of Japanese in 1924 created another shortage of cheap labor on the West Coast, and large farming interests saw Pilipinos as an easy replacement. As a result, economic realities saw to it that Pilipinos were exempt from the 1924 law by confirming them as "nationals"[34]—a designation sufficiently vague to permit their recruitment and migration to farming regions throughout California. As seasonal farm workers sought fishing and domestic jobs in the cities, "Little Manila" enclaves were established in Los Angeles and Long Beach, along with larger concentrations in Stockton and San Francisco.

By 1928, however, competition for scarce jobs led to race riots against Pilipino laborers throughout California and the West Coast. While Los Angeles was spared such violence, old timers recall those years with bitterness:

> The lives of Filipinos were cheaper than those of dogs. They were forcibly shoved off the streets when they showed resistance. The sentiment against them was accelerated by the marriage of a Filipino to a girl of the Caucasian race in Pasadena. The case was tried in court and many technicalities were brought in with it to degrade the lineage and character of the Filipino people.[35]

The nativist-racist coalition regarded the Pilipino influx as a "third wave of Oriental immigration" that had to be halted. But the Philippines were American territory, and as a final compromise, it was decided that future Philippine independence would settle the issue. After all, Pilipinos would be citizens of a sovereign foreign nation, and therefore subject to laws against the immigration and settlement of aliens in America. According to Carey McWilliams, "those who sought to bar Filipino immigration suddenly became partisans of Philippine independence."[36]

Unlike other large urban areas, Los Angeles has had not one but three Chinatowns. In 1909, Louie Quan raised $100,000 to build a market of 200 stores. When Union Station was built over his property, two Chinatowns emerged.

L.A.'s Chinatown merchants initiated a public relations campaign to turn around the negative public image of their community. On 25 January 1924, the Chinese Chamber of Commerce published the following resolution in the *Los Angeles Times*:

> Whereas, Chinatown has been made to suffer in the past because of the bad name generally applied to this district, the same being no fault of the Chinese residents, be it resolved:

First, that we, the merchants of Chinatown, use every opportunity to induce white people of the city and tourists to visit Chinatown; that we extend to visitors every courtesy on visiting our shops and places of interest.

Second, that we use every opportunity to spread the word that Chinatown is a safe place for women to come to, whether escorted or alone.

Third, that we use every opportunity to suppress rowdyism among the lower classes of white people visiting Chinatown; that the chop suey houses will see that any rudeness on the part of their guests be stopped and that order be kept if the same is not already being done.

Fourth, that we extend to Los Angeles an invitation to visit Chinatown on the celebration of the New Year and see for themselves the conditions that prevail here.

Ironically, in the midst of the cosmetic image-making, the original site and structures of Chinatown were systematically and deliberately obliterated. The process began in the late 1920s and early 1930s when Chinese residents were evicted from the Plaza area in order to permit a romanticized and commercial reconstruction of Olvera Street. In 1933, the city decided to build a new Union Station of a size and scale to serve as a contemporary metropolitan status symbol. It required the condemnation, evacuation and demolition of all that remained of the original Chinese residences and businesses in the area. But the Chinese business community was resilient. By 1938 they had constructed two complementary projects north of El Pueblo and the new Union Station: New Chinatown and China City. "These two Chinese quarters drew Chinese and non-Chinese alike into an orbit of business, pleasure and residence."[37] A metamorphosis occurred in Chinatown's leadership as merchants assumed control, dominated relations with public officials and the outside community and—with the encouragement of the L.A. Chamber of Commerce—sanitized the district's image from a vice den to an "all American" tourist attraction.[38] A major source of strength for L.A.'s Koreans lay in the strong network of Korean Christian churches which served as centers of political and social cohesion. The churches helped the community to survive the grim Depression decade of the 1930s, while "the Mutual Relief Society became almost insolvent and in 1934 the president of the hard-pressed Korean National Association resigned on account of funding difficulties."[39] On the eve of World

War II, a small but hardy core of Korean entrepreneurs included "thirty fruit and vegetable stands, nine groceries, eight launderies, six trucking companies, five wholesalers, five restaurants, three drug stores, two hat shops, one employment agency, and one rooming house."[40]

The 1920s saw a few Asian faces among the pioneers of the movie industry in Hollywood. Sessue Hayakawa and Anna Mae Wong[41] played leading roles on the silent screen, but they disappeared as the talking picture and images of Anglo supremacy took over the casting and script priorities of Tinseltown. Keye Luke was one of super-sleuth Charlie Chan's numerous offspring, but the role of the erudite Chan was never given to an Asian actor. Unknown to the general public, but increasingly respected by his professional peers was the keen eye of innovative cinema cameraman James Wong Howe. For Korean actor, Philip Ahn, the Depression years were lean: "I ate steamed cabbage for breakfast and potato for supper...all day I wandered looking for a job."[42]

For Japanese Americans, the Thirties was a particularly grim decade. As international tensions heightened between the United States and Imperial Japan over increasingly divergent policies in Asia, Japanese Americans were caught in the middle of a growing question concerning their identity and loyalty as Japanese or Americans. Throughout the 1930s their enemies increasingly called attention to the so-called un-American behavior of Japanese Americans—most of whom were American citizens by birthright. By the 1930s, the immigrant pioneer Issei ("first generation" Japanese in America) had produced a generation of American-born children, the Nisei (literally, "second generation"). However, the persistence of Japanese language and culture schools, the social cohesion provided by a network of Buddhist temples ("un-American" religion according to the Asiatic Exclusion League), and dual citizenship were used as evidence that both Issei and Nisei were consciously resisting acculturation into the mainstream of American society. Imperial Japan's attack, without an official declaration of war, on Pearl Harbor on December 7, 1941, exacerbated their accusations that *all* Japanese in America, irrespective of U.S. citizenship, could not be trusted.

JAPANESE AMERICANS AND WORLD WAR II

On the morning of 7 December 1941, aircraft carriers of the Imperial Japanese Navy launched a devastating attack on American naval and military installations at Pearl Harbor, Hawaii. There had been no prior declaration of war, and President Franklin D. Roosevelt declared it a day "which will live in infamy." Indeed, by the war's end in 1945 the Japanese Empire was destroyed. But for Americans of Japanese ancestry (Nikkei), it was a period of mounting fear and anxiety. For Nikkei, the real "day of infamy" would be 19 February 1942, when President Roosevelt signed Executive Order No. 9066: it authorized and directed "the Secretary of War and Military Commanders whom he may...designate...to prescribe...military areas...from which any or all persons may be excluded...."[43]

In the interval between Pearl Harbor and the President's decision, a climate of hysteria was created by local newspaper headlines and editorials, and radio commentators; and opportunistic businesses and politicians responded accordingly. In an editorial on 16 January, the *Palos Verdes News* complained that "we still have the Japanese farmers here cultivating the land immediately adjoining the ocean and military objectives...the Japanese are everywhere...."[44] Governor Culbert Olson inflamed suspicions about Nikkei loyalty in a broadcast on 4 February: "It is known that there are Japanese residents of California who have sought to aid the Japanese enemy by way of communicating information, or have shown indications of preparation for fifth column activities." On the following day the governor's patently false statements were exceeded by Los Angeles Mayor Fletcher Bowron: "right here in my own city are those who may spring to action at an appointed time in accordance with a prearranged plan wherein each of our little Japanese friends will know his part in the event of any possible invasion or air raid."[45] Some forty Japanese farmed 500 acres east of Point Vicente (known as Rolling Hills) on the Palos Verdes peninsula; on 13 February their leases were abruptly cancelled by the developer, A. E. Hansen.

Contrary to these irresponsible and unfounded charges, Japanese Americans—both citizen and alien—did not commit any acts of sabotage during the war. But even after weeks had passed without evidence of Nikkei disloyalty, Earl Warren—at that time California Attorney General and a gubernatorial candidate, appeared before a committee headed by California Congressman John Tolan on 21 February, and testified that the very *absence* of subversive activity was proof of Japanese American cunning: "I believe that we are just being lulled into a false sense of security and the only reason we haven't had a disaster in California is because it has been timed for a different date....Our day of reckoning is bound to come...." (Warren latter admitted that this was one episode where he was wrong.)   Moreover, said California's chief law enforcement officer, the American-born Nisei posed more of a threat than the alien Issei.[46]

A few days later, the *Los Angeles Times* and other local newspapers carried huge headlines about the "L.A. Air Raid." Shortly after midnight on 25 February, air raid sirens led panic-stricken anti-aircraft gunners to fire more than 1,400 shells into the early morning sky. Buried in the small print was the admission that no enemy planes flew over the city.

With few exceptions, other Asians were either ambivalent or unsympathetic to the plight of Nikkei. Some were fearful that they would be mistaken for Japanese and wore lapel tags that said "I am a loyal Chinese American, not a dirty Jap." A Pilipino boxer made the headlines of the sports page by beating up Japanese Americans on the street. Korean organizations saw little difference between Imperial Japan and Japanese Americans and supported the clamor for removal of all "persons of Japanese ancestry" from the Pacific Coast.

By the spring of 1942 the mass evacuation was well underway, supervised by U.S. Army troops replete with fixed bayonets. Their commander, General John L. DeWitt, declared: "A Jap's a Jap. They are a dangerous element...there is no difference whether he is an American citizen...he is still a Japanese, and you can't change him...."[47] Evacuees were assembled in local racetracks, livestock exposition facilities, and fairgrounds. Between 7 May and 27 October 1942, Santa Anita Racetrack housed 18,719 Nikkei in horse stalls and hastily constructed tarpaper barracks in the parking lot.[48] By early August 1942, the U.S. Army announced that 110,723 persons had beem removed from their homes throughout the West Coast and placed in temporary regional assembly centers while ten permanent camps were being constructed "inland."

It is now known that the evacuation could have stopped short of the subsequent movement to more distant "permanent" camps for the duration of the war. By the end of June 1942, U.S. military intelligence knew that the Battle of Midway had removed any serious threat to Hawaii and the West Coast. (Moreover, in Hawaii where the largest number of Japanese American concentrated, there was no internment inspite of the potential security problems because of the logistics involved.) Thus the autumn of 1942 saw the further mass movement of over 110,000 adults and children into ten U.S. War Relocation Authority concentration camps for the remainder of the war. With the exception of two camps in remote areas of California—Tule Lake near the Oregon border, and Manzanar in the Owens Valley, the camps were far removed from the West Coast: L.A.'s Nikkei were dispersed among all of the camps—Poston and Gila River in Arizona; Rohwer and Jerome in Arkansas; Minidoka, Idaho; Heart Mountain, Wyoming; Granada (Amache), Colorado; and Topaz, Utah. Five families were assigned to each tarpaper barrack; eating and toilet facilities were communal. Camp administrators earned regular salaries, but Nikkei doctors, dentists, teachers and other professionals received token inmate wages of $12-$19 a month. Personal supplies such as sanitary napkins had to be purchased from those meager allowances. Lack of privacy was a pervasive problem; as one former inmate recalled, "we lined up for everything—cheek to cheek, tit to tit, butt to butt."[49]

The evacuation orders were finally rescinded on 2 January 1945. Many Nikkei returned to their homes and found that household possessions had been stolen, while businesses and farms were stripped bare. Moreover, between 1944 and 1952 the returnees lost more land and money through escheat actions which the State Legislature supported by appropriating $200,000 to implement the program. The State encouraged county officials to cooperate by offering them one-third of the price when escheated lands were sold.[50]

Nikkei returnees to the West Coast were destitute and had to find shelter and jobs wherever they were available. In desperation, many families formed communal residences until they could afford their own homes and apartments. There was also the everyday battle to overcome both overt and subtle hostility. Returnees were turned away at markets and real estate offices; local bureaucrats found ways to deny and delay applications for business licences; insurance companies demanded that evacuees forfeit their original policies and begin paying premiums anew at higher rates; and both public and private employers refused to count the incarceration years toward retirement benefits. Threats of physical violence were commonplace. White males jeered and made obscene gestures at female returnees. Shots were fired at residences in the dark of night. Merchants received anonymous bomb threats. For these Americans who had been judged guilty for no other reason than their race, the long awaited homecoming became another chapter in the outrage which had begun in the winter and spring of 1942.[51]

The wartime diaspora "shattered the physical character of the California and Los Angeles area Japanese American community and altered its sense of ethnic cohesion, while strengthening its demonstrated and intense loyalty to the United States."[52] After the war, Little Tokyo would eventually rise again, much like the city's old and new Chinatowns, in the form of a commercial and tourist asset to the economy, and city image-makers' needs for illusions of international ambience.

TO MAINSTREAM MODEL MINORITY

The end of World War II was a turning point in the formerly negative perception of trans-Pacific Americans, as popular images moved from benign tolerance and acceptance to increasing admiration. The postwar shift to a more positive image reflected an easing of fears of a "Yellow Peril" for a variety of reasons. The highly publicized wartime heroism of Japanese Americans in Europe (442nd Regimental Combat Team) quieted questions about their loyalty. The occupation of Japan (1945-1950), and that nation's subsequent emergence as a Cold War ally reduced American fears. Although North Korean and Chinese Communist troops fought U.S. forces to a standsill in Korea (1950-1953), there was widespread sympathy for refugees from the war zone—if not the war itself. Equally important were the large numbers of

U.S. military personnel who served in Occupied Japan (1945-1950) and combat in Korea (1950-1953), and more recently in Vietnam and Southeast Asia. Many of them returned with positive impressions of Asian culture, and with Asian wives. The civil rights movement of the Fifties and the social and sexual upheavals in the Sixties and Seventies also saw a dramatic increase in multicultural outmarriages—particularly between acculturated Asian American women and non-Asian males.

The inexorable flow of inner city residents to suburban bedroom communities after World War II also included Asian Americans. With certain exceptions during the early 1950s, they were welcomed and increasingly dispersed throughout the basin.[53] The extent to which they were part of the suburban mainstream by the 1960s is reflected in the fact that an unprecedented (and largely un-noticed) number of them had been elected or appointed to suburban public offices. Except for Gardena (with Nikkei comprising 15-20 percent of the total population of 50,000) Asian Americans could not count on ethnic bloc voting to win, and the number of successful candidates therefore reflects their acceptance by broad cross sections of their largely moderate to conservative suburban communities.

Gardena voters have elected Nikkei to a number of offices since the 1960s, beginning with city councilman and later mayor Ken Nakaoka, councilman and later state assemblyman Paul Bannai, councilman Mas Fukai—who also serves as chief deputy to L.A. County Supervisor Kenneth Hahn, councilman Vince Okamoto, councilman Paul Tsukahara, city treasurer George Kobayashi, and city clerk May Doi. Torrance elected George Nakano as its first council member. Across the basin in the eastern suburbs, the late 1960s also saw Asians entering the politics of Monterey Park (decades before it became known as "America's first urban Chinatown"): councilman and mayor George Ige, a Japanese American; and Al Song, a Korean American who served as councilman and later two term state assemblyman and state senator. More recently, Chinese Americans have also been active in Monterey Park municipal politics: Mayor Lilly Chen, and mayor pro tem Judy Chu. In the City of Carson, north of the harbor, residents elected first Sak Yamamoto and later Michael Mitoma to the city council, and Helen Kawagoe as city clerk. In nearby Long Beach, Eunice Sato served as city council member and mayor. Tsuji Kato served as multi-term city councilman and mayor of Oxnard. The only Asian American from Southern California to serve in Congress was Dalip Singh Saund, a naturalized Asian Indian, who was first elected to a local judgeship in the Imperial Valley and later (1957) to two terms in Congress.[54] As Asian Americans moved from the inner city to the suburbs, the old Chinatown and Little Tokyo sections near City Hall underwent "urban redevelopment" to transform them into seductive targets for the tourist trade and new corporate skyscrapers. Older residents have been "relocated" as part of the ongoing inner city "gentrification" process, which replaces the aged and the poor with more affluent Yuppie tenants. Chinatown and Little Tokyo survive in official signs pointing to freeway offramps, but soon there will be little left from their original inhabitants. Laundry lines will no longer disturb the view from high-rise condominiums, corporate boardrooms, and upper floor offices of City Hall. Indeed, due to the bulldozer mentality of many urban planners, City Hall is for good reason described by old-timers as "Los Angeles' phallic symbol...sodomizing Chinatown and Little Tokyo in its shadow." An acculturated Asian American professional who now commutes to the central city from a home in an affluent suburb recalled childhood memories near City Hall before the war:

> There's nothing left to remind my well-fed, fashionably dressed, spoiled brat offspring of what it was to live here in the old days, before World War II and urban redevelopment. City Hall bureaucrats and the financial power brokers look down and see progress...lots of new stainless steel and glass skyscrapers
>
> ...No more immigrant old folks sitting in the sun in odd foreign costumes....No more hokey hand-painted storefront signs. The only old structures that are important to the dilettante historical preservation bleeding-hearts are the monuments to the heyday of Anglo autocracy. But I'm not mad. Living well is the best revenge. I got my college degree, got my big car, got my downtown office with plush carpets. I'm part of the new Asian America. I've made it. I'm the model minority.[55]

Koreans comprise one of the fastest growing Asian communities since the passage of the 1965 federal immigration law. Contemporary Koreatown is anchored by Hoover Street on the east, Crenshaw Boulevard to the west, Jefferson Boulevard to the south, and Beverly Boulevard to the north. Like its Chinese and Japanese counterparts, L.A.'s Koreatown is largely a business rather than a residential concentration. A 1983 study of Korean businesses in Los Angeles County found that "Koreans account for less than 1% of the county population but own 2.6% of the businesses," many of them in low-income areas where they are perceived as "unfriendly...and will not hire blacks." Of 4,300 Korean businesses in L.A. County in 1983, "about 40% are small retail stores...such as grocery or clothing stores, dry cleaners, gas stations, liquor stores and restaurants. Another 37%...are service providers, such as doctors or dentists, insurance salesmen or owners of building maintenance and janitorial services." Most Korean residences are scattered throughout the L.A. basin; therefore, the strongest community organization is the network of 430 churches, most of which are Protestant.[56]

In Artesia and neighboring Norwalk, an Asian Indian community has rapidly emerged in the last decade. Unlike the students or professionals of the 1960s and 1970s who came to Southern California to work as doctors, engineers and technicians at corporations such as Bechtel, the late 1970s and 1980s witnessed a second group of immigrants who were primarily the siblings and relatives of the earlier professionals. These newcomers are emerging as a new merchant class servicing both Asian Indian and non-Indian clientele. The businesses include Moni Syal's 1981 Norwalk eatery, which he proclaimed to be the "first Indian fast-food joint in California" serving take-out curried chicken and samosas. Syal moved his operations to larger quarters in Artesia Plaza in 1982 and in 1988, and hoped to build a second Reena Samosa Center in Cerritos. According to Rajen S. Anand, president of the Federation of Indian Associations of Southern California, "Artesia is *the* Indian shopping district" on the West Coast and the small, middle-class suburban city has become "the hub of the Indian community" which he estimated at 35,000 in an area stretching from West Los Angeles to Riverside to Mission Viejo. In the late 1970s, Asian Indian entrepreneurs saw the opportunities available in Artesia's depressed business district on Pioneer Boulevard; leases were cheap and available, and the area was easily accessible to the 12,000 Asian Indians in the surrounding communities. By 1988, some two dozen businesses were owned or managed by Asian Indians, many of whom emigrated from the Bombay area. An Indian Embassy spokesman in Washington said that "only Jackson Heights in Queens and Chicago's Devon Street" have more nativ stores and restaurants." Artesia's Asian Indians, however, have had to cope with growing resentment toward their success. Some local merchants have complained that the large crowds monopolize available parking and leave trash in the parking lots, thereby discouraging customers. Others claim that rents are raised because Asian Indians are willing to pay higher prices, and resent the fact that few Asian Indian merchants join local associations such as the chamber of commerce.[57]

The influence of Asian Indian culture is also highly visible in the recently completed Sree Venkateswara Temple in Malibu Canyon. The Hindu Temple Society of Southern California was formed in 1977 to raise the more than $3 million necessary to complete the 13,000 foot complex which sits on 4.5 acres. The largest Hindu temple built by Asian Indians in the United States, it was designed as a legacy to "future generations of Hindus who maybe would never get the chance to see similar temples. The Indian population was increasing, but we didn't have anywhere to meet. So we decided to build something that could follow in the Hindu tradition."[58]

MODEL MINORITY: MYTH VS. REALITY

During the Sixties and Seventies, as the civil rights movement turned increasingly violent, Japanese and Chinese Americans were hailed as "model minorities" and "quiet Americans" whose posture of self-help and self-effacing accommodation in the face of adversity should be emulated by more outspoken and militant minorities. This backhanded compliment continues to be applied to other trans-Pacific Asians.[59] Samoans are stereotyped as physically formidable but intellectually unimpressive, coveted by high school and college coaches for their prowress on the football field.[60] Tom Wolfe popularized the stereotype of huge Samoans and Pacific

Islanders in this passage from his 1971 nation-wide best-seller, *Radical Chic and Mau-Mauing the Flak Catchers*:

> The Samoans favored the direct approach. They did not fool around. They were like the original unknown terrors. In fact, they were unknown terrors and a half ....The thing you notice is not just that they're big but that they are so big, it's weird. Everything about them is gigantic, even their heads. They'll have a skull the size of a watermelon, with a couple of squinty eyes and a couple of nose holes stuck in, and no neck at all ....You get the feeling that football players come from a whole other species of human, they're so big. Well, that will give you some idea of the Samoans, because they're bigger...they start out at about 300 pounds and from there they just get wider....[61]

This image obscures severe economic and educational problems confronting Samoans and other recent trans-Pacific arrivals. In 1978, the *Los Angeles Times* reported that:

> The Centinela-South Bay has more Samoan residents than American Samoa....There have been no official counts or census taken of the Samoan population and estimates range from 60,000 to 90,000 in California, with at least half that total living in the Los Angeles Basin, primarily the Carson, Gardena, Compton, Wilmington and Harbor City areas....They come seeking better jobs (the average pay in American Samoa is less than $100 a week), education for their children and an improved standard of living.... Because of the language problem and educational disadvantages, they fare poorly on job interviews and examinations. The vast majority hold low-paying positions such as laborers or factory workers and the unemployment rate is high.[62]

The empathetic story emphasized that the application of the monolithic "model minority" stereotype to all Asian and Pacific residents was the cause of increasing frustration.

Indeed, a number of public and private studies have refuted the widely accepted but factually flawed belief that Asians have no problems, and require no public social services because they "suffer silently" and "take care of their own." For example: In 1985, the United Way reported that

> The Korean community here is growing so rapidly that social service agencies are not able to help quickly with such things as jobs and medical care for the newcomers....The fourth-largest Asian group in Los Angeles County grew 700 percent between the 1970 and 1980 census counts—from 8,500 to 60,618 people—and new estimates put the total at 250,000....The demographic study, centered on... Koreatown, found that transplanted Koreans are mostly young, many of them under 39;

with relatively low income levels, 40 percent of them earning less than $12,000 a year.

While city and county social service agencies may have become more aware of the situation, budgetary allocations are insufficient.[63]

The socio-economic characteristics of the recent trans-Pacific arrivals reflect both problems and potential. The newest arrivals include educated professionals from the Philippines, South Korea, India, Pakistan, Hong Kong and Taiwan; but the ignominious American military withdrawal from South Vietnam and Southeast Asia in 1975 created an exodus of entirely new Asians, linguistically and culturally different from the more acculturated Chinese and Japanese communities. Moreover, while the initial wave of refugees from war-torn Vietnam were often well-educated, urban and professional, the vast majority who followed included poor rural Vietnamese, Laotians and Cambodians lacking both basic education and marketable skills for entry-level jobs in the United States.[64] Many Southeast Asians remain isolated from the mainstream and, along with other refugees from Central America, are dependent upon exploitative employers:

> They have survived war, prison, famine, terrifying voyages across pirate-infested seas and long stints in refugee camps. Now, in the land of their dreams, thousands of Vietnamese immigrans spend long days hunched over sewing machines in sweatshops in suburban Orange County. Some earn as little as $1 an hour. Most are glad to get it....At least 400 sewing shops have sprung up in and around Orange County's Little Saigon, employing upward of 5,000 immigrants. In fact, the majority of the shop owners themselves are former boat people who have been in this country less than five years.[65]

A particularly poignant reminder of some things have not changed is the struggle of recent Vietnamese arrivals to enter California's commercial fishing. For example, in 1989 it was reported that:

> CITIZENSHIP LAW ENSNARES VIET FISHERMEN.... A federal judge...allowed the Coast Guard to resume enforcing a 200-year-old citizenship requirement against Vietnamese owners and pilots of commercial fishing boats in U.S. waters.

The Vietnamese Fishermen's Association, a 200-member group based in Oakland, filed an emergency appeal on behalf of the refugees who are in the process of applying for citizenship: "They fish for rockfish and hackfish and insist that they compete very little with the rest of the fishing industry."[66] Los Angeles' Vietnamese fishing fleet of fifteen vessels and 50 crew members is based at Fish Harbor on the eastern end of Terminal Island. Starting with a single vessel in 1981, they are now the second largest Vietnamese fleet on the West Coast after Monterey Bay.[67]

Even for the more established and affluent Japanese and Chinese communities, the "model minority" designation has proven to be extremely fragile and more myth than reality. In 1969, after receiving nationwide publicity for his autopsy of assassinated presidential candidate Robert Kennedy—Los Angeles County Chief Coroner Thomas Noguchi was summarily fired. Noguchi was eventually reinstated, but only after an ad hoc coalition of Japanese American community organizations drew public attention to the case through full page advertisements in the *Los Angeles Times*:

A PLEA OF JUSTICE, IF THIS CAN HAPPEN TO ONE OF US, IT CAN HAPPEN TO YOU....

A nationally known doctor and scientist was humiliated, disgraced and fired from a civil service post without a hearing, amid charges... bizarre...degrading and odious....Dr. Noguchi was accused of being mentally ill, in need of psychiatric care, and of excessive use of drugs....[68]

Old World War II racial epithets reappeared to haunt Japanese Americans at the height of the U.S. Senate Watergate hearings in the summer of 1973, when the attorney for President Richard Nixon's White House henchmen publicly slurred Senator Daniel Inouye as "that little Jap."[69]

While local Japanese Americans received racist phone calls and letters in the wake of this incident, Chinese Americans were shaken by the expose of a confidential memorandum distributed to all law enforcement agencies by State Attorney General Evelle J. Younger regarding the alleged threat posed by Chinese Benevolent Associations:

The present-day Chinese Benevolent Associations are believed...to operate under the facade of a mutual aid society...Although they tend to appear as a fraternal society involved in civic activities, the TONGS more closely resemble Mafia-like organizations....In viewing the involvement of many Chinese in illegal activities, the cultural differences must be considered. The Chinese's primary interest in coming into the U.S. is to make money and improve their lot. Some feel that an easy method is involvement in drug market . . . Drugs are a way of life in the Orient.[70]

The 1973 memorandum, which was exposed and circulated by a network of Asian American Studies faculty and students at public and private college campuses throughout the state,[71] bore a frightening resemblance to the hate literature circulated by racists and nativists at the height of the anti-Chinese movement a century ago, and it underscored the need for more middle class Asian Americans to get involved in politics. The time had come to demonstrate the enormous potential for financial contributions to candidates and organizations who were sensitive to their concerns. Broadly-based alliances had to be nurtured, for a continuing fact of life is that "even with a growing Asian-American population, unless the various ethnic groups band together, their numbers will be relatively small."[72] By the end of the decade, community activists among L.A.'s various Asian-Pacific communities had established a variety of informal coalitions with each other, and maintained contacts with elected officials in both major political parties. Protest movements have become an accepted activity, replete with pickets and press kits for the media, and range from pro forma support for mainstream left-of-center issues such as nuclear disarmament and women's rights,[73] to more specialized Asian American civil rights concerns which draw support from liberals and conservatives. The latter have included major lobbying efforts in support of "Redress" for Japanese Americans incarcerated during World War II,[74] and protests against alleged university admission quotas for Asian Americans at UCLA and Berkeley.

RETURN OF THE "YELLOW PERIL"

As in the past, American images of immigrants' homelands continue to directly influence their treatment here. With many Americans out of work, a severe trade imbalance, and our descent to debtor-nation status, there is a need for a scapegoat. And thus the popular appeal of "Japan-bashing."[76] Beyond this kind of self-serving scapegoating is the fact that, within the last few years, trade across the Pacific has surpassed commerce across the Atlantic. Moreover, two out of every five new immigrants now come from across the Pacific. The litany of loathsome epithets and propaganda images from our wars in Asia (from World War II to Korea and Vietnam) are circulating again as Americans fail to make a clear distinction between Asian Asians and Americans of Asian ancestries.

Fears of the old "Yellow Peril" are further fueled when the preference for Asian high technology products and automobiles is blamed for domestic unemployment and economic malaise. In the business and real estate sections of local newspapers and magazines, articles about investments by Asian-based corporations are consistently headlined to reinforce the "Asian takeover" theme. This pattern was identifiable as early as the September 1973 article by Art Detman in *Los Angeles Magazine* entitled "Banzai! Meet the New Owners of Southern California." More recent titles consistently echo, expand, and exacerbate this theme. For example, the article entitled "The Japanese Are Banking on Los Angeles, And It Means You May Never Use An American Bank Again, in the 26 July 1987 issue of *Los Angeles Times Magazine*, begins with this statement:

> Spread like financial Jesuits around the globe, Japanese bankers are finding that there are few places where they feel more at ease or have been more successful than in Los Angeles. Tokyo is divided into 23 wards; some say Los Angeles is the 24th.[77]

On 30 May 1989, the "On California" column by Robert A. Jones in the *Los Angeles Times* was entitled "Sayonara to the Best of California" and included this observation:

> The argument is made that the Japanese actually own far less of the American turf than do the Canadians or the British. Undoubtedly that is true. But neither the British nor the Canadians have this unerring knack for acquiring the best we have.[78]

Other repercussions of anti-Asian hostility and fears were discussed in December 1988 by the California Attorney General's Asian and Pacific Islander Advisory Committee. They concluded that "hate crimes and incidents of anti-Asian violence against Asian/Pacific Islander Americans are again on the increase."[79] Evidence of increasing Anti-Asian attitudes include epithets, graffiti, and vandalism. A 1986 report by the U.S. Commission on Civil Rights found bumper stickers in Los Angeles County which

read: "Toyota-Datsun-Honda-and   Pearl   Harbor"   and
"Unemployment Made in Japan."[80]

The growing number and diversity of Asian and Pacific
Americans has also meant the need for a more effective law
enforcement response to problems of criminal activity and
victimization of Asian and Pacific Americans. The Los Angeles
Asian Task Force was established in October 1975 to provide
linguistic and cultural expertise in police investigations. Two
storefronts were established by the Los Angeles Police Department
to service Asian-Pacific American communities. The storefronts
which are located in Korean and Chinese neighborhoods became a
reality only because "of organized community demand...and
subsequent donations from individuals and organizations within the
community who helped provide space and needed materials."[81]

The "outwhiting the whites" image has created problems for
Asians who have established highly concentrated communities in
both the inner city as well as suburban areas.   Some Asian
Americans have become targets of other minorities. The tensions
between Blacks, Koreans and Cambodians in the inner city have
been treated in newspaper articles with headlines such as: "TALE
OF 2 CULTURES: MURDERS REFOCUS SPOTLIGHT ON
TENSIONS   BETWEEN   KOREANS,   BLACKS"   and
"CAMBODIANS TRADE SHOTS WITH BLACKS AT
HOUSING PROJECT."[82] An ad hoc group of representatives
from the Korean and African American business communities was
formed to improve communications and seek additional community
and political support to resolve common concerns. The Black
Korean Alliance, formed after several Korean American merchants
were murdered in predominantly black neighborhoods in 1986,
contends that "greater economic cooperation is the only way to
warm relations between Koreans and African Americans in Los
Angeles...the way to improve relations is through joint ventures."[83]

The strong network of Korean churches has played a major role
in alleviating tensions between Korean small businesses located in
largely African American areas.[84]

Newly arrived Chinese in San Marino have discovered that their
affluence has not avoided the charge of being "block busters" in
communities traditionally reserved for the "best people" in the city.

Monterey Park has been described as the "Nation's 1st Suburban Chinatown," due to the intensive influx of businesses and investments from Taiwan and Hong Kong since the late 1970s, but the Asian population's increase from 14 to 40 percent of some 60,000 residents has not been without negative reactions. Mayor Lily Chen was swept out of office in the 1986 municipal election which some viewed as a racist referendum against the highly visible influx and influence of Chinese. [85]

Michael Woo's 1985 election as the first L.A. City Council member of Chinese ancestry focused attention on recent efforts to develop an Asian-Pacific Islander political support network. On 6 June 1985 the *Los Angeles Times* carried articles with the headings "Woo's Victory—Asians Come of Political Age," and "Woo: Asians Recognized as Growing Political Force." The *Times* headlines caused mixed reactions among Asian and Pacific Americans. Some, particularly those who savored the heady excitement of their first victorious campaign, celebrated. After a century and a half of being the victims of politicians, they had prevailed-and not from the outside, but by working from within the political system that had often misused and abused its power against them.[86]

"On the other hand," cautions a middle-aged Japanese American who remembers less positive times: Whenever one of our Asian homelands is

> too strong and whenever an Asian American is seen as too successful and acts too equal, watch out. We have the mark upon us...we become the 'Yellow Peril'.... and the 'Model Minority' quickly becomes the 'Indispensable Scapegoat.'"[87]

Nearly a century ago, historian Frederick Jackson Turner described the importance of the Western frontier as a continuing opportunity to revitalize democratic ideals and institutions. His assessment of the frontier and its promise of the American Dream has been given new life by Asian and Pacific immigrants who have journeyed to their "Far East," to America's "Far West" in Los Angeles, in search of the "second chance" and that perceived panacea, "upward mobility."

NOTES

Portions of this essay are drawn from the following publications by Don and Nadine Hata: "'That Little Jap': Such Epithets Revive the Old Internment Camp Mentality,"*Los Angeles Times*, 10 Aug. 1973, II:7; *Japanese Americans and World War II* (Forum Press, 1974); "The Far East in the Far West,"*California History* (Spring 1981): 90-91; "Asian and Pacific Perceptions of L.A."*Urban Resources* 4(Spring 1984).

1   The following statistics from the 1980 U.S. Census are in many cases inaccurate low for all groups except the Japanese. The forthcoming 1990 census is expected to confirm much higher numbers provided by local public and private surveys. EAST ASIANS: Chinese (94,521); Japanese (117,190); and Koreans (60,339). SOUTH ASIANS: Asian Indians (18,770); and Pakistanis (871). SOUTHEAST ASIANS: Filipinos (100,894); Indonesians (1,976); Thais (8,706); Vietnamese (27,252); Laotians (1,391); Cambodians (2,826); and Hmong (180). PACIFIC ISLANDERS: Hawaiians (6,126); Samoans (7,440); Tongans (615); Guamanians (3,596); Micronesians (296); and Melanesians (325). See: U.S. Department of Commerce, Bureau of the Census, *Asian and Pacific Islander Population in the United States: 1980* (1988).

2   Judy Tachibana, "California's Asians, Power from a growing population," *California Journal* (Nov. 1986): 534-543.

3   Elizabeth Aoki, "Which Party Will Harvest the New Asian Votes?"*California Journal* (Nov. 1986): 545-546.

4   Leon Bouvier and Philip Martin, "Population Change and California's Future," Population Reference Bureau, 1985; quoted in ibid., p. 546.

5   See, for example: Kenneth J. Garcia, "Sight to Behold: Ornate Temple in Malibu is Shrine Where East Meets West," *Los Angeles Times*, 25 Mar. 1988, South Bay Edition, B:1; Barbara Koh, "Tibetans in Southland Keep Faith. They Venerate Dalai Lama, Lead American Lives," *Los Angeles Times*, 20 Mar. 1989, II:1; David Haldane, "Modest Buddhist Temple Serves as Heart of Cambodian Community," *Los Angeles Times*, 23 Aug. 1987, South Bay Edition, B:6; Jonathan Peterson, "Filipinos—A Search for Community: Southland Rifts," *Los Angeles Times*, 24 May 1989, I:1; Mark Arax, "Asian Influence Alters Life in Suburbia: San Gabriel Valley," *Los Angeles Times*, 5 Apr. 1987, I:1; Kathleen Day and David Holley, "Vietnamese Create Their Own Saigon: Boom on Bolsa," *Los Angeles Times*, 30 Sept. 1984, I:1; David Holley, "Refugees Build a Haven in Long Beach. Along 10th Street, the city is known as the 'New Phnom Penh'—the capital of the growing Cambodian community in the United States," *Los Angeles Times*, 27 Oct. 1986, II:1; David Haldane, "Modest Buddhist Temple Serves as Heart of Cambodian Community," *Los Angeles Times*, 23 Aug. 1987, B:6.

6   "Success Story: Outwhiting the Whites," *Newsweek*, 12 June 1971, pp. 24-25.

7   William Mason and Roberta Kirkhart Mason, "The Founding Forty-Four," *Westways* (July 1976): 23.

8   Bill Mason, "Como se llama el Pueblo en Chinese?" *Society of Architectural Historians, Southern California Review* (Fall 1981): 8.

9   See: Mary Roberts Coolidge, *Chinese Immigration* (New York: Henry Holt, 1909), 30-31, 69-82; Elmer Sandmeyer,*The Anti-Chinese Movement in*

California (Urbana: University of Illinois Press, 1973), 43, 45; Leonard Pitt, "Beginnings of Nativism in California," *Pacific Historical Review* 30 (Feb. 1961): 23-24; Rodman W. Paul, "The Origins of the Chinese Issue in California,"*Mississippi Valley Historical Review* 25 (June 1938-Mar. 1939): 191; Lucille Eaves, *A History of California Labor Legislation* (Berkeley: University of California Press, 1910), 6; and Thomas Chinn, ed., *A History of The Chinese in California, A Syllabus* (San Francisco: Chinese Historical Society of America, 1969), 24.

10 Doyce B. Nunis, Jr., "The Demagogue and the Demographer: Correspondence of Denis Kearney and Lord Bryce," *Pacific Historical Review* 36 (Aug. 1967): 269-288; and Alexander Saxton,*The Indispensable Enemy, Labor and the Anti-Chinese Movement in California* (Berkeley: University of California Press, 1971).

11 Chester P. Dorland, "Chinese Massacre at Los Angeles in 1871," *Annual Publications of the Historical Society of Southern California* 3:2 (1894): 22-26; and Paul M. De Falla, "Lantern in the Western Sky," *Southern California Quarterly* 42 (Mar. 1960): 57-88.

12 Milton R. Konvitz, *The Alien and the Asiatic in American Law* (Ithaca, New York: Cornell University Press, 1946), 81.

13 Lucy Cheng, *et al.*, *Linking Our Lives: Chinese American Women of Los Angeles* (Los Angeles: Chinese Historical Society of Southern California, 1984), 3. For an excellent summary of the history of Chinese in America, see Shih-Shan Henry Tsai, *The Chinese Experience in America* (Bloomington: Indiana University Press, 1986).

14 Sucheng Chan, *This Bittersweet Soil. The Chinese in California Agriculture, 1860-1910* (Berkeley: University of California Press, 1986), 46-50, 115-159.

15 Chinn, *Chinese in California*, pp. 37, 40-41, 60. Also see Harris Newmark, *Sixty Years in Southern California, 1853-1913* (New York, 1916), 125.

16 Ibid., pp. 46-47; and Steve Padilla, "Site of L.A.'s 1st Rail Link to World Just a Name on a Map,"*Los Angeles Times*, 26 Nov. 1989, B:12. The official dedication was held on 5 Sept. 1876.

17 Roger Daniels, *The Politics of Prejudice, The Anti-Japanese Movement in California and the Struggle for Japanese Exclusion* (New York, 1969), 19.

18 Chan, *This Bittersweet Soil*, pp. 42-43.

19 S.W. Kung, *Chinese in American Life. Some Aspects of Their History, Status, Problems, and Contributions* (Westport, CT: Greenwood, 1962), 216-224; B.L.Sung, *The Story of the Chinese in America* (New York: Collier, 1967), 134-140; and Tsai, *The Chinese Experience in America*, pp. 45-55.

20 Tom Waldman, "The Korean Connection," *USC Trojan Family* 21 (Feb.-Mar. 1989): 21.

21 He died at the age of 92 on 27 Feb. 1986. "Leo C. Song, Pioneer in L.A.'s Koreatown," *Los Angeles Times*, 8 Mar. 1986, I:24.

22 Linda Shin, "Koreans in America, 1903-1945," *Amerasia Journal* 1 (Nov. 1971): 33-34.

23   Roger Daniels, *History of Indian Immigration to the United States, An Interpretive Essay* (New York: The Asia Society, 1989), 30. Also see Mark I. Pinsky, "The Mexican-Hindu Connection, In a Search for Their Roots, Descendants Discover a Moving Tale of Loneliness and Racism," *Los Angeles Times*, 21 Dec. 1987, V:1.

24   One of these was the San Francisco-based Gadar Movement, otherwise known as the "Hindu conspiracy;" see Joan Jensen, "The Hindu Conspiracy: A Reassessment," *Pacific Historical Review* 48 (1979): 65-83.

25   At the turn of the century, in the so-called "Insular Cases," the U.S. Supreme Court ruled that the Constitution and citizenship do not necessarily follow the flag.

26   For a history of early Japanese immigrants from "the perspective of the excluded," see Yuji Ichioka, *The Issei: The World of the First Generation Japanese Immigrants, 1885-1924* (New York: The Free Press, 1988).

27   Roger Daniels, *Asian America: Chinese and Japanese in the United States since 1850* (Seattle: University of Washington Press, 1988), 124-128; and Daniels, *Politics of Prejudice*, pp. 31-45.

28   Daniels, *Asian America*, pp. 135, 156.

29   See William M. Mason and John A. McKinstry, *The Japanese of Los Angeles, 1869-1920*, Contribution in History, No. 1 (Los Angeles County Museum of Natural History, 1969).

30   John Modell, *The Economics and Politics of Racial Accommodation: The Japanese of Los Angeles, 1900-1942* (Urbana: University of Illinois Press, 1977), p. 94.

31   Ibid., pp. 69-70.

32   Ibid., pp. 52-53. Also see, "Citizenship Law Ensnares Viet Fishermen. A judge uphold the enforcement of a 200-year-old sttute that threatens to put many resident aliens out of work," *Los Angeles Times*, 17 Oct. 1989, A:23.

33   Since the rise of Asian American civil rights movements in the 1960s, two terms, "Filipino" and "Pilipino," refer to the indigenous population of the Philippines; the latter being preferred by those who feel that "Filipino" was created by Spanish and American colonial rulers. See, for example, Royal F. Morales, *Makibaka, The Pilipino American Struggle* (Los Angeles: Mountainview Press, 1974).

34   In effect, "national" was an extremely ambivalent legal status meaning that Pilipinos were neither citizen nor alien.

35   Carlos Bulosan, *America In The Heart* (New York, 1946), 143; Morales, *Makibaka*, p. 48, cites another old timer: "Now you have a better life. In those days, there were no jobs and living around Los Angeles was demeaning." See also Benicio Catapusan, *The Filipino Occupational and Recreational Activities in Los Angeles* (San Francisco, 1975).

36   Carey McWilliams, *Brothers Under the Skin*, rev. ed. (Boston: Little, Brown, 1964), 242.

37   Christopher Salter, "The Chinese of Los Angeles," *Urban Resources* (Spring 1984). Mrs. Christine Sterling promoted "The China City" which opened in

June 1938 at the corner of Main and Macy streets. In addition to these two planned projects, there is a third community "along North Spring Street, between Ord and Macy Streets. A portion of the old Los Angeles Chinatown remains, composed of Los Angeles Street, the 400's block North, and Ferguson Alley." See Kung, *Chinese in American Life*, pp. 204-06.

38 Ivan Light, "From Vice District to Tourist Attraction: The Moral Career of American Chinatowns, 1880-1940," *Pacific Historical Review* 43 (Aug. 1974): 367-94.

39 Eui-Young Yu, Earl H. Phillips, and Eun Sik, eds., *Koreans In Los Angeles: Prospects and Promises* (California State University, Los Angeles: Koryo Research Institute, Center for Korean-American and Korean Studies, 1982), 17.

40 Tricia Knoll, *Becoming Americans. Asian Soujourners, Immigrants, and Refugees in the Western United States* (Portland: Coast to Coast Books, 1982), 123-124; Wayne Patterson and Hyung-chan Kim, *The Koreans in America* (Minneapolis: Lerner Publications, 1977), 34. Also see Hyung-chan Kim, ed., *Korean Diaspora* (Santa Barbara: Clio, 1977).

41 Edward Sakamoto, "Anna May Wong and the Dragon-Lady Syndrome," *Los Angeles Times Calendar*, 12 July 1987, pp. 40-41.

42 Yu, Eui-Yong, *Koreans in Los Angeles*, p. 17.

43 Executive Order No. 9066, 19 Feb. 1942, in *House Report* No. 2124, 77th Cong., 2nd Sess., pp. 314-315. The question of whether the Japanese attack was indeed a "surprise" or "sneak attack" is a matter of continuing controversy. See Ronald Lewin, *The American Magic: Codes, Ciphers and the Defeat of Japan* (New York: Farrar, Straus, Giroux, 1982); William L. Neumann, *American Encounters Japan, From Perry to MacArthur* (New York: Harper Colophon Books, 1963), 256-289; and Kemp Tolley, "The Strange Assignment of the U.S.S. *Lanikai*," *U.S. Naval Institute Proceedings* 88 (Sept. 1962)): 71-83.

44 Donald J. Young, *Wartime Palos Verdes* (privately printed), 10-11. Morton Grodzins, *Americans Betrayed, Politics and the Japanese American Evacuation* (Chicago: University of Chicago Press, 1949). Also see Michi Weglyn, *Years of Infamy, The Untold Story of America's Concentration Camps* (New York: Morrow, 1976).

45 Roger Daniels, *Concentration Camps USA: Japanese Americans and World II* (New York: Holt, Rinehart & Winston, 1971), 61.

46 Ibid.

47 Bill Hosokawa, *Nisei, The Quiet Americans* (New York: Morrow, 1969), 260.

48 See Anthony L. Lehman, *Birthright of Barbed Wire, The Santa Anita Assembly Center for the Japanese* (Los Angeles: Westernlore Press, 1970).

49 Donald Teruo Hata, Jr. and Nadine Ishitani Hata, *Japanese Americans and World War II*. (St. Charles, MO: Forum Press, 1974), 9.

50 California State Supreme Court decision in *Fujii v. State*; see Frank F. Chuman, *The Bamboo People: The Law and Japanese Americans* (Del Mar, CA: Publisher's Inc., 1976), 218, 220-222. In 1948 Congress passed the Japanese American Evacuation Claims Act, but this was only token compensation for evacuees' losses which the Federal Reserve Bank of San Francisco estimated at $400 million. The mere $38 million appropriated by Congress amounted to

less than ten cents for every dollar lost, with all claims settled without interest and on the basis of 1942 prices.

51   Audrie Girdner and Anne Loftis, *The Great Betrayal, The Evacuation of the Japanese Americans during World War II* (London: Macmillan, 1970), 433-434.

52   Martin Ridge, "Bilingualism, Biculturalism—California's New Past," *Southern California Quarterly* 46 (Spring 1984): 49. Also see *Personal Justice Denied. Report of the Commission on Wartime Relocation and Internment of Civilians* (Washington, DC: GPO, 1982).

53   Judith Michaelson and Richard E. Meyer, "L.A.'s Japanese-Americans: Breaking Into the Mainstream," *Los Angeles Times*, 19 Apr. 1982, II:1.

54   Northern California'a two Japanese Americans continue to serve as veteran members of Congress: Norman Mineta from San Jose, and Sacramento's Robert Matsui.

55   Hata, "Asian and Pacific Perceptions of L.A."

56   Penelope McMillan, "Koreatown: A Struggle for Identity," *Los Angeles Times*, 17 June 1984, I:1.

57   Steven R. Churm, "'Little India': Enterprising Immigrant Merchants Adding Spice to Artesia's Main Street," *Los Angeles Times*, 6 Apr. 1988, II:1, 4.

58   David Holley, "Legacy of Peace. Devotees Enact Rich Ritual at Festival as Work Progresses at Nation's Largest Hindu Temple,"*Los Angeles Times*, 27 Oct.1985, II:1, 4; and Kenneth J. Garcia, "Sight to Behold. Ornate Hindu Temple in Malibu Is Shrine Where East Meets West," *Los Angeles Times*, 25 Mar. 1988, II:1, 3. Television viewers may remember the "Korla Pandit Program" which was broadcast three times a week from 1949 to 1952 on station KTLA. Wearing a jeweled turban, Pandit never uttered a word during his 900 programs as he "took viewers on a musical journey around the world with an international repertoire of exotic interpretation of the classics." Kristine McKenna, "Korla Pandit Still Spreading Metaphysical Message," *Los Angeles Times*, 10 June 1988, VI: 8.

59   California Advisory Committee to the U.S. Commission on Civil Rights, *Asian Americans and Pacific Peoples: A Case of Mistaken Identity* (Feb. 1975).

60   Victor Merina, "Pacific Islanders Take Their Greatest Strides on Football Field: Athletes Find Prestige, Respect in Community Plus Opportunities for Higher Education," *Los Angeles Times*, 26 Nov. 1978, Centinela-South Bay , sec. XI: 1; "On Samoa, football players grow like coconuts,"*The Daily Breeze* (Torrance, CA), 2 Mar. 1985, sec. C:1.

61   Tom Wolfe, *Radical Chic and Mau-Mauing the Flak Catchers* (New York: Bantam, 1971), 128-29.

62   Jerry Ruhlow, "Culture Shock Traps Growing Samoan Colony," *Los Angeles Times*, 26 Nov. 1978, Centinela-South Bay, sec. XI:1.

63   "Korean influx strains social service agencies," *Daily Breeze*, 25 Jan. 1985, sec. B:2. Also see: Penelope McMillan, "Koreatown Social Services Lacking, Study Finds," *Los Angeles Times*, 24 Jan. 1985, sec. II:1. Some services are slowly becoming available: Bob Williams, "Libraries Expanding Services to Asians: Language Becomes Less of a Barrier as Collections Grow," *Los Angeles Times*, 14 Sept. 1986, sec. II:1; Lily Eng, "Refuge for Battered Asian Wives:

Shelter Helps Overcome Language, Cultural Barriers," *Los Angeles Times*, 10 Oct. 1986, sec. V:2.

64 See: Mark Arax, "Lost in L.A. Sang Nam Chinh's Tragic Odyssey Is the Story of a Generation of Vietnamese Refugee Youth Cast Adrift in America," *Los Angeles Times Magazine*, 13 Dec. 1987, pp. 10-14, 16, 42-46; Scott Harris, "Long Hoa, Vietnamese Version of Scouting, Marks 11th Anniversary," *Los Angeles Times*, 21 Dec. 1987, sec. II:1; David Haldane, "Culture Clash or Animal Cruelty? Two Cambodian Refugees Face Trial After Killing Dog for Food," *Los Angeles Times*, sec. II:1. Also see U.S. Commission on Civil Rights, *Recent Activities Against Citizens and Residents of Asian Descent*, Clearinghouse Publ. No. 88 (1986).

65 Sonni Efron, "Sweatshops Expanding Into Orange County. Garment Trade: L.A. no longer has a monopoloy on low wages and Third World conditions for immigrants," *Los Angeles Times*, 26 Nov. 1989, sec. A:1. Also see: Mark Arax, "Refugees Called Victims and Perpetrators of Fraud," *Los Angeles Times*, 10 Feb. 1987, sec. I:1; and Jane Applegate, "Indochinese Swelling Work Force. Majority of Orange County's Refugees Get High-Tech Jobs," *Los Angeles Times*, 2 Oct. 1984, pt. IV:1. Applegate reported: By some counts, 15% to 20% of [Orange] county's 60,000 Vietnamese residents are employed at high-technology companies. The majority work on assembly lines, but others are employed as test technicians, engineers, field service representatives, and supervisors. At some companies, as much as 25% of the work force is Indochinese.

66 See, "Citizenship Law Ensnares Viet Fishermen. A judge upholds the enforcement of a 200-year-old statute that threatens to put many resident aliens out of work." *Los Angeles Times*, 17 Oct. 1989, sec. A: 23.

67 Ashley Dunn, "Bucking the Tide. 200-Year-Old Law Makes Life Hard for Immigrant Fishermen From Vietnam," *Los Angeles Times*, 12 Nov. 1989, sec. A:3.

68 *Los Angeles Times*, 11 July 1969, sec. II:5. In a second case twenty years later, the coroner did not receive widespread community support and lost his position. See Dan Morain, "Supreme Court Refuses to Reinstate Noguchi," *Los Angeles Times*, 12 Mar. 1987, sec. II:1.

69 Don and Nadine Hata, "'That Little Jap:' Such Epithets Revive the Old Internment Camp Mentality," *Los Angeles Times*, 10 Aug. 1973, sec. II:7. During the 1987 joint Congressional hearings on illegal diversion of funds to Central America and guns for hostages schemes in Iran, Senator Inouye was again the target of racist hate mail.

70 California Department of Justice, "Triad: Mafia of the Far East," in *Criminal Justice Bulletin* (July 1973). The cover included the statement: "Confidential. Not to be released unless cleared by the Attorney General, Department of Justice, State of California."

71 By 1973 Asian American students had established campus organizations to support, and in many cases demand, ethnic studies courses and related programs at virtually every public and private campus in the L.A. region.

72 Tachibana, *California Journal* (Nov. 1986): 543.

73   John H. Lee, "Sex Harassment Case Called a First. Civil Rights: An Asian-American woman is awarded $30,000 in damages from the accounting firm she [Denise Okamoto] worked for," *Los Angeles Times*, 18 Nov. 1989, sec. A:35.

74   The following titles are representative of voluminous coverage of the subject: Karen Tumulty, "House Votes Payments for Japanese Internees. Bill Would Give $20,000 to Each Individual and Require U.S. to Apologize for Detaining Them," *Los Angeles Times*, 18 Sept. 1987, pt. I:1; Josh Getlin, "Senate Votes to Pay WWII Internees. Quick House Concurrence Seen for Reparations to Japanese-Americans," *Los Angeles Times*, 21 Apr. 1988, pt. I:1; "It's Official! Reagan Signs Bill. Ex-Internees to Receive $20,000 in Compensation," *Rafu Shimpo* (Los Angeles Japanese Daily News), 10 Aug. 1988, p. 1; and Josh Getlin, "Funds for WWII Internees Caught in Budget Squeeze; Delay in Payments Feared," *Los Angeles Times*, 7 May 1989, pt. I:1.

75   Dean Takehara, "Asian American Professor Wins Tenureship Battle," *Rafu Shimpo*, 26 May 1989, p. 1. Recent literature on allegations of institutional racism in college admissions policies is voluminous; see E. Gareth Hoachlander and Cynthia L. Brown, "Asians in Higher Education: Conflicts Over Admissions," *Thought and Action: The NEA Higher Education Journal* 5 (Fall 1989): 5-20; and Lauren Blau, "UC students allege racism. State legislators hear of recent incidents," *Daily Breeze*, 5 Oct. 1988, sec. A:6.

76   Walter Russell Mead, "Japan-Bashing, an Ugly American Tradition," *Los Angeles Times*, 4 June 1989, sec. V:2.

77   Joel Kotkin and Yoriko Kishimoto, pp. 1, 16-21.

78   Robert A. Jones, sec. I, p. 3.

79   See [California] Attorney General's Asian and Pacific Islander Advisory Committee, *Final Report* (Sacramento, CA: Dec. 1988): 43-44. The brutal murders of Chinese American Vincent Chin in Detroit in 1982 and Vietnamese American student Thong Hy Huynh in Davis, California in 1983 are among the more graphic examples of the rising tide of violence directed against Asian and Pacific Americans.

80   Commission on Civil Rights, *Recent Activities Against Citizens and Residents of Asian Descent* (1986), 40.

81   [California] Attorney General's Asian and Pacific Islander Advisory Committee, *Final Report*, pp. 60, 64-65. The committee noted that much of the existing literature on crime within Asian and Pacific American communities focuses on gang activity (see p. 60). For example: "Vietnamese Gangs Roam L.A., Orange Counties," *The Daily Breeze* (Torrance, CA), 3 Aug. 1980, sec. B:3; Ronald J. Ostrow, "Gangs Besiege Vietnamese in U.S., Crime Hearing Told," *Los Angeles Times*, 26 Oct. 1984, sec. II:1; Steve Emmons and David Reyes, "Gangs, Crime Top Fears of Vietnamese in Orange County," *Los Angeles Times*, 5 Feb. 1989, sec. I:3; and Kristina Horton, "Gang Values Divide Youth, Samoan Elders," *The Daily Breeze*, 5 Mar. 1989, sec. A:1. Also see Paul Pringle, "To serve and protect L.A.'s Asian community. Police task force handles cases involving cultural, language barriers," *The Daily Breeze* , 13 Jan. 1986, sec. B:1.

82   See for example: Marita Hernandez, "Tale of 2 Cultures: Murders Refocus Spotlight on Tensions Between Koreans, Blacks," *Los Angeles Times*, 18 May 1986, sec. II:1; and Nieson Himmel, "Cambodians Trade Shots with Blacks at

Housing Project," *Los Angeles Times*, 13 May 1988, pt. II:3. The U.S. Commission on Civil Rights briefly summarized the relations between L.A.'s Korean and Black communities in *Recent Activities Against Citizens and Residents of Asian Descent* (1986), 54-55.

83 Darrell Dawsey and John H. Lee, "Koreans and Blacks Seek Mayor's Help for Harmony," *Los Angeles Times*, 6 Oct. 1989, pt. II:2. Also see: Sophia Kim, "Seeking a Dialogue by Koreans, Blacks. Workshop Aims for Reduced Tensions With an Increase in Understanding," *Los Angeles Times*, 8 June 1984, pt. V:8; and Janet Clayton, "Tenuous New Alliances Forged to Ease Korean-Black Tensions," *Los Angeles Times*, 20 July 1987, sec. II:1.

84 John Dart, "Korean Immigrants, Blacks Use Churches as Bridge to Each Tensions," *Los Angeles Times*, 9 Nov. 1985, Pt. II:4.

85 "Monterey Park: Nation's 1st Suburban Chinatown," *Los Angeles Times*, 6 Apr. 1987, sec. I:1.

86 Alan C. Miller, "Political Newcomer's Bid for Congress Sparks Korean Community Involvement," *Los Angeles Times*, 15 Feb. 1988, sec. II:1; William Wong, "Asian Americans Shake Off Stereotypes, Increase Clout as Political Activism Grows," *Los Angeles Times*, 23 Feb. 1988, sec. II:7.

87 Hata, "Asian and Pacific Perceptions of L.A.," *Urban Resources* 5 (Spring 1984).

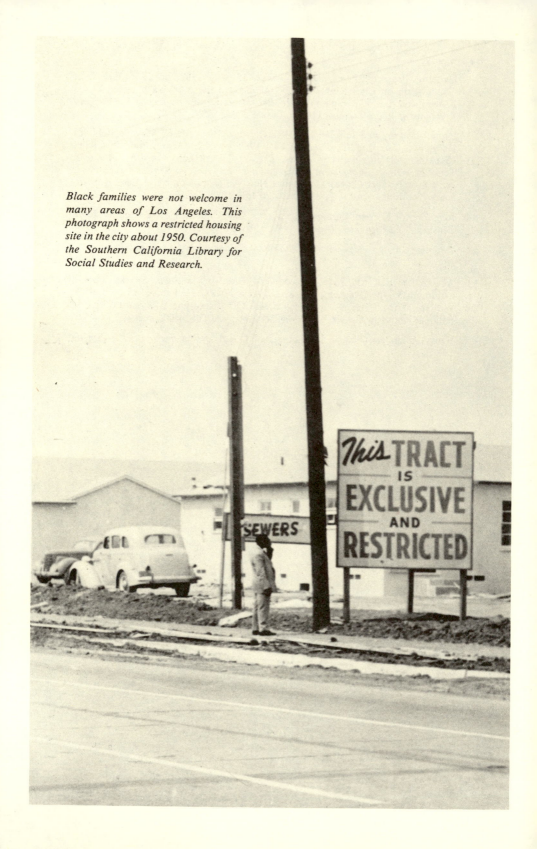

Black families were not welcome in many areas of Los Angeles. This photograph shows a restricted housing site in the city about 1950. Courtesy of the Southern California Library for Social Studies and Research.

Chapter 4

A PAST NOT NECESSARILY PROLOGUE:
THE AFRO-AMERICAN IN LOS ANGELES

Lonnie G. Bunch

In the Spring of 1913, W.E.B. DuBois, editor of *The Crisis* Magazine and the senior Black officer in the National Association for the Advancement of Colored People (NAACP) traveled to Los Angeles to encourage greater participation by Black Californians in the Civil Rights organization. DuBois, known for his jaundiced eye and sharp pen, was curious about the relations between the races in this land "of roses and orange blossoms." A procession of ten automobiles, filled with prominent Black Angelinos such as Robert C. Owens, J.A. Somerville, A. J. Roberts and C.S. Blodgett, delivered DuBois from the train station to the lobby of the YMCA at 8th and San Pedro, for the formal welcoming ceremonies.[1]

During the next several days, DuBois thrilled Black Los Angeles with a major address at Temple Auditorium to "2,300 people from the White, Yellow and Black races," and spoke to over one thousand students at Pomona and Occidental Colleges and the University of Southern California. Despite a hectic schedule, however, DuBois found time to take "automobile rides all about the surrounding country" and city.[2]

So impressed was DuBois that upon his return to New York City, he wrote "Los Angeles is wonderful. Nowhere in the United States is the Negro so well and beautifully housed, nor the average efficiency and intelligence in the colored population so high." Then DuBois summed up the lure of Los Angeles: "Out here in this matchless Southern California there would seem to be no limit to your opportunities, your possibilities."[3]

Ruby Johnson Braxton recently recalled how the possibilities and the promise of Los Angeles materialized for her family in the years prior to 1925. Located in Southern California since the return of the century, the Johnson family lived in the predominantly White neighborhood of Pico Heights. Mrs. Braxton remembers the Sunday afternoon drives, begun only "after attending services at First AME Church on 8th and Towne," where her family would ride through the city, waving at friends, heading towards the pass to the San Fernando Valley. As the car strained to climb the hilly grade, the family would marvel at the beautiful mosaic of orange groves and mountains, finally arriving at a small park where the children "were treated to oranges, ice cream and pony rides."[4]

Countless Blacks experienced the promise of better opportunity noted by DuBois or had a childhood similar to Mrs. Braxton in Los Angeles. For these individuals, the words of a recent migrant ring true: "I grew up in the deep south and we would have people visit us from California. We always had the impression that going to California was like going to heaven, there is no racism—you do what you want."[5]

Yet for thousands, Los Angeles became a place where the dream of a better life was shattered by the realities of de facto residential segregation, discrimination in the workplace and public displays of bigotry as the population increased dramatically during the 20th century. For these residents the pain and hatred they faced in Los Angeles mirrored the oppressive nature of racism found in any other American city: the involuntary creation of inner city ghettoes, the need to seek legal recourses to live in the home of one's choice and the inability of education to erase the stigma of race in employment interviews.

California has always been seen "literally and symbolically as America's golden share, its fabled region of hope and promise." California's call of hope and opportunity has had a powerful effect on Afro-Americans, a people who, at times, have had little more than faith, hope and dreams to sustain themselves. As one Black newspaper declared in 1913, "We [Blacks] are here like other people, to share these splendid conditions found in California, buying houses and contributing to our efforts to the common cause, that is, building up this great state."[6]

By 1895, Los Angeles had expanded upon the community and self-help organizations of the earlier decade and was poised to enter into an era where the California dream seemed accessible to many Black Angelinos, an era, where it appears J.L. Edmonds correctly analyzed the situation, when he wrote in *The Liberator* "the colored people in California are the best fixed in the United States."[7]

In 1911, a black newspaper editor declared "only a few years ago, the bulk of our present colored population came here from the South without money, in search of better things and were not disappointed."[8] This statement reflects the optimism and the sense of possible achievement that permeated the Los Angeles community during its Golden Era, from approximately 1900 until the stock market crash in 1929.

Although the numbers of blacks in Los Angeles increased dramatically, from 2,131 in 1900 to 7,599 by 1910 and 15,579 by the end of World War I, they still represented less than 3% of the total population in 1920.[9] The 1910 census does attest, however, to the lure of Los Angeles. For example, 83% of all Black Angelinos had migrated to Los Angeles while only 59% of White Angelinos were from outside of California. Also blacks who did migrate to California, preferred to settle in Los Angeles rather than Oakland or San Francisco.[10]

Several elements contributed to this period's label as the Golden Era. One of the most important was the ability of blacks to purchase homes in Los Angeles. Many a decision to migrate was influenced by the real estate ads that appeared in black newspapers, trumpeting the availability and moderate prices of homes; ads such as "For Sale-To Colored People, Fine Half Acre in Sierra Madre, California....Splendid chance out there for colored man and wife for steady work, fine climate"; or call "for bargains in cheap beautiful homes in any part of the city. Prices ranging from $200 to $500 cash"; and "Buy Lots now in Watts: where values are sure to double-where a five cent car line is started-where the price is within reach of all....Terms $10.00 cash and $5.00 per month".[11]

The high percentage of Black homeownership in Los Angeles is confirmed by the census of 1910 which revealed that 36.1% of Black Angelinos owned their own home. In New York city only 2.4% of blacks purchased their house; in New Orleans the percentage was 11%; in Dallas, 14.1%; in Oakland 29.5% and in Birmingham only 16.4%. The only areas to surpass Los Angeles were small towns such as Marshall, Texas at 37.5% and Atchison, Kansas with 53.6%.[12]

Inspite of the high percentage of Black home ownership during the Golden Era, communities resisted the trend to consolidate the black neighborhoods until the late 1920s. By 1910 there were several black areas of Los Angeles:

1.) West Temple Street-Occidental Boulevard
2.) 1st to 3rd Streets, San Pedro Street to Santa Fe
3.) 7th to 9th Streets, Mateo to Santa Fe
4.) Boyle Heights (1st to Broadway, Evergreen to Savannah)
5.) 35th Street and Normandie Avenue
6.) Pico Heights

Black Angelinos were proud of the diversity of their neighborhoods; "The Negroes of this city have prudently refused to segregate themselves into any locality, but have scattered and purchased homes in sections occupied by wealthy, cultured white people."[13] The quantity and quality of the black owned homes, all with, as Langston Hughes once wrote, great beauty and "miles of yard", was the central factor in designating this period as the Golden Era.[14]

Another element of the appeal of Los Angeles was the sense of community. Though the population had grown, it was still small enough in 1910 for citizens to feel that they knew their neighbors, yet large enough to provide business opportunities, some political influence through groups as The Afro-American Council and the Los Angeles Men's Forum, and the stirring of cultural life through concerts, recitals and educational organizations such as the Union Literary Society in Boyle Heights. To some residents the size of the community, plus the ethnic diversity of Los Angeles, mitigated against the severity of racism: "Perhaps the presence in this section of the country in large numbers of the representatives of every nation on the globe, has much to do with the success that has attended our men, as representatives of the so called 'backward races'; they have no monopoly of the embarrassing attention and prejudice so often directed mainly at them."[15] Whatever the accepted explanation, relatively speaking, the racism and bigotry that Black Angelinos faced paled in comparison with the institutional racism, codified discriminatory statutes and the lynching that southern Negroes faced daily.

Another aspect of the Golden Era involved the employment opportunities for Blacks in Los Angeles. While journals such as *The California Eagle* and *The Liberator* waxed defiantly that "The colored people of Los Angeles are not all laborers and white washers; that they are evincing a disposition to...go into business for themselves," and national magazines of color regaled the nation with tales of "Negro capitalists" such as Robert C. Owens, most Black Angelinos toiled in the service trades, as domestics or as unskilled laborers.[16] Black Los Angeles did maintain a number of prosperous businesses. Newer enterprises such as May's Ice Cream Parlor, the Dawson Cafe and the Golden West Hotel ("the largest colored hotel on the Pacific Coast") complemented nicely older, more established, businesses such as the real estate office of J.B. Loving, Los Angeles Van and Storage, Shackelford's Furniture Store and Donnell's Blacksmith Shop. Thus J. L. Edmonds could say in 1913, "the number of business establishment conducted by Negroes have increased and all seem to rest upon a solid foundation."[17]

Despite the gains made during this period, racism and discrimination were constant companions of the Black Angeleno. The ever perceptive W. E. B. Dubois wrote in the *Crisis* that "Los Angeles is not paradise...the color line is there and sharply drawn. Women have had difficulty in having gloves and shoes fitted at the stores, the hotels do not welcome colored people, the restaurants are not for all that are hungry." In 1904, the internationally known Jubilee Singers of Fisk University were denied the hospitality of the city's hotels and eateries. Even in the company of whites, blacks faced rejection. Delilah Beasley recalls the story of a white woman's anger when she realized the lunch counterwoman at Ralph's Grocery on Spring Street refused to serve her "colored maid".[18]

Although California had passed a civil rights act, the "Shenk Rule" in 1912/1913 had negative consequences for colored residents of the city. During the summer of 1912 a black businessman, C. W. Holden, was asked to join a white acquaintence for a beer. Once inside the salon, the bartender charged Holden a dollar for a beer while the white customer was billed a nickel. Holden's white colleague demanded that the mayor revoke the salon's license. City Attorney, John Shenk, after deliberation, ruled that the bartender was within his rights as "it was neither extortion or a violation of the Civil Rights Act to charge a negro more for an article than a white man." As a result of the "Shenk Rule", cafes and restaurants began charging Blacks excessive rates to deter their patronage. *The Liberator* led an unsuccessful battle to stop ice cream parlors, lunch counters and coffee houses from insulting "our women and girls by charging five dollars for a dish of ice cream."[19]

The color line also became apparent in business and residential accommodations. For many years, Black businessmen leased office space in downtown Los Angeles on an equal footing with their white contemporaries. In 1913 a group of white lawyers in the Copp Building complained about the black tenants in the office. "We...tenants in Copp building, do hereby most vigorously protest against your leasing...to colored tenants....Offices in the building are undesirable...so long as colored tenants are allowed."[20] As a result of this petition, the black residents were forced to vacate the premises.

Not all cases of discrimination, however, were lost by Black Angelinos. In 1907, Alva Garrott, the first black to practice dentistry in Los Angeles, purchased a lot in Glendale because the drier air would aid his wife who suffered from tuberculosis. While constructing their new domocile, the Garrott family slept in a tent house. After receiving a series of threatening notes addressed "to the only colored man in Glendale" that admonished him to leave "or suffer the consequences", Garrott slept with two loaded shotguns beside the beds."[21] Once the community realized that Garrott would not be intimidated, he was allowed to complete and occupy his new home. Another case of residential discrimination involved Miss Susie Anderson, whose only crime was relocating with her infirm mother to Hollywood. White "neighbors" pelted the house with bottles, rocks and dead animals. Initially, the police refused to grant her protection. Only after a group of Black women began standing guard at the site did the law enforcement officials respond.[22]

Rather than passively accepting this wave of discrimination, various strategies were developed to ensure that the fight against racism in Los Angeles became a collective struggle rather than an individual battle. Organizations as diverse as the Y.M.C.A. led by Thomas A. Green, the Sojourner Truth Club, the Women's Day Nursery Association, the NAACP, race papers like *The Liberator,* edited by J. L. Edmonds, and *The California Eagle*, edited by John Niemore (later replaced by Charlotta Bass), the Los Angeles Forum and a local chapter of Marcus Garvey's Universal Negro Improvement Association all joined to improve the lot of the Black Angeleno.

One of the most important Black organizations in Southern California was the Los Angeles Forum. This "club of intelligent colored men from the various churches of this city", was formed in February 1903 at the First A.M.E. Church, with the express purpose "of encouraging united effort on the part of Negroes for their advance and to strengthen them along lines of moral, social, intellectual, financial and Christian ethnics."[23] Founded by prominent Angelinos such as J. L. Edmonds, Frederick Roberts and Reverend J. E. Edwards,[24] the Forum, at weekly meetings held on Sunday afternoon at four, urged Blacks to develop a sense of pride in race and self; championed the need for laborers of color to buy land and encouraged businesses to hire Black's in non-menial positions.

The Forum's greatest contribution was fostering a burgeoning sense of community by providing an arena for public discourse, friendly debate and political dialogue. Even "the humblest citizen has access to these meetings and can state his grievance before the entire body."[25] Each meeting included lectures, debates and discussions of current events, while subgroups such as the "committee on strangers" helped the many new migrants adjust to the pace and tenor of Los Angeles. Soon the Form became the foremost "colored institution" assisting the newly arrived. One newcomer said, "one of the things they took me to when I arrived in Los Angeles was to the Forum."

By the 1920's, the Forum was at the apex of its power and influence: politicians—black and white—sought the support and votes that the Forum could provide. Even former Governor Hiram

Johnson came to a session of the Forum to solicit assistance in his bid for the Senate in 1922.[26] But the rapid growth of the black community mitigated against the continued effectiveness of the organization and as support dwindled, the group held its last meeting in 1942.

An organization created shortly after the founding of the Forum had an even longer existence. In 1904, a group of Black women, concerned about the moral environment faced by young working women of color, created the Sojourner Truth Industrial Club. Under the leadership of Mrs. Margaret Scott, the Sojourner Truth Club sought to protect the welfare of Negro women by establishing a Christian, yet non-sectarian, dwelling that would be a safe refuge. Mrs. Scott toured the east to find models for the group to emulate. After several years of fundraising, the club built a home "costing $5,200 with nine bedrooms, two baths, reception hall and library."[27] The Sojourner Truth Club, still functioning eighty five years later, was an important example of how the Black community in Los Angeles, especially during the Golden Era, worked collectively to effect change.

Another organization whose establishment was prompted by the worsening racial conditions in Los Angeles was the National Association for Advancement of Colored People (NAACP). In September 1913, after W. E. B. DuBois' visit to Los Angeles, several Black Angelinos, including E. Burton Ceruti, John Somerville, Charles Alexander and John Shackelford wrote to him soliciting advice:

> Problems and grievances arise constantly demanding attention and action by someone on behalf of the race. No one is charged with the duty and few can afford to take it singly....
>
> We begin to feel the necessity of an organization such as yours, supported by public spirited citizens and charged with this duty. Please advise.[28]

Later in 1913, Betty Hill, Reverend Joseph Johnson and W. T. Cleghorn joined with the authors of the above letter to found the Los Angeles Chapter of the NAACP.[29]

As the influence of the NAACP was on the rise, the story of one of the greatest fighters for Black rights was coming to an end, Jefferson Lewis Edmonds, "the Editor and Business Manager" of

The Liberator died on 4 January 1914. Commenting upon his demise, one newspaper wrote that his death "removes from the scene of action one of the most forceful writers of the race. He...seemed to fear nothing. He was an able thinker and a close reasoner and his editorials, through often keen and biting, always commanded attention."[30]

Edmonds, born a slave in Virginia, became a powerful voice for change among Black Angelinos. In the columns of *The Liberator*, whose masthead read: "devoted to the cause of good government and the advance of the Afro-American," Edmonds spared no one from his sharp pen.[31]   He gleefully attacked politicians, businessmen and dubious Black leaders always proclaiming "another great victory for *The Liberator*". Yet Edmonds was a pragmatic man who cared deeply about the lives of "the colored people", a fact attested to by the myriad of community organizations—from the Forum to the Afro-American Council— Edmonds joined during his life.

While Edmonds was best known for his battles against the Shenk Rule, his active involvement with the Los Angeles Forum and his dedication to protecting the rights of women (*The Liberator* led the fight to gain Black support for women suffrage in California in 1911—"the only Negro paper to come out for that amendment"), he was equally as important as a proponent and promoter of the lure of California. In his newspaper he eventually championed the idea that "opportunities for material advancement are greater in California" and that "the kindly feelings existing between the races in this city is no where surpassed."[32]

The decade of the 1920's was a time of change, a time of upheaval. To some Americans, President Warren G. Harding's pledge "to return to normalcy" was the perfect medicine; to others, there was a great need to challenge convention; while to still other citizens fear, bigotry and hatred shaped their response to the changes occurring around them. For Black Angelinos, the 1920s slowly brought an end to the Golden Era: the Ku Klux Klan found wide-spread acceptancefor their message of hate and fear among new and long time white residents of the city; more and more neighborhoods sanctioned the use of restrictive housing covenants;

and public facilities such as swimming pools further limited Black use.[33]

By 1920, the Black population of Los Angeles had doubled from the 1910 levels to 15,579; yet Afro-Americans represented only 2.7% of the total population of the city, just barely above the percentage of 1890. Unlike earlier migrations, the city, or rather the Black neighborhoods were unable to accommodate the influx. "Keep the neighborhood white" drives began the process that eventually led to the overpopulation of the Central Avenue community.[34]

Any discussion of the 1920s should begin with "The Avenue." The story of Central Avenue with its elegant neighborhood, jazz clubs, business districts and trolley cars full of Black faces has grown to mythical proportions. Some remember the "Avenue" as a miniature Harlem, where musicians and literati guaged the community's pulse by day and transformed that energy into rhyme and music by night; others recall with pride the offices of the Black physicians and dentists; the storefronts of Black businesses, and the fabled Dunbar Hotel; many, however, see only the overcrowded homes and apartments, the underside of the Avenue with its faded remnants of the dream.

The late 19th century brought the first Black residents into the area. By 1910 Central Avenue was the main thoroughfare of Black Los Angeles, with the central axis at 9th and Central, later moving south to 12th and Central. Soon "The Avenue" became an eclectic mix of stately homes representing the cream of Black society, rentals and apartments that housed the new southern migrants, and the business and professional offices of the Black middle class. In essence, "poverty and prosperity existed side by side" on Central Avenue.[35]

The Black businesses in the Central Avenue corridor were a continuing source of pride for Black Angelinos. As one walked south from 12th street, a myriad of businesses—Black and White owned—flashed by:[36] the offices of *the California Eagle*, the Lincoln Theater, the Kentucky Club, Blodgett Motors (with advertisements claiming "you can't go wrong with an Essex"),[37] the Elks Auditorium, the Central Flower Shop, and the Golden State Mutual Life Insurance Company were just a few of the many enterprises that graced this street. Just off the avenue was the 28th Street YMCA, the site of political meetings, social gatherings, as well as the leading organization working with Negro youth in the city, and the Dunbar Hospital. Located on 15th Street between Hooper and Central Avenues, the Dunbar Hospital, created in response to the discrimination against Blacks in health care, ministered to the needs of the community until the coming of World War II.

An example of the success of these businesses is the story of the Liberty Savings and Loan located near 25th and Central from its inceptance in 1924 until it ceased operations in 1961. Initially conceived and nurtured by a group of businessmen, including George Grant, A. Hartley Jones, Norman Houston, Dr. H. Claude Hudson and the Blodgett Brothers, the goal of Liberty Savings was to encourage thrift and to provide means to assist Blacks in achieving home ownership. By 1920, the company was hailed as "one of the outstanding marks of the race's business enterprises of the city...."[38]

But the jewel of Central Avenue was the Hotel Somerville, later renamed the Dunbar Hotel. This hotel, one of the most important landmarks in Los Angeles, was more than just a respite for weary travelers of color. The lobby, restaurant and conference rooms became the central meeting place for Black Angelinos, hosting a wide range of social and community events. The hotel, truly the symbol of Black achievement in this city, was the creation of John Somerville, a dentist in Los Angeles since the early 20th century. Somerville and his wife Vada were graduates of the School of Dentistry of the University of Southern California and active participants in the affairs of the Black community for over fifty years. One of the founders and early president of the Los Angeles branch of the NAACP, Somerville was keenly aware of the rising tide of racial discrimination.

In response to the fact that many Negro "visitors to the city would often suffer the embarrassment of being refused accommodations," Sommerville in 1928 decided to build a first rate hotel. Also a shrewd entreprenuer, he knew that the Pullman porters who resided in "flop houses" near the railroad station would provide a constant pool of lodgers. Located at 41st Street and

Central Avenue, the Hotel Somerville was completed in June 1928 at the approximate cost of $100,000 dollars. The Somerville contained "100 sleeping rooms" on the second, third and fourth floors, while the ground floor housed businesses such as a pharmacy, barber shop, beauty parlor and a flower shop. The lobby was decorated with murals, tapestries and exquisite furnishings, while a patio with "a fountain and potted palms faced the 41st Street entrance." The dining room, under the management of Fannie Burdette, seated one hundred and included a balcony for an orchestra.[39]

The opening of the hotel coincided with the annual National Convention of the NAACP held in the Philharmonic Auditorium. Thus the hostelry developed immediately a national reputation after housing W.E.B. DuBois, James Weldon Johnson, Lincoln Steffens, Mary White Ovington and Charles Chesnut. The Hotel Somerville was applauded as "the best hotel in the country." Even the taciturn DuBois gushed "and by all means, the Hotel Somerville."[40]

In 1929, Somerville lost the hotel because "the fate of my financial ventures could not withstand the crash of 1929....I went down with millions of other Americans." By July, the Lincoln Hotel Company acquired the property and changed the name to the Dunbar Hotel.[41] For years, the Dunbar Hotel remained the place to stay while visiting Los Angeles. Its register read like a "who's who" of Black America: Jack Johnson, Ethel Waters, Bill "Bojangles" Robinson and thousands of other Negroes called the Dunbar Hotel home.

Central Avenue was also home to a musical and literary movement that followed the patterns of the Harlem Renaissance, though on a much smaller scale. Groups like the Lafayette Players performed at the Lincoln Theater, bringing theatrical productions to the Black Angelinos. These shows were always well attended and usually well received, except by the theatre critic of *Flash Magazine* who wrote "I point with ill suppressed guffaws at the reign of the...Lafayette Players. This eminent company of mummers has offered theatrical fare that would give any normal child spiritual ennui."[42]

Literati from Langston Hughes to native son Arna Bontemps periodically spent time "in the ever enlarging artistic colony." Poetry readings by local and nationally known writers became standard Sunday fare at the 28th Street YMCA and in many residences throughout the city. While the literary output of Black Los Angeles pales in comparison to New York, further study is needed to assess properly the influence of the Harlem Renaissance on the literary productivity of the Black Angelinos. Only then will one be able to evaluate the charge made by Harold Forsythe in 1929 that the darker residents of the city were highly critical of Harlem Renaissance, so much so that "they may lay wake nights...over the depravity of Harlem, but [they] wreathe their countenances in beautiful smiles when contemplating the intellectual condition among the Afro-Americans of Los Angeles....Here reigns mediocrity,...ignorance, indifference to new ideas, love of God and hatred of beauty."[43]

For many Black Angelinos, the plethora of musical establishments jazz dens and nightclubs located in this area made Central Avenue the entertainment center of the city. While the club scene held sway along the avenue until the 1960s, this study is concerned only with the early evolution of this phenomenon. It was the jazz clubs that brought the evening crowds to Central Avenue, new migrants and established residents and "White Nordics" rubbed elbows on the dance floor. The Kentucky Club at 25th Street and Central with its racing decor; the Club Alabam; the Savoy at 55th Street and Central, where "Saturday night is whooperino nite....Everybody makes whoopee"; the Apex Night Club at 4015 Central Avenue, "where mirth, pleasure and happiness reigns supreme;" and many other establishments, all provided an opportunity for Black musicians to develop a following, and for patrons to have "cool, clean, scads of fun."[44]

One aspect of nightclubbing in Harlem that was also present along Central Avenue was "slumming." "Slumming" was the practice of Whites coming to Black clubs, lured by the music, the exotic notion of associating with Blacks and the desire to flaunt accepted racial conventions. In an article entitled "The Color Fad," Ruby Goodwin claimed "Negro night clubs of Los Angeles are filled to overflowing with prominent Whites who like dark atmosphere." Another observer of the jazz scene wrote that Whites "continue to pack in any place on the avenue that has a suggestion of a orchestra and two inches of dance floor." This practice was not meant to encourage better communication between the races for rarely did the two groups interact."[45]

Central Avenue was the home to many dreams—a fact that helps explain the historical significance of this community. The avenue was the center of the Black existence: "if you wanted to meet any of the people you...went to school with or had ever known, you could walk up and down Central Avenue and you would run into them." It "was the hub of Black life." One long time resident of the area expressed the importance of the street this way: "you didn't want to hit the avenue with dirty shoes."[46]

By 1930, racial lines had hardened as Black Angelinos suffered as a series of reverses that did much to dampen, though only temporarily, the lure of Los Angeles. In 1929 the California Supreme Court provided support and legitimacy to restrictive drives to "keep West Slauson White" and other "keep the neighborhood White drives" by declaring that residental restrictions on a tract of land as "to use and occupation" were valid. This was just one of several judicial decisions that left Black Los Angeles despairing of judicial remedies to racial discrimination. In 1926 a local court refused to force the city of Los Angeles to change a policy, adopted in 1925, that restricted the use of bath-houses and pools by "colored groups" to one afternoon each week.[47]

Racial discrimination soon found its way into the churches. The Rector of St. Matthews Protestant Episcopal Church in Brooklyn, William Blackshear, stunned the Black members of his congregation with this announcement: "The Episcopal Church provides churches for Negroes. Several of these churches are within easy reach to this locality. They are in need of the loyal support of all true Negro churchmen. Therefore the Rector of this parish discourages the attendance or membership in this church of members of that race."[48]

Even the annexation of Watts by the city of Los Angeles had racial overtones. While most Black migrants were funnelled into the regions surrounding Central Avenue, many had been drawn to Watts because of available inexpensive land deemed undesirable by the White residents. By the mid-1920s, Blacks were such a factor in Watts that many citizens, including members of the local Ku Klux Klan, feared that the community would become a Black town; already some residents of Los Angeles called the area "Nigger Heaven." To avoid the consequences of a Black mayor, many Whites sought to persuade Los Angeles to annex Watts: they were successful.[49]

The changes of the 1920s laid to rest any notion of the continuation of the earlier Golden Era. Although the conditions faced by Black Angelinos worsened during the "Roaring Twenties," many Negro residents barely noticed the rising tide of racism, as they participated in the prosperity of the era. No one—Black or White—was prepared, or could overlook, the consequences of the stock market crash in 1929 and the ensuing Great Depression.

The Great Depression stunned White America but it devastated Black America. Millions of Americans found themselves unemployed and unemployable—there were just no jobs. Many of these citizens took to the roads in search of a chance, an opportunity. Thousands saw California as the land where that change awaited them. Black Americans joined that stream of the California bound. These years saw a massive increase in the Black population from a previous high of 38,844 in 1930 to 63,774 in 1940.[50]

The need to improve the employment opportunities for Black Angelinos led to a pivotal event in the fight against discrimination in Los Angeles. Frustrated by the severity of the depression, and hindered by the oppressive nature of racial bigotry, Blacks in Los Angeles demonstrated a new militance by supporting Leon Washington's "Don't spend your money where you can't work" campaign. Washington, a former journalist on staff at the *California Eagle*, was the publisher of the *Los Angeles Sentinel*. Concern about the lack of Black employees in many of the businesses along Central Avenue, from 2nd to 40th Streets, especially because much of the patronage of these stores were Black, motivated the publisher to act. In January 1934, Washington parked his car in front of Zerg's Furniture Company at 4th and Central, with a sign proclaiming "Don't spend your money where you can't work." The police arrived and arrested Washington for unlawful picketing.

As word of Washington's arrest spread, several hundred demonstrators (probably drawn from the more than 20% of the Black community on the relief rolls) lined the street, calling for a boycott of all businesses that did not hire Blacks. In the 26 January 1934 issue of the *Los Angeles Sentinel*, Washington waxed optimistically that:

> With the incident as a spur, organizations interested in the success of the campaign were quick to lay plans for concerted action to bring home to the merchants...that refusal to employ Negroes will bring quick and decisive action.

Washington's actions were universally applauded by Black Angelinos. One resident commented later "through Mr. Washington's efforts thousands of Negroes are working."[51]

As the depression lingered, the Black residents sought solace and entertainment in a myriad of ways. The evangelical appeal of Daddy Grace and Father Divine garnered many of the faithful to Divine's "Heavens" or to Graces' "United House of Prayer". Others who looked towards the heavens were seeking a glimpse of the troupe of Black aviators known as the "Bessie Coleman Aero Club." Led by William Powell and J. Herman Banning, these pilots hoped to inspire "airmindedness" among the Black Angelinos by performing "feats of aerial daring" at Mine's Municipal Airport in Inglewood and at the Los Angeles Airport. These flyers were convinced that "the hopes of the Afro-American soars upward on the wings of an aeroplane." While these "Black birds" may not have converted as many Black residents as Grace and Divine, they nonetheless provided an important diversion from the hopelessness of the Depression.[52]

By 1940, the better days that movies and politicians claimed were "just around the corner," finally arrived, fueled by the struggles in Europe and in Asia. The requirements of a war-time economy revitalized the industrial sector of the nation, providing jobs for thousands of the unemployed. In California, this trend was accelerated by the number of war industries housed in the region. Until 1942, however, relatively few Blacks settled in Los Angeles due to the rampant discrimination in the war related industries. These companies claimed that introducing Blacks into the work environment was disruptive; therefore, they limited employment opportunities for people of color.

That policy weakened in 1942 when A. Philip Randolph, President of the Brotherhood of Sleeping Car Porters, demanded that the federal government guarantee Blacks equal access to jobs in the war industries. If President Franklin D. Roosevelt did not act, Randolph would call for "a march on Washington to publicize the grievances of the Afro-American." Roosevelt, concerned about the possible propaganda value such a march would have for the Axis Powers, issued Executive Order 8802, requiring defense contractors to eliminate discrimination in their companies. Coupled with this action was the growing labor shortage, brought on by the manpower needs of the military. Factories soon needed workers, regardless of color.

Between 1942-1945, some 340,000 Blacks settled in California, 200,000 of whom migrated to Los Angeles. These migrants were drawn by the possibility of jobs. Word had reached the south, via the state employment offices, that the shipbuilding industry needed laborers. Also, in March 1942 the Southern Pacific Railroad provided free transportation to three thousand Blacks who were hired as section hands. These recruitments also created unrealistic expectations of opportunities in Los Angeles for thousands of migrants, frustrated in their search for employment, were forced to accept public relief.[53] On balance, the movement to Southern California was beneficial for the rural migrants, at least they escaped the oppressive southern racism, but the influx had a negative impact on the established Black communities.

The greater the Black population grew, the more tightly enforced were the restrictive housing covenants. Though the Black community doubled in the 1940s, it remained confined by pre-war boundaries. The mayor of Los Angeles, Fletcher Bowron, called for federal assistance to build housing for the migrants; "we simply cannot throw these people into the streets."[54] The public housing authority could not, however, handle the sheer volume of the migration. Some members of the National Housing Authority, feeling the situation had reached catastrophic proportions, suggested limiting entrance into the city. Although this idea was rejected, that it received serious consideration speaks to the severity of the overcrowding.

As conditions worsened, racial violence occurred on the streets of Los Angeles. Students at Fremont High School, upset over the enrollment of Black students, went on a rampage in 1941. The White students threatened their Afro-American counterparts, burned them in effigy and displayed posters proclaiming "we want no niggers at this school." In 1943 a series of pitched battles occurred between Whites and Blacks on 5th and San Pedro Streets. Shortly thereafter, a riot occurred when the White owner of the Paramount Cafe on Central Avenue refused to serve a group of Blacks. Angered, the group wrecked the establishment.[55]

In spite of the violence and the worsening race relations, the Black Angelinos refused to accept second class citizenship. Continued pressure on the hiring practices of the war industries brought down racial barriers. California Shipbuilding and Consolidated Steel began hiring 7,000 Blacks in 1942; by August of that year, the Lockheed Company hired the first of its Black employees; and a lawsuit that culminated in the decision, *James* v. *Marin Ship* in 1944, eliminated segregated unions in a closed shop and paved the way for fuller union participation by Afro-Americans.

An example of one family's refusal to accept the racial strictures was the struggle waged by the Laws who arrived in Los Angeles in 1910 from Rosenburg, Texas. After living in a number of homes, the family settled in Watts about 1926, opening a restaurant in the predominately White and Mexican community. In 1936, the Laws family purchased property in the Good Year Tract, on 92nd Street in Watts. Mr. Laws knew that the land was restricted, that he could own the property but he could not live on it. In 1940, the family decided to challenge the law and live on 92nd Street. After three days in the house, the family received an eviction notice. As one member of the family remembers: "We were just ornery enough to say 'we're not going to get out of our house.'"[56] When a judge ruled that they had to vacate or go to jail, the family chose incarceration.

The *California Eagle* and Mrs. Bass initiated a campaign to assist the family in its fight against "the 92nd Street Outrage." After several years of litigation the NAACP urged the family to abandon their crusade, but the Laws recalled that: "we never decided to give up. We intended to fight the thing all the way through."[57] The Black churches, especially Clayton Russell's Peoples Independent Church, First A.M.E. Church and Second Baptist Church, raised funds and provided support for the family. In 1948, the case reached the Supreme Court of the United States where the court upheld the position of the Laws family. As a result of this decision restrictive real estate covenants became invalid and unconstitutional.

To ensure Black access to the war industries, the Victory Committee was formed in 1941. This organization, consisting of Black Angelinos such as Norman Houston of Golden State Life Insurance, Floyd Covington of the Urban League, Thames Griffith of the NAACP and Clayton Russell of Peoples Independent Church, took an active stand. In 1942, the Victory Committee marched on the United States Employment Service after hearing of a statement by a White official that Black women were not interested in employment in war industries. Because of this pressure, the federal agency issued a statement denouncing racial discrimination. The Victory Committee also used its clout to pressure the Los Angeles Board of Education to open vocational training centers in Black neighborhoods and to force the Los Angeles Railway to hire Black motormen and conductors.[58]

By 1950, the 170,880 Black residents of the city, comprising 8.7% of the total population, were almost all crowded into the traditionally Black neighborhoods. This community resided in the following areas: east of Main Street from 1st Street to Manchester Avenue; between Main Street and Vermont Avenue from Jefferson to Slauson; in Watts and in the West Jefferson District—from between Adams and Exposition Boulevards with the east-west borders being Vermont to Crenshaw. Although the Supreme Court outlawed residential covenants in 1948, this form of discrimination was not resolved effectively until the Open Housing Act of 1968.

While the postwar period was a harbinger of change, Black Angelinos had to wait until a future day brought integration and equal opportunity. As John Somerville so perceptibly wrote in 1949, "White supremacy may be scientifically dead, but its ghost still walks the streets of Los Angeles."[59]

It is clear that by 1960s, the black residents of Los Angeles, despite regional, color and class distinctions, had formed a cohesive community-one that had benefitted from the exertions and efforts of numerous earlier individuals and organizations. Black Angelinos, while still quite limited by the pervasive influences of racism, were optomistic that their sense of community, their political and educational organizations such as the NAACP, the Phyliss Wheatley Club and the Urban League, their business, professional and religious leaders and their defenders in the black press would stand them in good stead as they faced the future. A cursory view might suggest that except for the problems caused by the Watts Riot (known as the Watts Rebellion to the city's black residents), the black community has progressed admirably toward the realization of economic opportunity, political influence and racial harmony.[60]

After all, to many, the political ascendency of Tom Bradley marks the apex of black political power—as was the case with the election of black mayors in Newark, Chicago, Gary and the District of Columbia. Bradley's election must mean that Black Angelinos had a greater share of the political and economic spoils. That notion is an unsubstantiated myth. Part of Bradley's strength is his ability to triumph without overwhelming support of the black electorate. As the consummate builder of coalitions, Bradley had to temper his appeals based on race so not to alienate liberal white and Jewish support. While Bradley may be applauded for his ability to walk the political tightrope, his tenure should not be seen as a barometer of the success of the black community.

Obviously, the past is not prologue when it comes to the city's black citizens. By 1989, the cohesiveness of the black community that was built over a century, is a thing of the past. Looking at the many black communities in today's Los Angeles, it is easy to despair. Police estimates suggest that gang related crime has increased over 30% in less than a year, much of which occurs in the drug and turf-related war zones that house many of the city's citizens of color. Instead of the promised integrated schools that were to challenge and uplift black and Latino children, teachers and residents find that the real challenge is to find schools where substantive education occurs. Even in "good" areas of the city, homeowners resort to prison-like bars (regardless of how decorative they appear) to protect their property and themselves every evening. No longer does a black community contain a diversity of residents. Now the black middle class has fled to the hills of Altadena or to the "golden ghettoes" of Baldwin Hills or View Park or to one of several "integrated communities" outside of Los Angeles, leaving behind the less fortunate. And this new middle and upper class soon learns that race is still the central influence on the availability of affordable housing and upon career advancement.

This then, is the lot of black Los Angeles today. In some ways, life is better for certain segments of the black community than ever before; yet Black Angelinos appear to have lost much of the unique characteristics that have enabled blacks historically to endure the Sisyphean struggle against racism. This is not to suggest that during the period 1850-1950 Los Angeles was an oasis free of bigotry, but rather that the cohesiveness of the community, born from self-help organizations, church endeavors and the interaction of the needs and concerns of diverse social classes and articulated by various leaders, was the single greatest asset of Black Angelinos.

Clearly that connective tissue is missing in today's black community. Ironically, as racism and its outward manifestations retreated under the pressure for civil rights and affirmative action, the black community began to lose its sense of self. In a way, it was the bonds of racism that held the community together: restrictive housing covenants ensured that rich and poor shared the same residential spaces, stores that refused to allow black shoppers to try on shoes guaranteed that Afro-Americans would patronize black-owned enterprises, and the continued lack of political clout encouraged the support of community action or self-help organizations. When these bonds were stretched by the struggle for equal rights, the black populace's cohesiveness began to slip away, thus inhibiting effective communal responses to economic and social problems. It is, therefore, appropriate to discuss the impact of integration on the black citizens of Los Angeles.

Throughout much of the 19th century, integration was not the central focus of the Black American's struggle for equality. Few dared to broach the subject, which was then known as social equality, though many such as Frederick Douglass, Bishop Henry Turner, and here in Los Angeles, Biddy Mason and Robert C. Owens, struggled mightily for political rights and economic opportunity. In fact some African-Americans questioned the need for such "intimate" contact between the races. A quintessential example of the attitude was the speech delivered by Booker T. Washington to the Atlanta Exposition in 1894. During the address, Washington, then the most recognized Negro by White Americans, called for the races to work together in the area of economic development but "to be as separate as the fingers in all things purely social." A few years later, Washington and President Theodore Roosevelt dined together in the White House. After the meal, they were photographed still at the dinner table. While many blacks lauded these "social equality pictures," White America reacted with horror and disgust. To avoid political damage, Roosevelt promised never to invite Washington to the White House again. The furor that this event caused is illustrative of the attitude of most Americans towards even the casual mixing of the races. Not until the 20th century did blacks begin to see integration as synonomous with racial equality.

While this change can be attributed to several factors, one of the most important was the rise of W.E.B. DuBois and the NAACP. DuBois was a young, Harvard-trained historian who later was instrumental in establishing the NAACP and its publicity arm—*The Crisis* magazine. DuBois felt that racial prejudice in all arenas should be confronted, including social discrimination. Throughout the early years of the century, the NAACP battled for total racial equality from New York to Los Angeles. Eventually blacks throughout the nation rallied to the cause, discrimination in any area was wrong and must be eradicated. Another factor was the participation of African-Americans in both world wars. If blacks and whites could die equally in war, then blacks had the right to the same equality on the homefront. By the time that the Supreme Court issued its landmark school desegregation decision, *Brown* v. *The Topeka, Kansas, Board of Education,* in 1954, Black America was committed to making integration the rule, rather than the exception, in American life.

There is no denying that integration has dramatically changed the manner and attitudes of most Americans for the better. The benefits are too numerous to mention, yet there is a negative side to this wave of racial interaction. Integration, and black America's uncritical acceptance of all its aspects, has helped to destroy much of traditional black community life.

Talk with any Black Angeleno over the age of fifty and he will wax poetic about the richness of black life along Central Avenue, describing the plethora of homes, the wonderful atmosphere and music that flowed from the Club Alabam and The Apex Club, the economic promise of black businesses—whether a bakery, a newspaper or a beauty parlor, the pride in self that sprang from the bookstores, literary guilds and community organizations like the YMCA or Garvey's UNIA. Compare that passion with the spirit of resignation that accompanies his discussion about life along "the avenue" in 1989.

This is not just a Los Angeles phenomenum; this sense of decline, lose and spiritual ennui is replicated throughout black America. Almost every major urban center had its Central Avenue: in New York it was Lennox avenue and 125th street; Atlanta had "Sweet Auburn Street;" in Milwaukee it was Walnut Street; while the heart of black life in St Louis was Franklin Avenue; and Black Chicago was anchored by South Park Street. What happened to these communities was a combination of overcrowding caused by housing restrictions based on race, poverty and the impact of integration.

As soon as opportunity allowed, blacks quickly fled the constraints of areas like Central Avenue. Integration and equality now meant the freedom to shop at white department stores such as Robinson or The May Company; it seemed nonprogressive to continue to buy in black-owned establishments whose stock and prices could not compete with these other retailers. As one resident said, "there was something exciting about buying from the white stores." Soon black pharmacies, sweet shoppes, record stores, printing factories and hotels found that this rush towards integration too often resembled an exodus away from black enterprises. It is ironic that recent years have seen African American owned businesses develop advertising campaigns geared to convince the community "to buy Black," and that black leaders bemoan the paucity and fragile nature of the businesses that do exist. As these businesses declined, so too did the community.

Obviously, the advent of integration and fair housing legislation affected the residential composition of the community. As the middle class shattered the restrictions of housing covenants, more and more of its members left these eastside and south-central areas for more comfortable homes to the north and west. This limited the educational and economic diversity of the black communities. No longer did lower class citizens benefit from direct and indirect contact with black achievers; in many areas the only recognizable role models were individuals with less than sterling reputations. This is not an unimportant consideration. As long as these communities reflected every strata of economic achievement, children, though still exposed to the criminals, gamblers, drug addicts (the seamier side of life), developed a greater sense of career and educational possibilities. Also as the more affluent departed, the percentage of home ownership declined and the physical structures began to reflect the decay that often accompanies landlord neglect. And so begins the cycle that leads to poverty and despair.

Those Black Angelinos fortunate enough to escape the culture of poverty that gripped South-Central Los Angeles relocated to the newly opened (e.g. integrated) communities of View Park and Baldwin Hills. This process occurred slowly and cautiously, with a few families settling in the area of lovely homes and startling views of Los Angeles. Eventually the white residents departed leaving an elite class of blacks to populate these "golden ghettoes." While this enclave of doctors, lawyers and businessmen were able to distance themselves from their poorer brethern, scenic vistas and hilltop estates did not guarantee access to the halls of political and economic power. In some ways, this group was a classic example of the Afro-American communities that E. Franklin Frazier discussed in his work, *The Black Bourgoise*, who mimicked White patterns of behavior as a means to separate themselves from the rest of the black community.

This separation was so complete that this new "Black Bourgoise" created a series of social and cultural organizations such as "100 Black Men", "The Links", "The Jack and Jills" and "The

Circleletts" to service the needs of their class exclusively. On the surface this seems rather harmless, silly but harmless. Closer examination reveals that this desire to remain outside traditional black organizations undermines the effectiveness of these groups. Without the financial support and prestige of the black upper classes, old line pressure groups in the city such as the Los Angeles Forum, the NAACP, and the Phyliss Wheatley Club were much less effective. Thus the very vehicles that powered much of the social changes in the community were hampered, and in some cases destroyed, by the very forces of change that they had worked to unleash. While some transformation is beneficial, this flight from traditional black service and community organizations has eliminated effective tools in the struggle for civil rights. Today Black Los Angeles finds itself struggling to find a voice, an organization or an association that can help the citizens of color develop an agenda for the 1990s. This condition is because of the disharmony and isolation that is rampant among Black residents of Southern California and that stems, in part, from the changes sparked by the drive for integration.

Another factor that restricts the Black Angelinos in their campaign for equality, is the widening gulf between the lower and middle classes. Class conflict within the Afro-American populace is not new. Disagreements about the lifestyles, behavior, educational levels and contributions were apparent in Black Los Angeles as early as the late 1850s. These differences were moderated by the fact that all blacks—regardless of class—were relatively powerless and buffeted by the same winds of racism.

Today, residents of the inner city continually cry that they have been forsaken by the Black middle class. Rather than view this more affluent group as potential allies, they are seen as individuals who revel in a make-believe world of social gatherings while forgetting their common roots in the soil of racial oppression. "They just want to be white," said a resident of Watts recently. Meanwhile the middle class expresses concern that its less fortunate brethern are uninspired and uninterested in improving their lot, and more willing to accept crime, poverty and drugs in their neighborhoods. These comments reflect the antagonism that exists between the black social classes. Unless the black populace of Los

Angeles addresses the roots of this problem and begins to seek solutions, this chasm will become unreconcilable.

The black middle and professional class also faces difficult dilemmas that threaten to limit their future. As this group seeks to garner a greater share of the American Dream, it distances itself from the very community that has nurtured and supported those aspirations. Suggestions that this group has abandoned the race cuts deeply. Most of the black middle class, to its credit, feels firmly bonded to the race. They view themselves as examples of the "talented tenth" that DuBois felt would lead Blacks out of poverty and ignorance. With each achievement, they argue, "we are improving the lot of black folks". Yet the sense of isolation is strong, as if affluent Black Angelinos are struggling to keep one foot in the black world while the other foot is stepping gingerly into the white arena. One way that some address this sense of ambivalence is by sending their children or grandchildren to black colleges—to ensure that these Baldwin Hills babies will experience blackness in a way that is unlikely to occur in Los Angeles.

While issues of solidarity and class are the central challenges facing contemporary Black Angelinos, another important, though less obvious, consideration is the burgeoning power and influence of the region's Hispanic and Asian communities. Historically, the black residents of Southern California have accepted, generally, the diverse immigrant populations of the region. The oral history is ripe with stories of friendship and mutual assistance, such as Blacks and Mexicans working together in the 19th century pueblo and Japanese residents asking Afro-Americans to safeguard their belongings as they prepare for relocation.

Today, that era of good feelings has vanished. The African American community reacts with envy, distrust and, at times, anger, to the growing economic and political clout of the "new immigration". Part of the resentment stems from the perception that America embraces and encourages these new migrants to reach heights that are still unobtainable to most blacks. Why else, this argument posits, could the Koreans, for example, develop a monopoly of the small "mom and pop" stores in South-Central Los Angeles, a situation that has led to confrontation and violence in recent years. Why does the state government seem more response to the needs of the Hispanic community? Why does black political influence seem on the wane? Why do Black contributions to this region appear to have been forgotten.

This fear of being overlooked derives from a concern that the African-American has already had his moment in the spotlight. During the 1960s, the Negro was in vogue. There was an unrelenting flood of monographs (many quite awful) that chronicled every aspect of black life, from family structure to language to films. Television and movies (who could forget that "black private eye who was a sex machine with all the chicks—John Shaft") discovered that America was interested in watching its darker brothers and sisters. For a while it seemed that everyone wanted to revel in black culture. But the "law and order" administration of Richard Nixon signalled a new day.

Many blacks feel that they missed a opportunity to craft a society that more meaningfully and permanently permitted greater access to the promise of America. And now that other outsiders are demanding their share, many Black Angelinos worry that they will not have another chance to effect such farsighted change. As a Hispanic colleague noted, "blacks need to move over, it's now our turn."

Being ethno-centric is obviously not a trait restricted to the black citizens of Los Angeles. What is unfortunate, however, is the belief that each ethnic group is in competition with one another. This attitude prevents these political and economic outsiders from developing much needed alliances to expand their limited political clout. Thus, blacks see the recent migrants as contributing to their problems, rather than as potential allies.

So what does all this mean? Let me explain by way of an analogy. Recently I attended a convention of Science Fiction enthusiasts. With only a few exceptions, the authors' visions of the future did not include blacks, as if all voices of color would be silent in the next century. While I do not accept their future world of like-skinned residents, I do worry that Black Angelinos may become a voiceless minority, unless the community begins to address some of the serious issues confronting them.

This is not to suggest that the only problems facing Black America stem from their own community. Only the most naive or most racist of thinkers could believe that. The impact of integration is simply one of many hurdles facing Black Los Angeles, but it is a very significant factor. It is impossible to return to the past where Black Angelinos met every Sunday at Scott's Hall on Central or at the Los Angeles Forum to discuss issues of the day. But it is essential that the residents of color in this city rediscover and recapture the cohesiveness and strength of community that once existed. Unless Black Angelinos relearn to tap that wellspring of resiliency that is inherent in the African American experience, they may become simply silent spectators to the future.

NOTES

1   *The* [Los Angeles] *Liberator*, 16 May 1919, p.1.

2   *The Crisis*, Aug. 1913, p. 192.

3   Ibid, p. 193.

4   Oral Interview with Ruby Johnson Braxton, Sept. 1987.

5   Oral Interview with Kathy Perkins, Sept. 1987.

6   Claudia Jurmain and James Rawls, eds., *California: A Place, A People, A Dream* (San Francisco: Chronicle Books & Oakland: The Oakland Museum, 1986), 15; *The Liberator*, 31 Jan. 1913, p. 1.

7   *The Liberator*, 13 June 1913.

8   Ibid., 21 Apr. 1911.

9   *Negro Population in the United States, 1790-1915* (New York: Arno/New York Times, 1968).

10   Ibid. While the population of Black Los Angeles was 7,599 in 1910, Oakland listed 3,055 residents and San Francisco contained 1,642.

11   *The Liberator*, 23 May 1913; ibid, 22 Aug. 1913.

12   Ibid; *Negro Population in the United States, 1790-1915*.

13   Max Bond, "The Negro in Los Angeles," Ph.D. diss., University of California, Los Angeles, 1936, p. 24; *The Liberator*, Jan./Feb. 1904.

14   Arnold Rampersad, *The Life of Langston Hughes*. Vol. I: *I, Too, Sing America* (New York: Oxford University Press, 1986), 308.

15   *The Liberator*, 21 Apr. 1911.

16   *The Liberator*, 8 Aug. 1913; *The Colored American Magazine* (July 1905): 392.

17   *The Liberator*, Jan./Feb. 1904; ibid., 23 May 1913; and ibid., 17 Jan. 1913.

18   Ibid.

19   Ibid., 30 May 1913.

20 Edmonds had his revenge when John Shenk ran for Mayor. Edmonds marshalled the Black and disaffected White vote to ensure Shenk's defeat.

21 *The Liberator*, 20 June 1913.

22 *The Colored American Magazine* (May 1907): 387.

23 These cases were only a small number of the incidents reported in *The Liberator*.

24 *The Liberator*, Jan./Feb. 1904; *Los Angeles Times*, 12 Feb. 1909.

25 In 1904, the officers of the Forum were:

President, J. Thomas Norris
Vice President, F. H. Crumbly
Secretary, B. W. Sikes
Asst. Secretary, J. L. Edwards, Jr.
Recording Secretary, T. A. Green
Treasurer, J. H. Jamison
Chaplain, Reverend J. E. Jamison

26 *Los Angeles Times*, 12 Feb. 1909.

27 Ibid., p. 151.

28 Delilah Beasley, *Negro Trail Blazers of California,* Reprint (New York: Negro University Press, 1969), 132.

29 Emory J. Tolbert, *The UNIA and Black Los Angeles: Ideology and Community in the American Garvey Movement* (Los Angeles: Center for Afro-American Studies, UCLA, 1980), 34.

30 John Alexander Somerville, *Man of Color: An Autobiography of J. Alexander Somerville, a Factual Report of the Status of the American Negro Today* (Los Angeles: Morrison Printing & Publishing Co., 1942), 81.

31 Beasley, p. 259.

32 *The Liberator*, Nov. 1901.

33 *The Liberator*, 11 Apr. 1913; ibid., 7 Apr. 1911. J. L. Edmonds is an individual who deserves a book length study. His record of political consciousness is unsurpassed. See *The Liberator*, 6 Dec. 1912 for a poem that captures the importance of Edmonds to the Black Angeleno.

34 *Flash Magazine*, 27 July 1929, p. 23.

35 For an excellent study of this process, see Lawrence DeGraaf, "The City of Black Angels: Emergence of the Los Angeles Ghetto, 1890-1930," *Pacific Historical Review* 39 (1970).

36 Bond, p. 72.

37 There is a tendency to overstate the number of Black-owned business in the area. While many of the enterprises of the Avenue were owned by Whites, Black businesses were a small but significant segment of the business community.

38 *Flash Magazine*, 18 May 1929, p. 6.

39 Ibid., 9 Feb.1929, p. 21.

40 Somerville, *Man of Color*, pp. 125-128; *Flash Magazine*, 18 Jan. 1929, p. 20.

41 Somerville, p. 126; *Flash Magazine*, 18 Jan. 1929, p. 2

42 Somerville, p. 127; The Dunbar Hotel operated as a successful concern for many years. Today it houses a small museum and there are plans to restore the hotel so that it will once again be the jewel of Central Avenue.

43 *Flash Magazine*, 18 Jan. 1929, p. 24.

44 Ibid., p. 22; Joyce Johnson of California State University/Dominguez Hills and the author are both currently conducting research in this area.

45 *Flash Magazine*, 2 Mar. 1929, p. 15; ibid., 18 May 1929, p. 13; ibid., 18 Jan.1928, pp. 16-17.

46 Ibid., 31 Dec. 1929, p. 11; Ibid., 27 July 1929, p. 12.

47 Oral interview of Melvin Boulder by CAAM staff, August 1987; Oral interview of William Page by CAAM staff, Nov. 1987.

48 *Flash Magazine*, 18 Jan. 1929, p. 7; *George Cushnie v. City of Los Angeles, Board of Playground and Recreation Commissioners*, case #180780, Records of the County Court of Los Angeles.

49 *Flash Magazine*, 5 Oct. 1929.

50 Ibid., 18 Jan. 1929, p. 26; Bond's "The Negro in Los Angeles" and DeGraff's "The City of Black Angels" carry effective description of this process.

51 Bureau of the Census, *Sixteenth Census of the United States* (Washington, DC: GPO, 1942).

52 *Los Angeles Sentinel*, 26 Jan. 1934, p. 1; Somerville, *Man of Color*, p. 154.

53 Bass, p. 196; *Flash Magazine*, 1 June 1929, p. 14; For a discussion of the importance of early Black aviation see Lonnie Bunch, "In Search of a Dream: The Flight of Herman Banning and Thomas Allen," *Journal of American Culture* (Summer 1984); and Joseph J. Corn, *The Winged Gospel: America's Romance With Aviation, 1900-1950* (New York: Oxford University Press, 1983).

54 Gerald D. Nash, *The American West Transformed: The Impact of the Second World War* (Bloomington: Indiana University Press, 1985), 91-92.

55 Ibid, p. 95.

56 Ibid.

57 Oral interview with Pauletta Fears, Deloris Tropez and Anton Fears conducted by CAAM staff, 21 Sept. 1987.

58 Bass, p. 110; Ibid.

59 Ernest Anderson, pp. 180-192.

60 For more on the Watts Riot and other urban riots of the 1960s, see Henry F, Bedford, *Trouble Downtown: The Local Context of Twentieth-Century America* (New York: Harcourt Brace Jovanovich, 1978), ch. 5.

Chapter 5

WHEN THE MOBSTERS CAME WEST: ORGANIZED CRIME IN LOS ANGELES SINCE 1930

Richard Whitehall

The history of Los Angeles often sounds like the script for a Sam Peckinpah movie but with one essential difference, the good guys seldom won. In the beginning, there were the land barons who jealously possessed their real estate and wanted only to enhance its value. As the city grew to one million people by 1925, the attitude of its power elite remained unchanged. The idea of civic responsibility was not readily acceptable to the city leadership who were virtually governed by corporate interests. The organs of government were corrupted because the policies they followed were designed not to benefit or protect the population as a whole but to serve a set of special interests. Law enforcement selectively enforced the law and, thus, its whole purpose was corrupted. In Los Angeles, the police didn't fight crime; they protected it, controlling and directing vice and gambling. Since the basic philosophy of the city was that business interests took precedence, one can hardly blame the police for not exempting themselves from it.

Police protection of gambling and vice was standard practice. This is one reason why organized crime never became as deeply entrenched in Los Angeles as elsewhere. In 1936, when Benjamin (Bugsy) Siegel came west, the city administration under Mayor Frank L. Shaw and Police Chief James Davis was at its most corrupt.[1] It is thought Siegel came here with a specific directive to reorganize and expand mob interests in Southern California. Jack

Dragna, who ran mob operations here, was "very powerful and very well respected, but he got kind of lackadaisical"[2] and it was felt a more decisive leadership was needed. Albert Fried, in *The Rise and Fall of the Jewish Gangster*, offers a different view. He suggests Siegel came west because he hoped to make it in the movies.

With Siegel's smooth good looks, this is not an unreasonable assumption. On his arrival, he seemed to gravitate naturally towards Hollywood, giving the movie colony an opportunity to party with a *bona fide* gangster. The movie colony did not turn down this opportunity. Siegel was taken up by Countess Dorothy di Frasso, a rich American married to a minor Italian noble. She made a name for herself as one of Hollywood's most extravagant hostesses. Movies and mobsters mixed very successfully by the mid 1930s and the gangster film became a distinctive American movie genre. Siegel's friend, George Raft, who had hung around with Owney Madden's gang during Prohibition, gave the genre a touch of authenticity.

Raft made a strong impression in *Scarface* and had gone on to become a star at Paramount. When his contract expired at that studio in 1939, he moved to Warners where they made the best gangster films. At the Burbank studio he was very successful with his early films, *Each Dawn I Die* and *They Drive By Night*. However, he did not help his career by turning down the role in *The Maltese Falcon* which helped build Humphrey Bogart's screen persona to mythic proportions. "I feel strongly that *The Maltese Falcon* which you want me to do, is not an important picture," Raft wrote to Jack Warner.[3]

If Siegel wanted movie stardom, looks or lack of talent was not the major obstacle, but rather his past associations. Raft had traded on the slightly raffish romanticism of a bootlegging past, but how do you sell a brash young businessman whose business is murder? In his early twenties Siegel, with Meyer Lansky, formed the outfit known as "The Bugs and Meyer Mob" to carry out contracts, i.e. murders, for organized crime in New York and New Jersey. At first, Siegel and Lansky worked as freelancers. As their services became more valuable and expensive, they became partners in the Syndicate, and seven years later their outfit became the notorious

Murder Incorporated.   As a reward for their services and as appreciation of their participation, the mob gave California to Siegel as his fiefdom, and allotted Florida to Lansky.   Mickey Cohen, the best known of Angeleno gangsters, born in the Brownsville section of Brooklyn but raised in Boyle Heights from the age of two, said of Siegel: "Benny was part and parcel of New York on a par with anyone you could mention—Joe Adonis, Lucky Luciano, Frank Costello."[4]   Luciano's racketeering in New York vice had made headlines in 1936 when he was convicted on the evidence of prositutes.   Warner's, true to their policy of taking their stories from the headlines, made a strong film from this case, *Marked Woman* (1937).   It would hardly have been the appropriate time to make a movie star of Siegel, whose name and address was linked to Luciano's (they had both lived at the Waldorf Towers until Siegel came west).

Siegel's new territory presented challenges and difficulties different to those he had hitherto experienced.   Here the police department fulfilled the mob function of organizing crime.   Jack Dragna, who headed mob operations in Los Angeles, lacked clout in the organization.   Dragna, whose real name was Anthony Rizzoti, had come to America with his brother, Tom, in the early years of the century, and the family settled in California.   By the late 1920s, he was president of the Italian Protective League, a protection racket aimed at small businesses in produce, cleaning establishments, and barber shops.   Vice and gambling, the major profitable source of mob income in eastern cities, went into other pockets.   As Mickey Cohen remarked about the situation in which the newly arrived Siegel found himself: "There wasn't even a casino open."[5]   Siegel soon changed that.   Before long there was income from the Agua Caliente race track, from the numbers racket, from the Clover Club on Sunset Boulevard, from the Culver City dog track, and from a 15% interest in the gambling ships anchored out in the Santa Monica Bay.

The gambling ships were the brainwave of Antonio Cornero Stralla, once a cab driver in San Francisco.   During Prohibition, Stralla had changed from cabbie to bootlegger, running liquor across the Mexican and Canadian borders, making his first million by the age of 30.   In 1938, he earned himself a footnote to the social history of California by acquiring a steamship, the 'Rex', and anchoring it three miles off-shore from Santa Monica. Using a fleet of water taxis, Cornello had gamblers ferried out to his floating casino. It was not long before deputy sheriffs from Los Angeles County raided the ship. Pleading uncertainty as to their legal authority, the deputies arrested the gamblers but left the gambling operation intact.

Cornello countered this by moving his operation beyond the 12 mile limit and within a short time he had prospered to the extent that there were three gambling ships in operation. His business flourished for a year, until Earl Warren, then Attorney General of California, had the fleet raided and $100,000 worth of gambling equipment was dumped into the Pacific. In 1947, Cornello tried again with a decommissioned Navy mine-layer renamed the 'Lux'. The Coast Guard siezed the ship as a menace to navigation. After this setback, Cornello retired from California to Nevada, where gambling has been legalized since 1931. He died of a heart attack on 31 July 1955 while building the biggest resort hotel in the world, the Starlight (later renamed the Stardust) on the strip in Las Vegas.

Organized crime had prospered through its willingness to give the American public what it wanted, particularly if what the public wanted was illegal. Liquor was easily available during Prohibition, gambling in the years that followed, drugs in more recent days. The mobsters did not present themselves as public servants, although they sometimes acted as if that were their appointed function. "All I ever did was sell beer and whiskey to our best people," Capone once said. "If people didn't want beer and wouldn't drink it, a fellow would be crazy going around trying to sell it. I've seen gambling houses too in my travels, you understand, and I never saw anyone point a gun at a man and make him go in."[6]

The key to Siegel's success was gambling. He grasped and exploited new opportunities to part the public from its money. This resulted in his greatest achievement: the creation of Las Vegas. But the road to Las Vegas was taken by way of the race-wire service and the war that raged around it in the 1940s. This struggle for control seemed like the scenario for a Warner gangster film, *The*

Roaring Twenties. This was one story Warner's did not take from the headlines. Only one film has touched on the subject, watered down and wildly distorted, making a B movie from an A subject. *711 Ocean Drive* (1950) set in Los Angeles, fritters away its opportunities, although its producers claimed they had received threats from the mob.[7] This was a publicity ploy to sell a bad movie and it can hardly be taken seriously.

As late as 1951, the U.S. Senate's Kefauver Committee, in its massive investigation of organized crime in America, found that, while the city of Los Angeles was now actively investigating criminal elements, the county was more tolerant. What the committee referred to as "the vice squad pattern" was in full operation. "The police department bosses set up a vice squad composed of a chosen few directly accountable to them. They instructed the remaining law-enforcement officers to stay away from gambling and vice and to channel any complaints to the vice squad for action or, in most cases, inaction. By this device, a small clique frequently controls the collection of the protection pay-off. It directs police activity against operations that conflict with those that are 'in' or those slow to recognize their responsibilities to purchase 'official tolerance' to operate." As an example of how this pattern works, it was found that in Los Angeles County even the vice squad didn't move freely without instructions from Captain Pearson.[8] In the case of one raid, Captain Pearson wrote a note to the sergeant in charge of the squad saying: "Make your raid specifically at 10 o'clock. At that time the gambling tables will be covered. Observe the girl show and then leave. During that time there will be no gambling conducted so your officers will not be embarrassed." Captain Pearson admitted the note was in his handwriting.[9]

By 1950, the race-wire service war had been settled. The Kefauver Committee reported in 1951 that "Of all the forms of gambling, the one showing the greatest degree of organization and syndication, the one which depends most on interstate commerce and interstate communication, is bookmaking." Until fairly recently, race-track betting was surrounded with rules. In 27 states, it was legal within the enclosure of the race-tracks. However, in every state except Nevada off-track betting was illegal.

Such rules were made to be broken, and broken they were. The Kefauver Committee report, a mine of information on how organized crime was organized, spent a great deal of time investigating the race-wire service. "Big-time bookmaking, operations largely monopolized by the big mobsters with their rich returns, cannot be carried on without the rapid transmission of racing information and information about other sporting events. We find that to conduct successful bookmaking the operators must have information in excess of that which can be obtained through regular news and radio channels. Accordingly, there has grown up a specialized wire service which has for its principal purposes the dissemination of detailed racing information within a matter of minutes after the occurrence of the actual events. This information includes details of track conditions, betting odds, jockey changes, and other facts occurring immediately prior to the running of the race and the results thereof. These wire services sell this information to bookmakers who in turn use it in conducting their business."[10]

Nationwide, a race-wire service developed by Moses Annenberg, became a lucrative monopoly during the 1920s and 1930s. Its purpose, the transmission of information, was not illegal but as the information was passed from its initial source (the race-tracks, not all of which cooperated) to Nationwide and then to the regional distributers who sold directly to the bookmakers, there were grey areas in the operation. Formerly the circulation manager of the Hearst newspapers and magazines, Annenberg was a veteran of the bloody and violent circulations wars fought by rival newspapers. The operation and selling of the race-wire service required similar tactics, certainly in the beginning, and Annenberg brought into his new business a seasoned group of veterans. His chief aides were Edward McBride and James Ragen.

In 1939, Annenberg ran into trouble with the authorities over his income tax returns and eventually went to jail. During the investigation, Annenberg literally walked away from Nationwide, accepting one dollar for his 50% interest and abandoning the business. On 15 November 1939, Nationwide went out of business. Five days later, Continental Press Services owned by McBride and Ragan came into existence. "The old management closed the door and a new management walked in and sat down and started operating."[11] Eleven years later, the Kefauver Committee was intrigued and baffled by the business procedures whereby a profitable and visible company could be made to change hands. "Continental Press Services continued to operate without serious trouble until about 1946. During this period Ragen and McBride operated it as partners. There is no indication on the record that during this period it was dominated by any out-and-out gangster element although, beyond any doubt, Continental Press enjoyed amicable relations with the gangsters who were building up large-scale bookmaking operations in the bigger cities of the country."[12]

Then, mysteriously, a new race-wire service appeared to challenge Continental's monopoly. The new service, Trans-American Publishing and News Services, had been organized by one of Continental's sub-distributers, R and H Publishing Company. R and H was controlled by Tony Accordo of the Chicago mob. Ragen tried to buy out his rivals but was asked an astronomical price. Then he threatened to go to the FBI and tell all he knew about the Chicago syndicate, saying that the wire service could not tolerate a gangster element or it would itself be put out of business. He did approach the District Attorney of Cook County, Illinois, saying his life had been threatened and that he fully expected the threats to be carried out. If he were killed, he said the probable killers would be Accardo, Jake (Greasy Thumb) Guzik, and Murray (the Camel) Humphreys, top names of the Chicago mob.

Siegel had money in Trans-America and began to direct its western operations. There were difficulties though in Los Angeles. The manager of Continental there was Russell Leonard Brophy, Ragen's son-in-law, with powerful connections into City Hall. Confident of his alliances, Brophy ignored threats, persuasion or business offers. Finally Siegel called in Mickey Cohen, which meant strong-arm tactics. Cohen was nothing if not direct. He began to break up bookie joints, using the Continental service and finally, with another hoodlum, Joe Sica, Cohen led an attack on Continental's main office on the ninth floor of the Newmark Building downtown.

According to Cohen, Brophy was on the phone when he and Sica burst into Brophy's office.[13] On the other end of the line was John Roselli who had strong links back to east coast crime. Roselli had heard of Cohen's plan and ordered him not to break up Brophy's office. But Roselli was not part of a Siegel association and Cohen was. "So we tore that fucking office apart. In fact, we busted Brophy's head open pretty good because he got out of line a little bit. But actually the instructions were to knock him in pretty good anyway."[14] For this attack Cohen and Sica were arrested, tried, given suspended sentences and fined, Sica $200, Cohen $100. "The Nationwide wire service war was really something," Cohen remembered nostalgically in his autobiography.[15]

Not long after this Ragen, in Chicago, was shot from a moving car. Hospitalized but not killed, the mob finally got to him. He was given a lethal dose of poison. Continental passed to McBride's son, then a young law student at Miami University. The Kefauver Committee questioned McBride who complained he knew nothing about the business he was supposed to own, and that he could not even even name the people who were supposed to be working for him. The race-wire service war plainly demonstrated that two opposing factions were attempting to control organized crime in Los Angeles. Dragna might be working under Siegel but felt no loyalty toward him. "The worst thing you can do to an old-time Italian mahoff is to harm his prestige in any way, and that's what took place when Benny came here", Cohen said contemptuously of Dragna, dismissing him as a "moustache Pete". Cohen's allegiance was to Siegel not to Dragna or Roselli, and after Siegel's death it was Cohen's attempt to take over Siegel's position that led to gang war. Dragna opposed Cohen. The mob violence and murder, as they struggled for territories and prestige, was one element in the eventual appointment of William Parker as chief of police, in 1950.

After Pearl Harbor, Los Angeles became a boom city once again, with its defense industries working around the clock. Suddenly, there was a great deal of money and not much to spend it on. Benjamin Siegel had also become a public figure well known outside the restricted circles of mob and Hollywood society. In 1940, he was indicted for murder but the charges were dismissed at the request of the District Attorney. Later it came out that the

D.A.'s campaign fund had benefitted by a $30,000 contribution from Siegel. The D.A. said he knew nothing about the contribution but was going to give the money back. Mickey Cohen swore he did not. In 1943, Siegel was arrested for illegal betting and fined $250. Hollywood producer, ex-newspaper columnist Mark Hellinger, testified that Siegel was a man of "good moral character".

That his name and history made the front pages did not hurt Siegel's social standing at all. Police Chief Clint Anderson later said that it helped put Siegel on the "A list" for Hollywood parties and premieres. "Friends at the police department even drove him home from the races, often with the siren wide open," Anderson said. "No gangster in criminal history ever had such open association with the big names of the town."

In 1942, Siegel turned his attention to Las Vegas, acquiring an interest in two casinos, the Golden Nugget and the Frontier Club, and increasing the cost of the race-wire service-it was rumored to be two-thirds of the take from bookmaking. Whether his ambitions in Las Vegas began then or later, he had to wait until after the war to put them into operation. In December 1945, groundbreaking took place for the construction of the Flamingo Hotel, supervised by Siegel and financed with mob money.

Reno was then Nevada's popular gambling resort. Las Vegas, with a population of little more than ten thousand, was a small desert town with a nucleus of gambling halls at its center. Siegel bought land seven miles from downtown to build his hotel casino, a prototype of many more to come. It cost $6,000,000, reputedly including the purchase of scarce materials on the black market at inflated prices, the assistance of Senator Pat McCarran in the granting of building priorities, the disastrous opening on 26 December 1946, and the closing down of the hotel within a month. Still uncompleted, the Flamingo reopened on 1 March 1947 with guests waiting to check into rooms still without furniture, and the hotel suffered an operating loss over its first six months of $774,000.

To cover his losses, Siegel again raised the rates on the race-wire service to the consternation of his customers. And then, on the night of 20 June 1947, Siegel was shot down by two mob gunmen as he sat on the couch in the Beverly Hills living room of his mistress, Virginia Hill. Minutes after Siegel's murder in Beverly Hills, representatives of the Cleveland mob walked into the Flamingo and announced they were taking control of the resort. No one argued with them.

The transfer of power in Los Angeles was less smooth. Mickey Cohen had strong-armed his way into a position of authority. "When I really became a power was when Benny turned everything over to me", Cohen boasted in 1945, when Siegel began to spend more time in Las Vegas than Los Angeles. After Siegel's murder, control of Las Vegas passed into the hands of the Chicago, Cleveland and the east-coast mobs but Los Angeles was, Cohen thought, his territory. The newspapers agreed with him. He was fleshy and flashy and always good for a headline in the tabloids. He looked like a mobster and behaved like one. In a city so responsive to image, he seemed the very embodiment of what he claimed to be.

When Dragna and his adherents contested Cohen's claim to leadership, Los Angeles had its taste of a gang war. Not on Chicago's scale, but it employed sufficient gun-power to get itself labelled "The Battle of Sunset Strip". Cohen took most of the attention when the Kefauver Committee came to Los Angeles, where he was treated as the comptroller of local organized crime. Dragna did not show up to argue differently.

In the end, Cohen helped deflect attention from organized crime in Los Angeles precisely by drawing media attention to his own presence at the expense of that which he represented. With a strong resemblence to Al Capone, Cohen aped Capone's expansive style, night clubbing with girls from the strip clubs and sitting ringside at the Olympic Auditorium for the fights. He also turned his haberdashery shop on Santa Monica Boulevard into a highly visible headquarters and brawled publicly with Dragna's men. If Los Angeles lacked the range of conflicting gang leaders Chicago had in the 1920s, Cohen sought to make up for it by acting as if he were Al Capone and Dion O'Bannion rolled into one.

The stories, inevitably, got back to the Kefauver Committee: "Cohen's tendency towards strong-arm tactics is evidenced by the treatment he administered to Jimmy Utley in broad daylight in a Los

Angeles restaurant. It has been related how Cohen pistol-whipped Utley in the presence of numerous patrons of the place but none of them, including Utley, would testify about what they had seen."[16] The restaurant in question was Lucey's on Melrose and across the street from the Paramount Studios and a popular hang-out with executives, directors and writers from that studio. Cohen and Utley had already battled outside another popular restaurant, the Brown Derby on Vine. Utley was a Dragna lieutenant and Cohen accused him of being a stool-pigeon, suspecting that Utley had been responsible for an attempt of Cohen's life outside Sherry's Restaurant on Sunset Strip in 1949. "There was a little panic and people started hollering as they watched this stool-pigeon scream," Cohen remembered.[17]

This unexpected bonus of mob violence with their lunch wasn't of much practical value to the Paramount executives. Even though Paramount had more or less created the gangster film in 1927 with *Underworld*, the studio no longer specialized in the gangster genre. The studio most closely identified with the gangster film was Warner Brothers in Burbank. This, too, was Cohen territory. For ten years he ran a Las Vegas type casino operation in the city. On the surface, the Dincara Stock Farm was a stud farm and stables, highly respectable and perfectly legitimate. It was also a front for a massive gambling operation. "Blanie Matthews, who was with me on certain things, was the chief of police at Warner Brothers Studio," Cohen remembered, and the Dincara Stock Farm was run for Cohen by a retired police captain, Jack Dineen. The operation of Dincara showed just how deeply organized crime infiltrated the area. A popular hang-out for Warner's studio employees, its contacts started with the Burbank police department and reached right up into the attorney general's office in Sacramento. Cohen paid top rates for corruption. He believed in "making a man anxious to keep the joint open" and for years it paid off. He boasted that he had newspaper people on his payroll, well paid not to mention Dincara.

In the end, Cohen became, like Capone, too much of a public figure. Alarms sounded as reform movements began to move through Southern California's police departments. Dincara closed when reform reached Burbank. The authorities got Cohen, as they did Capone, for income tax evasion. He went through two trials and was sentenced to fifteen years. Released in January 1972, after serving eleven years, part of it on Alcatraz, Cohen came back aging and ill but still seeking to make headlines. In the early days of the Patty Hearst kidnapping, he gained attention by claiming she was hiding out in Cleveland. It was his last bit of publicity until his obituary, dying at 61 of complications from an operation for stomach cancer.

Dragna had died in 1956. Cohen may have sneered at him as a "moustache Pete" but, like most of his generation of mobsters, he cultivated his privacy, kept his distance from the headlines, and died a natural death. He also left a legacy. An outfit which could be handed on, and was. Frank diSimone took over from Dragna. He too kept a low profile, although probably not as low as he would have liked. DiSimone represented California mob interests at the Apalachin conference of the leading mafiosa on 14 November 1967, a meeting rudely interrupted by the New York State Police.[18]   In connection with his participation in that meeting, diSimone was charged and convicted of conspiracy to obstruct justice and sentenced to four years. His conviction, along with those of two dozen other mafiosa present at the meeting, was later overturned.

DiSimone died suddenly of a heart attack in January 1968, and the organization passed to Nick Licata. Licata was fingered in 1967 as the head of the California Mafia by Joseph Valachi but, since so many better known mob figures were being exposed, Licata kept his anonymity. In a way he only lost it when he died in 1974. One hundred fifty mourners attended the funeral service at St. Peter's Roman Catholic Church downtown but they were observed, as *The Los Angeles Times* reported on 24 October 1972 by "almost half that many intelligence officers and newsmen". The most visible contingent came from the San Diego D.A.'s office and "manned cameras behind the partially covered windows of a brightly painted camper van". For the general public, organized crime had ended with the conviction of Mickey Cohen. However, there is still much more to be said about organized crime in Los Angeles.

The Hollywood that Ben Siegel (no one with a sense of self-preservation ever called him 'Bugsy' to his face) came to in 1936 was a company town, run by and for the major film studios. Collectively they wielded great power within the economic, political and social framework of the city. Film people might not be allowed to join certain country clubs and Pasadena might look down its nose at them but the money in Hollywood made the film people formidable friends. Heads of publicity had tremendous clout, and scandalous stories could be spiked, star escapades smoothed over with the police. Each studio had its own police force for internal security, and cultivated strong relationships with law enforcement.

The studio chiefs with their Friday night poker games formed a kind of Mafia family of their own, making and breaking reputations. They shared a solid belief in the sanctity of private enterprise but many industry practices were in restraint of trade. They especially disliked the unions. The Motion Picture Industry Council may have beaten back the challenge of Upton Sinclair, but in the studios their crafts were organizing. And in the mid 1930s, the IATSE (International Alliance of Theatrical Stage Employees) began to mount a powerful threat. Willie Bioff and George Browne were the heads of IATSE. And behind Browne and Bioff were the Chicago mob as organized crime had begun to move in on organized labor.

Like the wire-service war, the studio shakedown had its origins in Chicago. In 1932, a minor hoodlum, Willie Bioff, who had been selling "insurance" (i.e. protection) to kosher butchers met up with George E. Browne, business agent for Local 2 of the IATSE. Their operation began in a small way. Of the 400 members of the union, 250 were out of work. Browne and Bioff began a soup kitchen. Their employed members paid 35 cents for a meal, leaving enough profit for a free meal for an unemployed member. Handled by voucher, the system allowed the unemployed to eat without the public stigma of charity. What came out of the system was good publicity (even the Capone organization ran soup kitchens for the unemployed), a profit for Browne and Bioff, who 'persuaded' local merchants to donate food, and a system with endless possibilities for corruption.

Bioff, the brains of the duo, soon had the idea of selling votes and favors to politicians in return for donations to the soup kitchen. Shortly thereafter, he thought of the even more interesting idea of approaching Barney Balaban, head of the 400 Balaban and Katz movie theaters in the Chicago area, and asking him to donate $50,000 to the kitchen in return for trouble-free labor relations. Balaban bargained the donation down to $20,000, and paid. Browne and Bioff were in business.

Neither Browne nor Bioff were tied to organized crime. It did not take the Capone mob long, though, to sniff out a profitable racket. Browne and Bioff soon had silent partners with whom they had to split the take 50/50. The fortunes of one small local were of no interest to the mob, however; they thought beyond that to control of the entire union with Browne and Bioff as their agents. The next IATSE convention was to be at Louisville in June 1934, and George Browne was put on the ballot for president. The mob did their work well and the 800 delegates raised no dissenting voice against Browne's election. Within a year, the policies of the new president were made manifest. In July 1934, Browne was called in to smoothe over a labor dispute between the union and two of New York's largest theater chains, RKO and Loews (the exhibition arm of MGM). Browne took a $150,000 pay-off, and the union membership took a 10% pay cut.

Hollywood was not insulated against labor problems. Some technicians, cameramen and sound men had already organized. The Screen Actors Guild was being formed. The writers were organizing and preparing to battle the company union being foisted on them, particularly at MGM. The directors were getting together under Frank Capra. In March 1933, the Motion Picture Producers Association under the chairmanship of Louis B. Mayer, proposed another pay cut, this time of 50 percent. The studio employees, who had voluntarily accepted a pay cut of the previous year, were outraged. The cameramen met in the gymnasium of the Hollywood Athletic Club and voted solidly to strike. They had confidence in their position as highly skilled professionals who couldn't be replaced by scab labor. And they knew that if the cameras weren't turning, production would grind to a halt.

Most of the craft unions and the projectionists were affiliated with IATSE, and all the unions stood firm. The Motion Picture Producers Association had to climb down, but it was a defeat that strengthened Mayer's anti-union position and his attempts to break the union.[19] The labor spokesman for the Producers Association was Pat Casey. One of his associates from 1933 on was John Roselli, Jack Dragna's associate and, by his own admission to the Kefauver Committee, a strong-arm man for Gene Normile who operated the Nationwide wire service for Annenberg in Los Angeles in the mid-1930s. The Kefauver Committee was intrigued that a monopoly operation needed muscle to sell their service to a clientele who could not operate without it. One thing is clear: in the 1930s organized crime had influence on both management and labor.

The struggle in the studios centered on highly skilled craft personnel, outside the studios IATSE seemed much more vulnerable, less open to persuasion. Browne and Bioff had one invaluable asset though; they had the projectionists. On 30 November 1935, Browne and Bioff demonstrated their power. At 8 p.m. that evening, every Paramount theater in Chicago went dark as the projectionists left their booths. St. Louis was next, followed by San Francisco, New York, Indianapolis, Philadelphia and Boston. The walk out did not last long. Close the theaters and you closed off the source of the film industry's prosperity, the box-office. Decisively and dramatically, Browne and Bioff had shown their power and made their point. They had no trouble with the film companies after that.

The strike was only the beginning. The major film companies at that time, until the antitrust consent decree of 1949 which forced the five companies which owned theaters to sell their exhibition interests, were vertically integrated into production/distribution/exhibition. The system was susceptible to attacks from a number of points, and Browne and Bioff had exposed one of them. To keep the system running smoothly, Browne and Bioff informed the companies, in April of 1936, that they would have to pay $1,000,000 in installments. This was a 50% reduction from the original demand of $2,000,000, but they had listened to Nicholas Schenck, president of MGM, that "nobody can take that much out of any corporation today." The levy was $50,000 a year from the four major companies, (MGM, Paramount, Warners, 20th Century-Fox) and $25,000 from each of the others. The money, Bioff insisted, must be paid over in $100 bills. Shortly thereafter Nicholas Schenck and 20th Century Fox's Sidney Kent took a taxi to the Waldorf, each with $50,000 in $100 bills concealed beneath his overcoat. After the delivery, they waited around in Room 1065 while Browne and Bioff counted everything out to make sure they were not being shortchanged. The Chicago mob, by this time a rumored if not exactly visible presence behind Browne and Bioff, had raised their percentage from one half to two thirds.

The understanding thus reached might have continued indefinitely. Browne and Bioff never allowed the studios to forget who was pulling the strings. When RKO, then in receivership, was unable to meet its annual payment by the set date, the studio sweetened Bioff by providing him with $5,000 worth of drapes for his Westwood home in return for an extension. When Columbia did not pay promptly, a one day strike was called against the studio, ostensibly on behalf of make-up artists. John Roselli interceded with Browne and Bioff on behalf of Harry Cohn.

In the end, that old federal reliable, income tax fraud, caught up with Bioff. Anxious to acquire a ranch property in the San Fernando Valley, Bioff persuaded Nicholas Schenck to launder $100,000 of Bioff's money by giving it the appearance of a genuine loan. The real estate deal did not go through, but attention was being paid to Bioff's activities, he being the brains and principal manipulator in the partnership. Columnist Westbrook Pegler attacked Bioff in his syndicated column of 23 November 1939, and was to win a Pulitzer Prize for his exposes of labor racketeering. The Treasury Department began to look into tax frauds both by Bioff and Nicholas Schenck.

The Loews executive had won a great deal of money, undeclared for tax purposes, on the 1936 Presidential election. The accountants, examining Schenk's financial affairs, found the $100,000 which had passed between Schenck and Bioff. While investigating Bioff's finances, the tax investigators found he had a declared income of $7,206 in 1937, however they traced $69,000 back to him. In March 1941, Schenck went on trial for perjury and tax fraud, was found guilty, and sentenced to three years. Once in jail, he began to cooperate with the federal authorities in hope of lessening his sentence. In return for his help, he did win a reduction of his sentence to a year and a day, of which he served four months. There was more than enough in Schenck's story to deeply implicate Browne and Bioff. In May, they were indicted for extorting over a million dollars in violation of the Federal Anti-Racketeering Statutes, and later, with stealing one and a half million dollars from the union. Put on trial, they were each sentenced to eight years.

Browne and Bioff served three years of their sentence. They also told the authorities what they knew and became the principal witnesses in the 1943 trial in which the Chicago mob was indicted and convicted "for conspiring to obtain by use of force, violence, and coercion, the payments of almost of one million dollars from a certain group of persons and corporations in the motion picture industry designated as 'victims'." When the trial opened on 5 October 1943, the men in the dock represented the top echelon of Chicago organized crime figures. The only big name missing was "Frank Nitto alias Frank Nitti" who had committed suicide immediately after his indictment. (Nitti's death at the hands of Elliot Ness in Brian de Palma's *The Untouchables* is pure fiction.)

Willie Bioff took nine and a half days to present his testimony. It was a complete account of how each shakedown had been organized, starting from the very beginning, the soup kitchen. "People of my calibre don't do nice things", he answered to one question. The defense attempted to turn the indictment back on the film companies themselves, alleging this was a case of bribery and not of extortion. The Assistant U.S. District Attorney, Richard Kostelanetz, countered with the statement: "The Government holds no brief whatsoever for the officers and companies that made these payments. They should have been more courageous. But it is a fact that they did yield to persuasion and that is why the case is being tried here today".

All the defendants were found guilty, and most of them received the maximum sentence, ten years and a $10,000 fine. Some stockholders, outraged by the evidence presented at the trial, filed suit against those officials and corporations that had knuckled under to Bioff, demanding that all the monies lost should be repaid by the officials concerned out of their own pockets. The suit against Paramount was used as a test case and the stockholders got short shrift from the courts.

Browne and Bioff served their three years. After being released, Browne dropped from sight, perhaps to a farm in Illinois or Wisconsin. Bioff changed his name to Al Nelson and moved to Phoenix. His identity was a badly-kept secret and, on 15 November 1955, his jeep blew up when he pressed the starter. Browne's death, a few years after Bioff's, was not even noted in the press.

John Roselli, another mobster also in the 1943 trial, returned to Hollywood after his release in 1947. In 1950 he appeared before the Kefauver Committee to answer counsel Rudolph Halley's questions.

Q: Since 1947 what have you been doing?

A: Since 1947 I have been in the picture business. I came home and worked as an assistant purchasing agent for Eagle Lion Studios. I later was assistant producer to Bryan Foy and associate producer with Robert B. Kane Productions.

Q: Associate producer? How did you get into that?

A: I have always had some knowledge of the picture business. When I came home on parole I went to work at Eagle Lion Studios. I know I couldn't live long on any $60 a week without having to borrow money. Mr. Foy thought I had the ability to become a producer.

Q: What was your occupation before you went to prison?

A: ...I was with the Pat Casey Enterprises. I was in the insurance business. Pat Casey is a labor-relations man in the (film) industry.

The U.S. Immigration and Naturalization Service eventually claimed that Roselli was not American citizen. He was actually Filippo Sacco born in Esteria, Italy. He was to spend a great deal of time in the 1950s and 1960s fighting their attempts to deport him.

His name was linked in two bizarre incidents in the 1960s and 1970s. First, was the Friars Club card-cheating scandal in 1967. Roselli had been sponsored for membership of the private club by Frank Sinatra and Dean Martin in 1962 and, five years later, he became the central figure in the cheating case. Spy holes in the ceiling allowed an observer to signal a confederate seated below with an electronic device concealed beneath his trouser leg. A lot of money changed hands and many high-rollers were taken.

Second, Roselli was alleged to have been recruited by Salvatore (Sam) Giancana, the Chicago mobster, into a CIA backed plan to assassinate Fidel Castro in the early 1960s. Castro had closed the lucrative gambling concessions in Havana when he took control in Cuba, impounding $450,000 in funds. In return for their help, the principal participants would be granted immunity from prosecution for crimes committed in the United States. The full story has never been told, as the two chief players were forcibly removed from the scene. Giancana was silenced by seven bullets from a .22 caliber automatic pistol in the basement of his Chicago home on 19 June 1975. Roselli disappeared on 28 July 1976, the day he reportedly left his sister's home in Broward County, Florida, to play golf. The next month Roselli's body was found in a chain-wrapped metal drum floating in an arm of Biscayne Bay. Both murders have been added to the long list of unsolved gang-related killings.

By the end of the 1980s, the Mafia seemed to be in deep trouble. After a decade of successful prosecutions against Mafia families, law enforcement was confidently predicting an imminent demise. Rudolph Guiliani had become as visible a prosecuting attorney through the 1980s, as Thomas Dewey had been in the 1930s. Indictments and convictions threatened to leave the Organization virtually without leaders. John Gotti, alleged head of New York's Gambino Family, was one of the few to survive, with an enhanced prestige after a Brooklyn jury found him innocent of racketeering charges in 1987. The power and wealth of Colombian drug dealers, the Medellin Cartel, was superior to that of the Mafia. The old law of *omerta* (silence) was less and less observed by younger mobsters who, as Ronald Goldstock, head of the New York Organized Crime Tast Force, said: "Is no different than any other Yuppie. He's in it for himself." The old sense of loyalty to The Family had diminished. The threat of long prison sentences seemed more intimidating than the justice of the Dons, and increasingly Family members were willing to testify against the Family. Some of the original evidence against Gotti was secured by a trusted Family member wired for sound.

Similar methods were used to obtain evidence against the Los Angeles Mafia, an organization by now so lacking in clout that L.A. Police Chief Daryl Gates dismissed it as "Mickey Mouse Mafia." However, the Mafia was still a source and center of local corruption. It was headed by Peter Milano, a vending machine operator from the San Fernando valley. New York and Chicago interests were attempting to muscle in on Milano's territory. As with Families across the country, there seemed to be a shortage of suitable recruits. The Fiato Brothers, Anthony and Lawrence, were recruited and, like Dominick Lofaro in New York, they came wired for sound with body recorders. The subsequent indictment of Milano covers familiar ground; the attempt to shake down bookmakers, "tribute payments" from drug dealers, and the promise of labor peace on Hollywood film productions. On 29 March1988, Milano and six associates pleaded guilty, although all of them denied any affiliations with a Los Angeles Mafia, which the FBI claimed Milano had headed since 1984. A week later, on 6

April 1988, three more alleged members of this Mafia Family pleaded guilty to extortion, conspiracy, and a labor conspiracy involving payoffs to a Teamsters Union official for smoothing labor relations on a Hollywood film production. Richard Marks, prosecutor in the case, was quoted by The *Los Angeles Times* as saying on 30 March 1988: "We indicted what we believe to be the hierarchy of the La Cosa Nostra family in Los Angeles, so we have effectively put them out of the business."

The optimism of law enforcement is perhaps premature, although not without basis. The Crips and the Bloods, black street gangs in Los Angeles, get far more notice than the Mafia has received since the high days of Mickey Cohen. *Colors* is a film of contemporary violence and corruption, whereas the old gangster genre of filmmaking has become as historical as the western and has, perhaps for that very reason, lost its appeal to a ahistorical generation of filmgoers. Since The *Godfather I* and *II*, and the *Untouchables*, the major crime films, have largely concentrated on the period aspects of the genre. Only the remake of *Scarface* tried to update the genre, with Miami rather than Chicago as its setting, drugs instead of booze as its focus. Yet the Mafia control of certain areas of urban life—the construction industry in New York, for example—is still strong. Dewey thought he had broken the power of organized crime when he sent "Lucky" Luciano to jail. Chicago law enforcement thought it had dealt the Chicago syndicate a mortal blow when it prosecuted seven of its leaders in 1943. The Los Angeles police are convinced that organized crime has been driven out of their city. As long as society feels the need for certain surreptitious activities, than a Mafia still have a function to fulfill.

NOTES

1   William G. Bonelli, *Billion Dollar Blackjack* (Beverly Hills, CA: Civic Research Press, 1954). I have never seen an original edition of this book but the Los Angeles *Underground*, an alternative newspaper, issued a microphoto reprint as a complete issue in the late 1960s (Vol. 1, No. 16). Bonelli launches a frontal assault on the Los Angeles *Times* that is raucously over-written. A run-off candidate for mayor against John C. Porter in 1929, Bonelli had served as president of the Los Angeles city council. In 1931 he was elected to the California State Board of Equalization, which controlled the issuance of liquor licenses. The *Kefauver Report*, p. 98, is highly critical of him and the sources of his campaign funds, but Bonelli knew the intricacies of the city power structure.

2   Mickey Cohen, *In My Words*, as told to John Peer Nugent (Englewood Cliffs, NJ: Prentice-Hall, 1975), 41

3   Letter from George Raft to Jack Warner, in Rudy Behlmer, ed., *Inside Warner Brothers* (New York: Viking, 1986), 151. Raft rejected four roles subsequently played by Bogart: *Dead End* (1937), *High Sierra* (1941), *All Through the Night* (1941), and *The Maltese Falcon* (1941). Bogart was removed from the cast of *Manpower* (1941) and replaced with Edward G. Robinson after Raft refused to work with him. Warners saw them as similar types and *Casablanca* was acquired by the studio in 1941 as "a good vehicle for either Raft or Bogart" (Behlmer, p. 196). This was a role Raft wanted but Bogart got.

4   Cohen, p. 41.

5   Ibid.

6   Fred D. Pasley, *Al Capone* (London: Faber & Faber, 1968), 312-313. First published in 1931, this biography, hardly admiring of its subject, follows Capone's rise to power and influence but was written before the decline and the federal jail sentence.

7   *Variety*, 21 June 1950.

8   U.S., Congress, Senate, *Second Interim Report of the Special Committee to Investigate Organized Crime in Interstate Commerce*, (Washington, DC: G.P.O., 1951), 96. This body is generally known as the Kefauver Committee, since it was chaired by Senator Estes Kefauver of Tennessee. The report is a remarkably comprehensive study of the subject.

9   *Kefauver Report*, p. 96.

10   Ibid., p. 15.

11   Ibid., p. 18.

12   Ibid., p. 19.

13   Cohen, p. 62.

14   Ibid.

15   Ibid., p. 61

16   *Kefauver Report*, p. 97.

17   Cohen, p. 131.

18   The story of the Apalachin meeting at the home of Joseph Barbera is told in Frederic Sondern, Jr., *Brotherhood of Evil: The Mafia* (New York: Farrar, Strauss & Giroux, 1959). The screen rights were acquired by MGM and a script was written by Ben Hecht. The film, however, was never made. The film rights to the Dean Jennings' biography of Ben Siegel, *We Only Kill Each Other* (Englewood Cliffs, NJ: Prentice-Hall, 1967), were acquired by Tony Curtis, with Paramount to produce. By 1972 the production was reaactived by Zanuck-Brown at Universal, with Peter Bogdanovich to direct. The film was never made. Neither was Mickey Cohen's autobiography which had been sold for filming soon after publication.

19   Herbert Aller, *The Extortionists* (Beverly Hills, CA: Guild-Hartford, 1972). Aller was with IATSE for 36 years, starting as Assistant Business Agent for Local 659 in 1932.

Police brutality contributed to the eruption of racial violence in the Watts area in August 1965. Almost every store in this block of 103rd Street was damaged severely. Courtesy of the Los Angeles County Fire Department.

Chapter 6

BEHIND THE BADGE: THE POLICE AND SOCIAL DISCONTENT IN LOS ANGELES SINCE 1950

Martin J. Schiesl

No public agency has attracted more attention in the evolution of Los Angeles during the post-World War II era than has the Los Angeles Police Department. Several television series have portrayed the LAPD as a calm and impartial guardian of law and order in the city. The actual conduct of the department, however, seldom conformed to this image. Operating in an environment of extensive social change, the LAPD developed a highly partisan system of policing which, while serving well the interests of white residents, caused considerable discomfort and hardship for the city's racial minorities. There was also little sympathy and tolerance on the part of the LAPD with regard to political activism and organized dissent. Consequently, controversy and conflict arose over questions of police accountability, citizen control, and preservation of basic civil liberties. Resolving these serious issues led eventually to the enactment of important reforms designed to ensure that law enforcement was carried out fairly and impartially for all inhabitants of the city.

Internal corruption was the biggest problem for the LAPD at the end of the 1940s. The Los Angeles *Daily News* uncovered evidence of protected vice operations and turned over its findings to the county grand jury. Sergeant Elmer V. Jackson, a member of the vice squad, had provided protection for a known prostitute in return for information about the activities of a few eastern gangsters visiting the city. Apparently, Chief C. B. Horrall knew about

Jackson's prostitution racket in 1948 and had decided not to take any disciplinary action against him. Mayor Fletcher Bowron was not so tolerant as he had ridden into office as part of a reform crusade against police corruption and subsequently devoted much of his time to keeping local law enforcement free from scandals. He started to look for a new chief. The Los Angeles Police Commission forced the retirement of Horrall, secured the resignations of two senior officers, and discharged three members of the vice squad for alleged extortion.[1] Mayor Bowron decided to have an outsider undertake reforms and, consequently, appointed William A. Worton, a retired Marine Corps general, as interim chief. Worton dismantled many of the unsavory associations developed during Horrall's tenure and restored morale. Important bureaucratic changes were also instituted in the department. Worton separated the training and personnel divisions, but his boldest innovation was a new bureau of internal affairs responsible for good order and discipline. It was authorized to investigate charges of police misconduct, report its findings to the chief, and administer appropriate punishment.[2]

Few persons seemed better suited to direct the internal affairs bureau than William H. Parker. Parker joined the LAPD in 1927 and attained the rank of captain in 1939. During World War II, he served for two years in the army in Europe where he helped draft police and prison plans for the Allied occupied areas and established police systems for several German cities. He advanced to a LAPD inspector in 1947 and won command of the traffic division. Two years later Worton promoted Parker to deputy chief and placed him in charge of the internal affairs bureau. Barred from staying on as chief on a permanent basis, Worton stepped down and joined the police commission where he was able to insure that his protege would succeed him. The commission appointed Parker chief on August 2, 1950.[3]

Building upon Worton's reforms, Chief Parker converted the LAPD in the early 1950s from an inefficient and unreliable organization into a national model of a professional police department. He launched a tough selection and training program which included a thorough character investigation, comprehensive examinations, and a long probation period. He placed special emphasis on science and technology in crime prevention and created a planning and research division to analyze crime patterns, budgets, and department resources. Extensive reorganization accompanied these innovations. Parker relied heavily on the managerial principles of Orlando W. Wilson, a widely respected police administrator and scholar. Wilson advocated that police departments be arranged along semimilitary lines so as to maintain strict command and control. The LAPD copied the military model almost literally. Communication and responsibility flowed up and down the organization, but all lines eventually led back to Parker, who spelled out the duties of each administrative level and defined the limits of authority and discretion. The result was a highly centralized, impersonal, and very arrest-conscious department.[4]

Such reform brought a different style of law enforcement. In the 1940s the police had patrolled city blocks on foot and knew personally the residents of the area. They developed neighborhood connections and used selective judgment in making arrests. Parker took the police off the beat, put them in radio-equipped cars, and ordered around the clock surveillance to discourage criminal activity. He also insisted that all laws be strictly enforced and without exception.[5] These "preventive" patrols seldom caused problems in white communities; few of the residents used the streets in ways that aroused police suspicion. In black neighborhoods, where teenagers and young adults spent a good deal of their time on the streets, preventive patrols meant continual harassment and intimidation. Also, most officers were white and came from working-class backgrounds that had fostered the notion of racial supremacy. Since they seldom distinguished between innocent and troublesome citizens, they treated the majority of ghetto dwellers as potential criminals. They regularly broke up groups of youth congregating on street corners and lectured them in uncivil and insulting language. Many middle-class black adults were routinely stopped for interrogation and sometimes rousted because their prosperous appearance prompted the officers to suspect that they might be involved in bookmaking, narcotics, or prostitution. The police also made illegal searches of minority residences and stopped cars indiscriminately in the ghetto.[6]

More disturbing were incidents of physical brutality. The local chapter of the National Association for the Advancement of Colored People (NAACP) received written statements from some people who had witnessed assaults on black residents by certain patrol officers. "The technique is the same," Everette R. Porter, a member of the NAACP's legal redress committee, noted. "After a citizen has been brutally beaten by the policemen, they book him on some trumped up charge, usually drunkenness and resisting arrest."[7]

Similar abuse was occasionally meted out to Mexican American residents. Especially nasty was the "Bloody Christmas" incident in December of 1951. Two patrolmen entered a downtown bar to break up a brawl and were attacked by several patrons, one so badly that he had to be taken to the hospital. Several officers arrived later, arrested seven young Chicanos, and took them to Central Station where the police were celebrating Christmas Eve. A rumor spread through the station that the hospitalized officer was going to lose an eye. Angry and drunk policemen hauled the boys out of their cells and beat them viciously. Stories of the assault prompted Mexican American councilman Edward Roybal to charge the LAPD with systematic brutality. While Chief Parker denied the allegation, some 300 officers were interrogated, with 200 taking lie-detector tests. Parker turned over their testimony to a police board of rights and the county grand jury. Eight officers were indicted, two others were dropped from the force, and another thirty-six received official reprimands.[8]

These actions, however, did little to discourage the mistreatment of minority citizens. Jimmy Witherspoon, a nationally famous blues singer, was stopped by two officers for drunk driving in early 1952. He asked them for a sobriety test but was not given one. They handcuffed the singer, threw him into their car, and pounded him in the stomach and the knees. He filed a $100,000 damage suit against the LAPD charging excessive use of force.[9] The police commission decided to hold a public hearing on law enforcement in nonwhite neighborhoods. Among the witnesses were members of the police relations committee of the Los Angeles County Conference on Community Relations, an organization representing different ethnic groups, churches, and various civic associations.

"We suspect that there are altogether too many police officers who are persuaded that some groups in Los Angeles must be kept in line," the committee bluntly observed, "and that some others believe that the people of certain groups ought to be struck regularly, like gangs." Complaints about such behavior brought little redress. The committee reported that the department's internal affairs division did not allow complainants to have counsel and usually interrogated them in an antagonistic manner. It recommended that one police commissioner be present at every division hearing to ensure fair and objective review of citizen complaints. The committee also proposed the establishment of police-citizen committees in ghetto and barrio neighborhoods and urged that police recruits be given adequate instruction in the area of minority relations.[10]

Only the latter proposal won the support of the LAPD. Chief Parker assigned responsibility for racial matters to Inspector Noel McQuown, who was in command of the Newton Street Division located in the heart of the ghetto. McQuown drafted a program on race relations and integrated it into the curriculum of the police academy. The recruits were required to read various pamphlets which described prejudice against nonwhite groups and listed racial stereotypes. There were also classes devoted to ethical matters, the enforcement of civil rights laws, and social problems in minority communities. Police conduct in 1954 indicated that some officers easily forgot these items once they were out on the streets. One close observer of the LAPD reported that leaders of minority organizations believed that many white patrolmen continued to see most black people as predisposed to violent crime and used "antagonistic expressions" when conducting field interrogations. The officers also did not enforce various laws as vigorously in white districts as they did in minority communities.[11]

None of this was of great concern to Chief Parker. He believed that effective law enforcement in the ghetto required a large and aggressive concentration of police power to cope with high levels of criminal activity. Police work in a big city, Parker reported to a meeting of the National Conference of Christians and Jews in 1955, was heaviest in minority areas because "certain racial groups" accounted for a "disproportionate share" of the total number of crimes. "In deploying to suppress crime, we [LAPD] are not interested in why a certain group tends toward crime," he stated, "we are interested in maintaining order. The fact that the group would not be a crime problem under different socio-economic conditions and might not be a crime problem tomorrow, does not alter today's tactical necessities."[12]

Many patrol officers, however, acted like an occupation army. Stories of unprovoked police assaults appeared regularly in the black press in 1957. The experience of one couple was particularly appalling. Hosie Tenner and his pregnant wife, along with some other people, left the home of a friend and stopped on their way to their cars to watch two officers cite a motorist for a traffic violation. As the officers were leaving the scene, someone in the group made critical remarks. The police returned and placed Tenner under arrest. When his wife protested that he was merely an on-looker and had not said anything, she was knocked to the ground and a knee pressed into her stomach. She was taken to the hospital and later suffered a miscarriage. The NAACP reacted angrily and held a mass meeting to focus critical attention on law enforcement in the ghetto. Eason Monroe, the executive director of the Southern California branch of the American Civil Liberties Union (ACLU), brought with him ACLU files on police-minority relations and provided the audience with detailed descriptions of various examples involving harassment and physical abuse. "Maybe if we would get off the dime and get a plan to change police practices in Los Angeles," Reverend Maurice A. Dawkins, local NAACP president, told the audience, "we could then have a police department to be proud of."[13]

There was little the police commission could do to help the ACLU as it did not have the authority to investigate personnel matters black residents believed to be discriminatory. Chief Parker felt that the commission had no business interfering with the general policies and administration of the department. The controversy over the enforcement of gambling laws revealed the discrimination against minorities. Judge David Williams, a black man, charged in 1958 that the vice squad raided only black gambling games and allowed gamblers in other areas of the city to operate freely. The few white people arrested, he noted, were usually playing in games in the ghetto. Black commissioner Herbert A. Greenwood asked Parker for the vice squad's statistics on gambling arrests, but received no information.   Parker also would not allow the commissioners to interview officers accused of systematic mistreatment. "We don't tell him. He tells us," Greenwood angrily referred to the chief shortly before resigning from the commission in 1959.[14] Making things worse, the internal affairs division usually resented the complaints of minority citizens and made them feel that they, and not the accused officer, were on trial.   The division, moreover, after investigating a complaint, could—and often did—bring charges against the complainant for filing a false report.[15]

One remedy to this disturbing situation appeared to lay in the direction of more civilian control of police practices. ACLU officials, backed by the NAACP, proposed a five-member police practices review board to be appointed by the mayor, with the council's approval, from lists of names submitted by superior court justices, college and university faculties, and local political party organizations. It would investigate charges of police misconduct and submit its findings and recommendations to the police commission and chief for "appropriate action." The board could also file criminal charges and retain special counsel to prosecute the accused officers. Such authority, in the judgement of the ACLU and NAACP, would restrain those patrolmen who routinely misused their power, provide minority residents with redress, and ensure an impartial investigation of citizen complaints.[16]

Chief Parker and his staff strongly opposed the notion of a review board because it threatened the integrity and professional autonomy of their department. People with little or no experience in law enforcement, they cried, would sit in judgment on police officers! The review board idea, moreover, was described as a communist plot. Captain Edward M. Davis, vice-president of the local Fire and Police Protective League, presented this argument to the industrial security section of the Los Angeles Chamber of Commerce in the spring of 1960. Davis described review board campaigns in Los Angeles and other cities as a "national conspiracy" to undermine law enforcement and asserted that they "did not displease the Communist party" since one of its goals was to "render the police ineffective."[17] The *Los Angeles Times*, a strong supporter of the LAPD, contended that a review board would demoralize the police and give special interests control of local law enforcement. The city council, in the face of all these arguments, rejected the ACLU proposal in the summer of 1960.[18]

Police conduct continued to be controversial. In the 1961 mayoral election, Samuel Yorty, former member of the state legislature and the U.S. House of Representatives, forced Mayor Norris Poulson, a strong defender of the police, into a runoff. Yorty's spirited campaign charged that Poulson was a tool of downtown business elites and that Chief Parker and the police commission were insensitive to minority group problems. He promised the city's nonwhite citizens a change in police management. Shortly before the election, a disturbance involving 75 policemen and 200 minority teenagers took place at Griffith Park and ended with many blacks arrested, dozens injured, and several hospitalized. The black community saw the melee as one more example of excessive police brutality. Their votes, in combination with a large turnout in the East Los Angeles barrio, gave Yorty a comfortable victory. His choices for the police commission gave some hope that there would be an improvement in police-minority relations. Among them were a black attorney who had headed the NAACP's complaint division, a Mexican American physician, and a liberal professor of public administration from the University of Southern California, but they had little inclination to closely monitor department operations. They respected Chief Parker, apart from his insensitivity to racial issues, and did not want a major confrontation over the character of local policing.[19]

Such deference gave Parker little incentive to change the department's policies toward black residents. He stepped up patrols in the ghetto to undermine the growing influence of militant groups who he saw, without any real evidence, as enemies of the state. His major target was the local Black Muslim sect. Consisting of men and women from the most alienated segments of ghetto society, the sect advocated black pride and black power through the development of autonomous institutions such as businesses, churches, and schools. It also stressed paramilitary training and threatened armed resistance to police repression. An opportunity for the latter came tragically in April of 1962. Several patrolmen stopped two burglary suspects near the Muslim Temple, exchanged gunfire with some militants, and then entered the building, shooting wildly. When the smoke cleared, one black was dead, another was permanently disabled, and four others were seriously wounded.[20]

The shootout aroused considerable resentment. Malcolm X, a dynamic Muslim preacher, accused the police of murder and claimed that Parker was fostering racial hatred, while Roy Wilkins, national head of the NAACP, limited himself to charging the officers with extreme brutality. The United Clergymen of Central Los Angeles called Parker "anti-Negro" and requested an independent civilian review board. They also asked that Mayor Yorty personally investigate some of the complaints of black residents against certain patrol officers. He firmly turned down their request. He blamed Black Muslims and subversive groups as chiefly responsible for the brutality charges and saw publicizing minority grievances as a communist plot to "secure endless publicity for every charge brought against the police department, no matter how frivolous."[21]

Conditions in the ghetto did not support the mayor's extreme views. The California Advisory Committee to the U.S. Civil Rights Commission visited Los Angeles in the fall of 1962 to investigate law enforcement practices in nonwhite communities. "A situation is being created in which the claim by minority groups of police brutality and the counterclaim of police agencies of minority group resistance to police authority are beginning to be self-fulfilling prophecies," John Buggs, executive director of the Los Angeles County Commission on Human Relations, told the committee. Such tensions escaped the attention and consideration of Chief Parker. He assured the committee that no "difficult problem" existed between his officers and minority residents and charged that certain elements were always trying to inflame the black community with false stories of police abuse. The testimony of several civil rights activists, however, provided the committee with evidence of much discriminatory law enforcement in the ghetto and in local barrios. The police often scolded residents with discourteous and derogatory language, arrested blacks and Mexican

Americans for minor offenses (ignored when committed by white people), and frequently used excessive force in a large number of arrests.[22]

Complaints about these practices seldom found redress. ACLU lawyers reported that the internal affairs division continued to be unsympathetic to stories of racial abuse, harassed minority citizens at their homes and jobs, and threatened them with criminal prosecution if their complaints were not sustained. Making things more difficult was the lack of contact between civil rights groups and the chief's office. NAACP officials and representatives of the Community Relations Conference of Southern California, an organization composed of civic associations, various churches, and labor unions, informed the committee that Parker appeared to have little interest in minority problems and refused to meet with them to discuss ways to improve police conduct in nonwhite areas.[23]

New agitation over racial issues kept law enforcement on the front burner. In the spring of 1963, the ACLU and NAACP teamed up with the local chapter of the Congress of Racial Equality to establish the United Civil Rights Committee. Headed by Reverend H. H. Brookins, one of the city's most respected black ministers, the committee organized a conference with leading white officials and business executives to discuss the serious inadequacies in housing, employment, and education. Police attitudes and conduct were also on the agenda. "Negroes do not receive equal treatment at the hands of law enforcement officers in the city and county," Thomas G. Neusom, a prominent black attorney, bluntly observed. "Persons guilty of this conduct may be a small minority, but unchecked as they are, except in very flagrant cases, the community continues to suffer and long smoldering resentment continues." He and other civil rights activists demanded a civilian review board and urged more emphasis on human relations in police training programs. Personnel policy was also of considerable importance to them. The number of minority officers was very small and most of them were confined to patrol work. Black leaders called for the removal of discrimination in employment and promotion procedures. None of these items concerned the LAPD brass. Chief Parker reiterated his strong opposition to outside supervision of police conduct and told the audience that the internal affairs division provided adequate redress on those unfortunate occasions when a citizen suffered police mistreatment. Employment and promotion of blacks, Parker insisted, operated on an "equal basis" throughout law enforcement in the city. He would not adopt any "special considerations" for them because the "morale" of his department would be greatly weakened.[24]

The United Civil Rights Committee organized several demonstrations in the summer of 1963. Large numbers of people from different walks of life participated and demanded an end to racial discrimination in public schools, private business, and various municipal agencies, including the LAPD. Parker greeted them with anxiety and resentment. Any attack on the establishment or on the police as protectors of the establishment, he believed, represented a serious threat to civil order. His intelligence division had compiled dossiers on alleged radicals and subversives and supposedly found several such people in the civil rights movement. Inspector Edward Davis claimed to know of a number of "second generation communists on the racial picket lines."[25] Furthermore, a relatively low turnout of black residents in the demonstrations convinced Parker that civil rights activists were out of touch with most of the ghetto population. The city of Los Angeles, he assured a group of local journalists in the fall of 1963, would never become "part of the battleground of the racial conflict that is raging in the United States today." He told them that it was "ten years ahead of other major metropolitan areas in assimilating the Negro minority."[26]

Daily life in Watts revealed that the chief was a poor sociologist. The number of blacks in Los Angeles County had grown to 650,000 in 1965, most of them crowded into the southcentral part of the city including the Watts area. Unemployment became routine, especially after the 1961 recession; by 1965 four of ten families in Watts lived below the poverty level. The housing in the area, most owned by absentee landlords, was very old and badly needed sanitary and structural improvements. Savings and loan associations involved in mortgage finance refused to provide loans to families wanting to live outside the steaming ghetto. Transportation was another problem. The people who found work spent long hours on overcrowded, expensive buses in order to get to their jobs. Police violence also rose dramatically in ghetto neighborhoods. Sixty blacks were killed by patrolmen from 1963 to 1965, of whom twenty-five were unarmed and twenty-seven were shot in the back.[27]

All of these conditions contributed to the outbreak of massive rioting in the Watts district. On the sweltering evening of August 11, 1965, a highway patrol motorcycle officer stopped a young black named Marquette Frye for speeding and reckless driving on a main thoroughfare near Watts. He ordered him to get out of the car and take a sobriety test. Frye failed the examination and was told that he was under arrest for drunk driving. The officer radioed for a patrol car to carry the youth to jail. Several people gathered around the vehicles, including Frye's brother and mother. They scuffled with the police and were also arrested. The crowd prevented the patrol car's departure, forcing the officers to summon reinforcements. Local and state police slowly left the intersection surrounded by an angry mob of about 1,000 persons. The mob proceeded to throw rocks and bottles at unsuspecting whites driving through the area. More rioting, accompanied by arson and looting, occurred in other parts of Watts the following day. The police could not penetrate to the center of the disturbance and failed to restore order. California national guardsmen arrived on the scene the third evening, moved en masse through the district, and started clearing the streets of rioters and looters. By August 15 the riot was over. It had covered about 46 square miles and left thirty-four persons, mostly blacks, dead, 1,032 wounded, and 3,952 arrested. Property damage amounted to $40 million, with over 600 buildings damaged or destroyed.[28]

Much of the immediate reaction centered on the role of the LAPD. Black leaders blamed Chief Parker, not only for previous police brutality, but for his intemperate language and conduct during the disturbance. He had branded the rioters as "monkeys in a zoo" and refused to consult with local black ministers and officials, claiming that they had little power to alleviate the situation. Civil rights leader Martin Luther King, Jr., after a tense meeting with the chief, declared that he showed a "blind intransigence and ignorance of the social forces involved." Councilman Billy Mills requested an investigation of the LAPD and studied the possibility of deposing Parker. State assemblyman Mervyn Dymally was not so patient and demanded the chief's replacement. Parker responded with typical belligerence. He accused the Black Muslims of provoking racial hostility and keeping the riots going when they might have died out with little bloodshed. He also claimed that two agitators with loudspeaking bullhorns kept inciting the rioters during the disturbance. Councilman Tom Bradley, a 21-year veteran of the LAPD, wanted some evidence of this activity and demanded that Parker identify any outside agitators in the ghetto. The chief resented Bradley's request and charged that he and other minority leaders were "trying to put the blame" on his department by engaging in a "sham" discussion of police brutality.[29]

Governor Edmund G. Brown worried about the possibility of more racial violence in Los Angeles. He appointed a commission to investigate the riots and named former CIA director John McCone to head it. The McCone Commission consulted numerous experts in the field of race relations and heard testimony from over 500 witnesses, some of whom had participated in the rioting. Its final report, entitled *Violence in the City—An End or a Beginning?*, documented serious deprivation suffered by the ghetto in housing, jobs, schools, and transportation. The commission, however, minimized the extent of riot participation among the black population and recommended few economic and social reforms.[30] Chief Parker and his department were also absolved. "Despite the depth of feeling against Chief Parker expressed to us by so many witnesses," declared the commission, "he is recognized, even by many of his vocal critics, as a capable Chief who directs an efficient police force that serves well this entire community." It dismissed the charges of systematic police brutality as highly exaggerated and naively concluded that the problems in police-minority relations were mostly the result of misunderstanding rather than mistreatment. However, the commission did point out that there was a "deep and long standing schism between a substantial portion of the Negro community and the Police Department." It advocated the strengthening of the police commission to improve its ability to supervise the department and proposed the establishment of an inspector general's office outside the police hierarchy to review citizen complaints. It also called for an expansion of the department's community relations program and recommended the hiring of more black and Mexican American officers who, taken together, constituted less than eight per cent of the police force.[31]

Parker paid little attention to these proposals. The city's white majority, deeply shaken by the Watts uprising, supported the chief and expected him to keep a tight lid on any suspicious activity in the ghetto. His intelligence division increased surveillance of black neighborhoods, discovered some members of the Communist party working with activist groups, and concluded that they were behind the ghetto hostility. As a result, he urged the state assembly to pass stricter measures against rioting and incitement to riot. He also asked the city council to double the police force and demanded more shotguns and other antiriot equipment. These requests were denied.[32]

Parker died suddenly of a heart attack on July 16, 1966, while being honored by the Second Marine Division Association. Civil rights activists and black politicians joined with white officials and newspaper editors in praise of the deceased chief and stressed his personal integrity and strong devotion to the city.[33] Few of the former group, however, were sorry to see him go. His long tenure, while bringing efficient and uncorruptible law enforcement, had also produced major and persistent problems. They included a paramilitary style, invasion of civil liberties, and unnecessary aggravation of racial discontent.

It was not easy to replace Parker. Inspector James G. Fisk, head of the department's community relations bureau, scored the highest on the chief's examination. Fisk had participated in a dialogue of sorts with the NAACP and other liberal groups in the early 1960s and earned the respect of much of the city's black leadership. The police commission, dominated by white conservatives, passed over him and named Thomas E. Reddin to the chief's post. Reddin had joined the LAPD in 1941 and moved up to the position of deputy chief in charge of techical services at the time of his appointment. He retained the military model and continued most of Parker's administrative policies and procedures.[34]

Chief Reddin also took it upon himself to determine what constituted a threat to civil order and was prepared to use all available methods in dealing with a potential danger. One major threat to the status quo was antiwar protest in the city. President Lyndon B. Johnson was to attend a fund raising dinner on the evening of June 23, 1967. The Peace Action Council, a loose confederation of fifty groups seeking an end of the Vietnam War, organized a mass demonstration to coincide with the president's visit. Several thousand people, most of whom were white, gathered in a nearby park to hear speeches by leading antiwar activists. They then marched from the park in an orderly manner down the Avenue of the Stars toward the president's hotel, chanting and singing in protests against the Vietnam conflict. Waiting for them were 1,300 policemen outfitted in helmets, guns, and nightsticks. Fearful that "outside agitators" might rush the hotel and harm the president, the officers moved quickly to disperse the crowd. They turned the demonstration into a police riot, violently clubbed hundreds of men and women, and left many of them with serious injuries. The following day Chief Reddin, responding to charges of excessive brutality at a press conference, claimed that the march developed into an unlawful assembly and reported that the department's "beautiful plan" to disperse large crowds had been "well executed."[35]

Developments in law enforcement in the ghetto proceeded along far different lines. Reddin was determined to ameliorate the LAPD's unpleasant relationship with black residents and sought to provide them with more flexible and sensitive policing. He increased the community relations unit from four persons to 120 and instructed them to establish community councils in all of the department's seventeen geographical divisions. Each council met with a group of officers on a regular basis and discussed various law enforcement practices. Out of their meetings came some recommendations which won the support and approval of Reddin. He made the police wear nametags for easy identification and ordered them to fraternize with minority residents. They were also to issue warnings instead of citations for minor "mechanical violations" of the vehicle code, an important concession in poor black neighborhoods. Certain activity was implemented to build more confidence between the police and minority citizens. Reddin put many officers back on foot patrol and used some black ex-convicts in police-community liaison work. He also reinstituted a variety of youth-related programs and stepped up the department's effort to recruit black and Mexican American officers. In addition, Reddin created the office of inspector-general, as recommended by the McCone Commission. The new executive supervised the internal affairs division and reported directly to the chief rather than to the head of the special services bureau.[36]

These reforms, while admirable and long overdue, accomplished little change in the attitude and behavior of the police toward black residents. ACLU officials, never satisfied with the LAPD's complaint procedures, had opened a police malpractice complaint center in Watts in late 1966. Anyone who suffered police mistreatment was urged to come forward and get assistance for lodging grievances with the LAPD. By the end of the next year, the center had received and filed numerous complaints charging certain patrol officers with verbal harassment and occasional physical abuse.[37] These conditions aroused new militancy in the ghetto. Most resentful of the police was the Black Panther party. The group first appeared in Oakland, California, in late 1966. Huey Newton and Bobby Seale, two young black militants, formed the Black Panther Party for Self-Defense to promote political nationalism and contain police activity. The party organized a system of patrol cars and filled them with guns and lawbooks. Whenever black people were stopped by the police, armed Panthers were on the scene, making sure that their constitutional rights were not being violated. The next stop was the Los Angeles ghetto. Panther leaders teamed up with the local chapter of the Student Non-Violent Coordinating Committee, a group of black nationalists, and opened an office on Central Avenue in late 1967. They attracted many young blacks with a mixture of Marxist-Maoist dogma and advocacy of resistance to the police and other symbols of white authority in the city. Each of them was required to have a gun and enough ammunition to protect themselves and their homes. They sometimes trailed squad cars through the ghetto and threatened citizens' arrests of brutal officers.[38]

Chief Reddin believed that the Black Panthers represented a major threat to the safety of his officers and their authority on the streets. He also recognized, however, that their views reflected the dissatisfaction of many ghetto dwellers with law enforcement and thus deserved to be taken very seriously. "Sitting down to talk with militants of whatever persuasion does not mean an automatic compromise of position or giving in to pressure," Reddin declared in early 1968. "It means very simply that conditions in society today demand that we communicate with all segments of the community." He often met with Panther officials and discussed with them, sometimes in heated exchanges, different ways to improve police conduct and performance. However, their meetings aroused much resentment among many patrolmen. All militant groups, in their eyes, were the enemy of the police and had to be firmly resisted, if not suppressed.[39] They kept leading Panthers under constant surveillance and looked for the least little opportunity to provoke a confrontation with them. One gun battle in August of 1968 left two officers wounded, three Panthers dead, and parts of the black population in an uproar. Governor Ronald Reagan, hearing rumors of the possibility of another Watts riot, sent Lieutenant Governor Robert Finch to investigate the situation. Mayor Yorty met with Finch and assured him that there was little chance of a major racial disturbance in the city.[40]

Little noticed in the preoccupation with the Panthers was growing ethnic consciousness and activism in the East Los Angeles barrio. The civil rights movement and black nationalist program made many Mexican Americans cognizant of how they shared similar problems with the black community and showed them how change could be pursued through mass organization and mobilization. Out of this recognition came the establishment of new social and political organizations strongly committed to racial pride and solidarity. Particularly influential was the Young Citizens for Community Action (YCCA). Founded by a group of Chicano high school students in early 1967, YCCA, among other things, participated in Mayor Yorty's Youth Advisory Council and joined forces with other local groups to elect Julian Nava, a Mexican American professor of history at San Fernando Valley State College, to the Los Angeles Board of Education. It also opened a coffee house in East Los Angeles called La Piranya and held discussions and classes in Mexican culture and history. Los Angeles County Sheriff's deputies greeted this activity with much disdain and routinely harassed the group. YCAA grew more belligerent, adopted military garb, and changed its name to the Brown Berets. The Berets strongly promoted cultural nationalism and threatened armed resistance against any unwarranted police aggression in the barrio. Their militancy met with considerable opposition from the sheriff's department and the LAPD. Both agencies, acting on the belief that the group was capable of inspiring violent behavior in other barrio organizations, authorized raids on the Berets' headquarters, planted informers in their ranks, and worked to discredit them in the eyes of the Mexican American community.[41]

None of this repression, however, could divert attention away from the barrio's serious educational problems. Most of the public high schools were very overcrowded, employed few Chicano teachers, and paid little attention to the cultural values and rich heritage of Mexican people. There was also a lack of programs to reduce the high dropout rate. Seeking to draw attention to these inequities, the Brown Berets organized student boycotts at five East Los Angeles high schools in March of 1968. School officials requested police and sheriff's deputies to come to their campuses and prevent possible vandalism and violence. The officers foolishly treated the protest as a mass insurrection, roughed up many students, and arrested those who got in their way. Shortly afterwards, a county grand jury found sufficient evidence that the walkouts had been carefully planned and indicted Sal Castro who taught at Lincoln High School, seven Brown Berets, and five other people on various charges, the major one being conspiracy to disturb the peace. Their indictment and arrest aroused protests from top minority officials and leaders of civil liberties associations, including Walter Bremond, head of the Los Angeles Black Congress, state senator Mervyn Dymally, and Eason Monroe, the ACLU's executive director.[42]

Prominent residents of East Los Angeles were more apprehensive over law enforcement practices. The U. S. Civil Rights Commission visited San Antonio, Texas, in December of 1968 and held public hearings on employment and educational problems facing Mexican American people. Police behavior also received considerable attention. Armando Morales, a social worker and chairman of the police community relations committee of the California Unity Council, talked about "growing friction between law enforcement and the Mexican American community" in Los Angeles and attributed this condition largely to the fact that the barrio was "much more aggressive as to its demands, its social needs." Similar sentiments were voiced by Reverend John P. Luce, rector of the Epiphany Parish in East Los Angeles. He expressed great concern over the possibility of a major "police-barrio confrontation" and pointed out that the LAPD and sheriff's department refused to "talk with...a whole variety of activist people who want change."[43]

Racial activism became the leading issue in the 1969 mayoral race. Tom Bradley, a critic of police mistreatment in minority areas since his election to the council in 1963, took the high ground and talked about problems of urban renewal, rapid transit, ecology, and business expansion. Mayor Yorty conducted a nasty campaign, linking Bradley to the Black Panthers and contending that his election would persuade many police officers to quit. Chief Reddin decided to resign and provided timely justification for the mayor's warning. Yorty's shameless appeal to the fears of white voters won him the election by a comfortable margin. Again, James Fisk got the highest score on the chief's test. The police commission, reminded by Yorty of Fisk's previous ties with civil rights activists, passed over him and appointed Edward Davis to the top post.[44]

Chief Davis had little patience with any militant group and attributed their program and tactics to communist propaganda and infiltration. Any major disruption of the peace, he warned, would be met with swift and forceful resistance. One opportunity came with new antiwar protest in response to President Richard M. Nixon's decision to invade Cambodia in May of 1970. This set off demonstrations on college and university campuses across the nation. The biggest one in Southern California took place at the University of California at Los Angeles. Adding to the tension on the UCLA campus was the celebration of Cinco de Mayo, the Mexican national holiday, by Chicano students. They also had drafted proposals which, among other things, provided for the expansion of certain Mexican American programs and demanded that they be implemented as soon as possible. School authorities felt that it was an inappropriate time to discuss them and chose not to meet with the students. Their decision led some militant Chicanos to join forces with a number of white student activists. They smashed the glass doors of two classroom buildings, broke many windows, and destroyed several display cases. The university administration called upon the Los Angeles police to restore order. Two-hundred officers marched onto the campus and took 74 persons into custody. Chief Davis congratulated his men on their performance in a "pressurized situation" and declared that they had rendered "an excellent service to the citizens of Los Angeles."[45]

Many students and faculty members sharply disagreed. They charged that the police had used excessive force and arrested people indiscriminately. Chancellor Charles C. Young shared their concerns and appointed a commission to investigate the disturbance. The commission examined numerous photographs, reviewed newspaper accounts, and interviewed scores of witnesses. Its final report revealed that student violence was dying out by the time the police arrived on the scene. However, officers wandered about the campus, physically attacked innocent persons, and arrested people who had not damaged any school property. Among them were several blacks, Chicanos, and other minority students. The police, in this instance, went well beyond their instructions, personalized the issues, and graphically showed partisanship.[46]

Developments in the Eastside barrio also brought much tension and conflict with law enforcement agencies. Students at Roosevelt High School attacked unequal conditions at their school and walked out in March of 1970 in protest. After several days of demonstrations, school authorities called upon the Los Angeles police to maintain order. KMEX, the local Spanish-language television station, filmed the beating of many students, and several officers stormed into the station in an effort to keep the pictures off the air. The behavior of the sheriff's department was equally repressive. Particularly disturbing were unprovoked assaults by deputies on prisoners in custody. Six Mexican Americans died at the East Los Angeles sheriff's station in the first five months of 1970, three of whom hung themselves. Their deaths aroused great concern among community residents and led to demonstrations against police brutality. One took place in front of the sheriff's station on the Fourth of July and ended with one Chicano shot and 21 others arrested.[47]

The breaking point in police-community tensions occurred on July 16, 1970. Five LAPD officers and two San Leandro policemen raided an apartment in downtown Los Angeles in search of a murder suspect and shot and killed two cousins, Beltran Sánchez and Guillermo Sánchez. The suspect was nowhere around and no arms were found in the apartment. LAPD officials defended the shooting as an unfortunate case of "mistaken identity" and pointed out that the two men had entered the country illegally. Neither consideration carried any weight among leading members of the Chicano community. Congressman Edward Roybal, a longtime critic of police violence in the barrio, urged the police commission to take some action against the officers involved in the shooting, while directors of the Mexican consulate issued a harsh statement denouncing the killings. Further controversy came at the hands of Rubén Salazar, a well-known reporter for the *Los Angeles Times* and news director at station KMEX. He interviewed two survivors of the attack and uncovered evidence showing certain discrepancies in the LAPD's account of the shooting. Some officers paid him a visit and demanded that his television coverage be toned down. Such publicity, they insisted, was only intended to arouse more hostility among barrio residents toward the police. Salazar ignored their admonition and continued to publicize law enforcement abuses in the barrio.[48]

The war in Vietnam joined police repression as another issue that brought the community closer together. Chicanos accounted for some nineteen per cent of all servicemen from the Southwest killed in action from 1967 to 1970, although they comprised only about twelve per cent of the total population in the region. The National Chicano Moratorium, a coalition of groups strongly apposed to the Vietnam war, conducted huge protest marches in Los Angeles in December of 1969 and in February of 1970. Another demonstration occurred on August 29 in Laguna Park and attracted between twenty and thirty thousand people from across the country. During the afternoon some trouble broke out at a liquor store across the street. The incident turned into an assault by sheriff's deputies on the people in the park and ended in a major riot. Clubbings, rock and bottle throwing, and looting led to considerable property losses in the nearby business district. Many people were seriously injured and three deaths occurred, the most controversial being the slaying of Rubén Salazar. He and his T.V. crew had captured some of the action on film and retired to the Silver Dollar Cafe located a few blocks away. Shortly afterwards, a group of deputies surrounded the bar, supposedly looking for a man rumored to have a rifle. One of them fired a tear gas projectile into the bar and it struck Salazar in the head, killing him instantly. District Attorney Evelle Younger, after reviewing the verdict of a coroner's jury in which only three of nine jurors voted in favor of accidental death, decided not to indict the deputy. His decision angered the Chicano community and led to several demonstrations. The biggest one took place in front of Parker Center in early 1971 and resulted in a police riot and the arrests of 42 people.[49]

Such conflict diverted attention away from another side of local policing which promised to be sensitive and responsive to the needs of the city's racial minorities. The military model in law enforcement, according to Chief Davis, was not that suitable for the times. He subscribed to a postbureaucratic philosophy of policing that placed emphasis on local initiative and cooperation in coping with different kinds of criminal activity. "The most technologically advanced, best financed, best staffed police department in the world is never going to solve the problems of crime and disorder," Davis told the Captains' School in 1969. "That is because our police have not given reality to the truth that the public are the police. Our police must communicate to the citizens that solving these problems is their job, their obligation." Similar sentiments appeared in a speech given by Davis to the International Association of Chiefs of Police in 1970. He reviewed the LAPD's community relations programs and concluded that most of them contributed little to the "resolution of mutual problems." If anything, he added, they aroused "heightened tensions" and widened the existing gulf between many citizens and the police, especially in minority neighborhoods.[50] The remedy to this disturbing situation appear to lay a system that could enable the police to develop and maintain broad support in all segments of Los Angeles society.

Davis presented the Basic Car Plan as the best way to obtain such support. Local residents, he felt, would be more concerned with crime prevention if they could meet with the police in their neighborhoods. He assigned car teams, composed of five senior officers and three less experienced officers, to specific geographical areas. It was expected that each team would learn their area's particular crime problems and form close relations with its inhabitants. Division commanders, meanwhile, contacted the leaders of different ethnic groups and persuaded them to select an advisory committee for each car district. The committees invited local residents to meet with the police once a month and discuss with them common crime problems, but few barrio and ghetto dwellers accepted the invitation. One reason for their absence was that team officers were under strict orders not to discuss police harassment and brutality. This restriction made little sense to black teenagers who complained about mistreatment from certain patrolmen and stayed away from the meetings in protest against their behavior.[51]

The Car Plan received more favorable attention in 1972. Some of the team officers got to know their areas very well and won the trust and respect of residents; the meetings evolved into coffee klatches in individual homes and apartments within housing projects. Anti-burglary "neighborhood watch" programs were also organized and included young people as well as adults. This cooperation greatly impressed Chief Davis and led him to extend team policing a little further. The Team 28 Experiment, as it was officially titled, brought together numerous officers experienced in various fields of law enforcement and gave them complete responsibility for policing a large portion of the Venice district, which was home to low-income minorities and middle and upper-income white groups. The team conducted numerous neighborhood meetings, informed the participants of crime problems, demonstrated different kinds of police equipment, and educated residents in specific methods of self-protection against burglaries and other criminal activity.[52]

Team 28 operations were extended to a few more areas and provided additional evidence that the police and local residents could work together if a common interest existed between them. Davis decided in 1973 to implement the program throughout the department and instituted Neighborhood Action Team Policing to accomplish the task. Each of the department's seventeen areas were divided into three to six team districts. The teams included patrol, traffic, and investigative officers who met once a week to identify the most serious crime and traffic accident problems. The teams also met regularly with individual citizens and representatives of various community organizations. They and the police concentrated on major criminal activity and developed specific programs to increase the safety and security of different neighborhoods. The result of all this activity was greater public cooperation in law enforcement and a lower crime rate, particularly in parts of the ghetto and barrio.[53]

These accomplishments, however, did not signify a radical change in LAPD conduct on the streets. Some black residents in 1972 and 1973 made the same complaints about patrol officers that had been made in the 1960s. The attitudes and behavior of the department toward political activism and dissent hadn't changed at all. Davis in late 1970 had replaced the old intelligence unit with the Public Disorder Intelligence Division (PDID) and staffed it with a large number of officers experienced in undercover operations. PDID investigated and collected files on a wide range of activists and organizations in the city, including certain officials of political parties, civil libertarians, socialist and communist groups, and minority leaders critical of police misconduct. This surveillance went on with little or no supervision from the police commission. Davis seldom consulted with the commission on intelligence-gathering policy and kept it in the dark on much of PDID's activity. Since most of the commissioners were supportive of the police, they contented themselves with routine administrative matters.[54]

The 1973 mayoral election ended this cozy relationship. Tom Bradley, running on a law and order platform, defeated incumbent Sam Yorty by a wide margin. Shortly after the election, Chief Davis met with the new mayor and pledged his cooperation and support. Bradley assured him of a cordial relationship to insure that

Los Angeles residents received the best possible law enforcement. He also wanted to recapture a measure of community control over LAPD operations and appointed five liberal-minded professionals to the police commission to achieve this goal. Among them were retired deputy chief James Fisk, Samuel L. Williams, former prosecutor with the state attorney general's office and later the first black president of the Los Angeles County Bar Association, and William A. Norris, a prominent lawyer and former member of the state Board of Education.[55] The commission sought to find out whether PDID had any guidelines to distinguish between criminal conduct and political activity. It soon learned that PDID's intelligence-gathering net extended beyond private political groups to elective officials, civic-minded organizations, and even members of the police commission. The commissioners in early 1975 ordered the destruction of nearly two million intelligence files, some of which went back to the 1920s.[56]

Next, the commission drafted tentative guidelines for PDID personnel to follow in intelligence operations. One rule stipulated that files would be maintained only on those individuals and organizations who "threaten, plan, attempt or perform acts disruptive of public order." Another required that files on political activists not expected to cause "bodily injury or property damage" be destroyed after a few years. These guidelines were hotly debated at a public hearing held by the commission in late 1975. Fred Okrand, legal director of the ACLU, saw no good reason to maintain records on nonviolent political groups for any time period and argued that this surveillance constituted a blatant violation of their constitutional rights and liberties. Similar criticism was voiced by representatives of the Legal Aid Foundation, NAACP officials, and the county Bar Association. They considered the guidelines to be arbitrary and warned that PDID would continue to violate the rights and privacy of individuals under a cloak of official secrecy. During 1976, the commission reexamined these concerns and enacted more detailed rules for the collection and maintenance of intelligence materials. PDID could only investigate potential criminal acts that might result in physical or property damage. Two commissioners would audit the division's files on a regular basis and periodically review major sources of intelligence information.

Names were also to be removed from PDID files after five years if there was no evidence of any involvement in criminal activity. The ACLU, not convinced that the police would follow these regulations, teamed up with the American Friends Service Committee and formed the Citizens Commission on Police Repression in early 1977. Representing some forty-five community groups in the city, the organization pledged to keep a close watch on intelligence operations.[57]

An escalation of police violence gave the police commission another opportunity to expand its influence and authority. Eighty-seven people were shot to death by patrol officers from 1975 to 1977, of whom a large number were unarmed minority residents. Mayor Bradley, upset with the killings, instructed the commission to hold hearings on the LAPD's firearms policy. Some members of the Coalition Against Police Abuse, a citizens group very critical of officer-involved shootings, attended the hearings and testified that suspects were often shot if they appeared to be reaching for weapons or fled from the scene of the crime. The latter criteria, in the commission's opinion, was too harsh and showed a callous disregard for the value of human life. It decided to draft new and tougher rules on the use of guns and ordered that they be integrated into the department's training programs. One of them forbid an officer to shoot at a fleeing felon unless the person had committed a violent crime and presented a "substantial risk of death or serious bodily injury to others." Another rule authorized the use of deadly force only when "all reasonable alternatives" had been exhausted. The police, moreover, were not to draw their guns for protection against assaults not likely to have serious consequences. Chief Davis strongly objected to these restrictions and charged that his officers would be "walking into situations with their guns in their holsters and bullets in their heads." Commissioner Stephen Reinhardt strongly disagreed. He praised the new guidelines as "reasonable and moderate" and contended that the chief was inflaming the police force unnecessarily. He and his colleagues rejected requests from Davis to modify certain parts of the rules and instructed him to make sure that they were being fully implemented throughout the department.[58]

Such actions, coupled with the new restrictions on intelligence gathering, convinced Davis that the police commission had moved far in the direction of being master of the LAPD rather than its booster. He decided to retire in 1978 and was succeeded by Daryl F. Gates, a dedicated professional who commanded a large internal following. Gates had joined the LAPD in 1949, rose rapidly through the ranks to hold various administrative positions, and was serving as assistant chief at the time of his appointment. The role of the police commission, he conceded in an interview shortly after being named chief, was to set "broad policy guidelines" and make sure that they were being followed throughout the department. Gates pledged full cooperation with the commissioners on various matters and promised to "heed their counsel" to insure that the city had the best police force possible.[59]

Law enforcement in the ghetto indicated that some officers did not share his sentiments. "Many black leaders view the police in Watts as an 'occupying army,' the *Los Angeles Times* noted in August of 1978, "and this perception, while it may be considered an extreme view, cannot be dismissed altogether." The statistics on police shootings certainly justified their position. One-hundred and one people were shot by patrolmen in 1978, of whom 57 were black residents. Some of them had not displayed or threatened to use a weapon immediately preceding the shooting.[60] Chief Gates saw this violence as a sad but unavoidable result of much criminal activity in certain black neighborhoods. "South Central Los Angeles has never been easy to police," he declared in an editorial in the *Times*. "It has always required an aggressive effort by the department in order to cope with a crime level that is a plague upon those who live in the area."[61] The senseless killing of Eulia Love did not exactly fit his explanation. On January 3, 1979, an employee of the Southern California Gas Company came to Love's home, presented her with an unpaid $22 bill, and proceeded to shut off the gas at the side of the house. She became upset and hit him with a shovel. He went to a company office nearby and telephoned the police. Two officers accompanied the man's supervisor to Love's house and stood by while he turned off the gas. In a fit of anger, she threw a kitchen knife at the officers and they opened fire, emptying twelve rounds into her body. Gates anticipated much controversy in the black community and quickly instructed the department's shooting review board to investigate the incident. It justified the shooting on the grounds that the policemen were confronted with a "life-threatening situation" and concluded that their actions complied in "all respects" with department policies concerning the use of deadly force.[62]

These findings did not satisfy local black leaders. Councilman Robert C. Farrell, in whose district Eulia Love had lived, persuaded the police commission to hold a public hearing on the shooting. At the hearing Farrell, other minority officials, and several black ministers and civil rights activists denounced the LAPD defense of the killing as a "whitewash" and demanded the creation of a civilian review board to ensure that cases of excessive brutality were investigated independently of the department bureaucracy. Commissioner Samuel Williams shared their resentment and made reference to a special report on the incident written by Deputy Chief Marshall L. Anderson, a member of the shooting review unit. It accused the officers, among other things, of using "faulty judgment and poor tactics by placing themselves in a position that necessitated the use of deadly force." Further criticism came from Mayor Bradley. He described the woman's death as a "terrible tragedy" and saw an urgent need for some forceful reassertion of the firearms policies of the department.[63]

The commission strongly agreed. It devoted three months to an investigation of the shooting and put its findings in a detailed report that largely discredited the department's evaluation. Commissioner Stephen Reinhardt, reading parts of the document to a meeting attended by LAPD executives, top city officials, and black leaders, pointed out that the findings of the shooting board were based on "erroneous and misconstrued facts" and dismissed its explanation mainly on the grounds that all available evidence had not been obtained and assessed. The two officers, he noted, made "serious errors in judgment" and drew their guns "before all reasonable alternatives had been exhausted." Their actions, as a result, were in direct violation of departmental policies on the use of deadly force.[64] The next item on the agenda was the way in which shootings were investigated by the LAPD. The commission renamed the shooting review unit as the Use of Force Review

Board and ordered that its reports be submitted to the chief. He, in turn, had to review the board's findings and provide the commission with his own explanation and evaluation of the particular shooting. The commission would then either adopt the chief's findings and recommendations or conduct an independent review to make sure that important evidence was not being overlooked. Its report and that of the chief were to be available to the public.[65]

Further hearings and inquiry conducted by the commission portrayed the police as being not "sufficiently responsive to minority needs." Representatives of various black and Chicano organizations expressed strong dissatisfaction with departmental procedures for handling citizen complaints and charged that the LAPD brass did not always hold officers accountable for any major wrongdoings. Subsequently, the commission in early 1980 recommended that the training program include greater emphasis on the use of minimal force and directed the department to evaluate the need for retraining veteran officers with regard to shooting policies. It also proposed monthly tests in defense and disarming tactics, urged more research on the use of nonlethal weapons, and ordered the department to develop a crisis intervention program for all field officers, particularly those assigned to stations in black districts. The commission also instructed the department to include in the training program panels of officers and minority leaders who would discuss social and economic problems in ghetto neighborhoods. Moreover, it ordered a review of the methods by which policemen were assigned to stations in black areas and directed the department to treat the assignments as a special duty. Another innovation was the creation of a steering committee designed to reduce tensions in the ghetto. The commission appointed prominent black professionals to the committee and assured them the cooperation of the LAPD in dealing with police-community matters. Some consideration was also given to complaint procedures. The commission ordered that the department provide a formal and detailed response to any citizen who complained of police mistreatment, complete with the results of the particular investigation.[66] "We do not read in the report any hostility to the police," the *Los Angeles Times* observed. "Rather, the police commission's reforms should help police perform a job that is admittedly difficult. How well that job is done has a direct effect on the entire community, and is the entire community's concern."[67]

Concern with intelligence operations flared again. PDID personnel usually ignored the commission's guidelines on surveil-lance and sought to undermine a number of politically active organizations. Members of the Coalition Against Police Abuse came across a partial list of PDID personnel and discovered that one of them had served for a time as the group's secretary. They gave the list to the Citizens Commission on Police Repression who, in turn, distributed it to several liberal and leftist organizations. Among them was the Alliance for Survival, an anti-nuclear organization, Young Workers Liberation League, and the Campaign for Democratic Freedoms, an educational outfit which sponsored forums on abuses in federal law enforcement. Some of their members were revealed to be PDID officers with much experience in undercover work. Leaders of the three groups took this information to the ACLU in 1978 and requested that a lawsuit be filed on their behalf against the LAPD for illegal spying and invasion of privacy.[68]

Joining them as co-defendants were various social activists, radical groups, and minority organizations in the city. The successful campaign of civil liberties associations in other big cities to curb police spying led them to push for strict controls on the intelligence activity of the LAPD. They filed lawsuits against the department in 1981 and 1982 charging that certain officers and civilian informants had infiltrated their activities and unlawfully collected information on private conversations and political meetings. The LAPD, to its chagrin, was ordered by the court to release some 6,000 pages of intelligence documents to the ACLU and its clients. The documents revealed that PDID officers, among other things, kept close tabs on campaigns calling for a civilian review board, infiltrated black and Mexican American organizations on college campuses, and reported on the appearance of city council members at meetings of groups critical of local law enforcement. More disturbing than that were some 2,500 pages of "captains' briefing notes" which chronicled the lawful activities of left-leaning political advo-cates, police critics, and various public officials. Prepared for the chief of police, the documents suggested that the LAPD's top brass had sanctioned the collection of such information.[69]

Making things a lot worse was the activity of Detective Jay Paul. Paul had joined the police force in 1968, worked as a photographer for PDID, and spyed on various radical groups in the 1970s. He also developed a personal intelligence library, stocking it with newspapers, magazine articles, public documents, and private reports. His library received some embarrassing publicity in January of 1983. A public school official told the *Los Angeles Times* that he had been offered police intelligence files on school personnel that should have been destroyed. PDID personnel were ordered to return any files they had in their possession. Paul gave his superiors a box which contained information about school desegregation in the city. Shortly afterwards, two LAPD investigators, armed with search warrants, went to his house and discovered some 15 additional cartons of intelligence documents. They contained, among other things, dossiers on some judges, liberal councilmen, and three members of the police commission. Paul then led the offices to 50 boxes of materials hidden in a private garage in Long Beach.[70]

This indiscriminate surveillance, along with the lurid stories springing from the spy suit, exhausted the patience and tolerance of the police commissioners with PDID. They appointed a committee of top LAPD officials to investigate the division and propose some changes in intelligence gathering. It reported that the division suffered from poor management, had collected a lot of worthless information, and could not be effectively reformed. The commission, acting on the committee's recommendations, voted unanimously in the spring of 1983 to disband PDID and established a new Anti-Terrorist Division (ATD) with strict controls and tighter management. It placed responsibility for ATD directly with the chief and held him accountable for its conduct and performance. The commissioners also gave themselves more authority to oversee police surveillance and ordered that they and the district attorney's office be given monthly briefings on all intelligence activity. Linda Valentino, former director of the Citizens Commission on Police Repression and member of the ACLU's committee on police-community relations, found much to praise in these actions but added that she still felt "cautious about reforms that take the form of guidelines rather than a law or a court decision."[71]

The resolution of the spying lawsuit ended her anxiety about future intelligence operations. Two members of the ACLU legal team, Paul Hoffman, a professor at Southwestern University School of Law, and Robert Newman, former president of the local chapter of the National Lawyers Guild, drew bits and pieces from anti-spying settlements reached in other cities and integrated them into a comprehensive out-of-court accord designed to provide more civilian control of undercover operations. They and other ACLU lawyers entered into negotiations with the police commission and the city's legal team and persuaded them to present the accord to the city council for approval. Council members, worried about a costly and sensationalist trial, voted in favor of the agreement in the winter of 1984. It required that the city pay $1.8 million in damages to 131 plaintiffs, of whom 23 were specific organizations. The settlement also established the most stringent guidelines on police intelligence in the nation. Two members of the police commission had to authorize any undercover operation by ATD officers. In addition, the commission would periodically audit the records of the division and make certain information on its operations available to the public. The accord also spelled out in detail the evidence necessary for starting a surveillance and required that there be a written record of all participants in a particular investigation.[72] These controls were of little comfort to Chief Gates, who characterized them as bureaucratic "foolishness" and raised the possibility of disbanding ATD if "we are spinning our wheels." Mayor Bradley provided a more intelligent and accurate assessment. He pointed out that the guidelines would "balance the needs of the police department for legitimate gathering of intelligence while at the same time protecting the civil rights of all our citizens."[73]

Further troubles for the LAPD came at the department trial of Jay Paul. After a exhaustive internal investigation, Chief Gates relieved Paul of duty and charged him with several counts of police misconduct. The department's board of rights conducted hearings in the winter of 1984 and listened to extensive testimony on the intelligence activities of PDID. One of Paul's former supervisors testified that he had given him permission to keep sensitive intelligence documents at home and other places.   He also authorized him to feed confidential police information to Western Goals Foundation, a right-wing organization that was building a massive data base on the activities of political liberals and leftists. Paul told the same story to the trial board and added that his outside surveillance work was known to most of his superiors.   The board concluded that he could not be held solely responsible for violations of intelligence-gathering guidelines, absolved him of most of the misconduct charges, and ordered that he be suspended from duty for ten days.   Shortly afterwards, the city council hired a local law firm to investigate the LAPD's intelligence network.   The firm closely reviewed the transcripts of Paul's trial, scores of PDID files, and numerous depositions taken in connection with the ACLU's police spying lawsuit.   Its report charged that Chief Gates and other high-ranking police officials withheld vast amounts of intelligence documents from the police commission and misled city officials about PDID's extensive surveillance activity.   Gates angrily denied these allegations and described the report as being "riddled with unsupported speculations based on substantive errors."[74]

Such controversy over intelligence gathering was not the only major embarrassment for the LAPD in regard to its internal operations.   Minority discontent with police policy surfaced again and attracted much attention in the local press.   The issue this time revolved around mobility and advancement within the department itself.   LAPD executives, after battling civil rights activists and feminist groups in the courts for several years over the question of equal opportunity, entered into a consent decree in 1981 in which they agreed to hire a certain percentage of woman and minority officers.   By 1986 both groups accounted for about 25 per cent of the department.   The *Los Angeles Times* decided to investigate their working conditions and uncovered considerable evidence of racial and sexual bias.   Twice as many blacks had resigned before completing their first-year probation.   Most of the training officers were excessively critical rather than educational and usually misrepresented certain incidents in their written reports.   The experience of Lewis Ellis was particularly unpleasant.   Ellis, a former bus driver for the Southern California Rapid Transit District, joined the LAPD at the age of 53 and looked forward to a rewarding career in law enforcement. He graduated from the Police Academy in May of 1985, amid a lot of department publicity and media attention. Five months later he resigned from the department, citing racially-motivated harassment at the hands of two white training officers. The department's employment opportunity and development division received similar complaints from veteran black and Mexican American officers. They charged that certain white officers, some of whom were their partners, periodically insulted them with all kinds of racial slurs and sexual jokes.[75]

Several coveted assignments were also beyond the reach of many minority people and usually went to white males. These included various managerial posts, planning and research work, and high-profile detective positions. "Some places you are just not wanted," bluntly observed one 18-year black veteran officer. The statistics on the metropolitan division, the most elite unit in the department, strongly supported his contention. Two hundred and twenty officers worked in the division, of whom ten were blacks and 28 were Mexican Americans. Another complaint concerned the social geography of the police force. The Oscar Joel Bryan Association, an organization representing black officers, had issued a report in 1983 in which they called for some relocation of minority police to areas where they were severely underrepresented: "Black officers know that full acceptance of their equality means an equal opportunity to serve in all areas of the city and all assignments within the department." The ethnic makeup of the police in 1986 in the predominantly white San Fernando Valley indicated that LAPD executives paid little attention to these concerns. There was one black officer in the area for every 42 members of the force, while at the same time blacks accounted for one of every four officers assigned to the south-central city ghetto. Disproportionate numbers of Mexican American officers also worked in Eastside barrio neighborhoods.[76]

Law enforcement in all three districts, however, while occasionally marred by needless verbal and physical abuse, was more flexible and impartial than that found on the streets of downtown Los Angeles. The area's homeless population became the new target of police repression. A severe lack of cheap housing, few decent employment opportunities, and various psychological problems forced thousands of poor men and women to wander aimlessly across the city in search of temporary refuge. Some 2000 people occupied downtown shelters and another 1000 slept on Skid Row streets.   Central City East, a business association representing about 40 companies on Skid Row, were quite upset with this situation. It complained about certain criminal activity and unsanitary conditions and persuaded city officials to authorize raids on the homeless community. Dozens of police officers and some street maintenance crews in February and March of 1987 swept into sidewalk camps, tore them apart, and loaded clothing, furniture, and other items into dump trucks. Several activists who protested against the raids were carted off to jail.[77] Three months later Chief Gates, backed by Mayor Bradley who was concerned about health and fire hazards, informed the homeless that they had a week to clear the streets and threatened mass arrests if they did not comply with his order. "Jailing the homeless," Nancy Mintie, director of the Inner City Law Center, pointed out, "is not going to make the homeless problem go away." The crackdown turned out to be an exercise in futility. Most of the homeless, having gotten word on the street that the police were coming, picked up their possessions and escaped into alleys and behind nearby buildings. Some officers arrived at the camps and handed out vouchers for publicly-subsidized hotel rooms to a handful of people.[78]

Homeless persons suffered greater abuse at the hands of the LAPD in the following year. Considerable criticism of police behavior from political activists, social workers, and ACLU lawyers led the city council to adopt policies to regulate raids on the encampments. The police were ordered to notify the council in advance of major sweeps and give the homeless ample time to remove their belongings. Both guidelines were ignored in a raid conducted in June of 1988. Several officers and some street maintenance workers, without advance warning, swept through two camps near city hall and carted away blankets, clothing, medicine, and other materials to a landfill in the San Fernando Valley. The items belonged to forty people, many of whom had just finished breakfast at nearby missions when the raid occurred.

LAPD officials explained that the gathering was too small to be considered a camp and labeled most of the belongings as simple trash. Michael Dear, a close and sympathetic student of the plight of the homeless in Los Angeles and other cities, saw no justification for any of this action. "The private property of homeless persons is not trash," he reminded Chief Gates and his force. "Just because people are homeless, they do not surrender their civil rights."[79]

Far more serious and menacing for the LAPD was the escalation of gang violence in the city. The years from 1986 to 1988 saw more than 400 people killed in the fighting between members of rival street gangs. Some of them were innocent bystanders who were standing in the wrong place at the wrong time. The LAPD responded to this senseless violence as if it was going into battle against a foreign army. Dubbed as "Operation Hammer," Chief Gates, on a weekend in April of 1988, deployed 1000 officers in a full-scale assault on youth gangs and drug trafficking in south-central Los Angeles. He instructed his officers to be "gentle with the citizens, so they won't feel their neighborhood is under siege." The results of the sweep indicated that this consideration was not always respected. Some 600 people were arrested, of whom only half were affiliated with gangs. The experience of one black construction contractor was particularly embarrassing. Two officers arrested him on his front porch as he attempted to pay his employees. "It's good what the police are doing, but they are harassing innocent people," the man's mother told a *Los Angeles Times* reporter. "Just because my son is black, and had that kind of money on him, doesn't make him a drug dealer." The following night 200 persons were taken into custody, many of whom did not possess illegal drugs. The police, like patrol officers in the 1960s and 1970s, found it difficult to distinguish between law-abiding people and known defenders and mistook respectable blacks for gang members.[80]

Little attention was given to this situation by Chief Gates, however. Pressured by church leaders, civic groups, and various elective officials, he stepped up the battle against illegal drugs and authorized raids on certain dwellings in ghetto neighborhoods. The biggest one occurred in August of 1988 and aroused much resentment in the black community. Eighty-eight officers, ostensibly searching for cocaine and other drugs, broke into four apartments, ransacked the premises and personal belongings, and roughed up some of the tenants. Thirty-three people were taken into custody, with only one of them being charged with possession of drugs. They filed a lawsuit against the city accusing the police of systematic brutality. The department's internal affairs division closely investigated the raid and concluded that a number of the officers had caused "excessive" damage during their search of the apartments. It also uncovered evidence of other infractions and recommended strong disciplinary action. Twenty-five policemen were suspended without pay for three weeks, three received official reprimands, and two others were forced to resign from the department. "The officers were trying hard to do the right thing— to solve the gang problem, to solve the narcotics trafficking problem," Gates pointed out in June of 1989. "Unfortunately, while doing the right thing, they were doing it in the wrong way."[81]

His comments suggest that the 1990s will be a very difficult and troublesome period for the police force. The postwar decades saw the development of much social discontent and highly organized protest in Los Angeles. In the face of such turbulence the LAPD, under the direction of strong-willed and imposing chiefs, often confused professional responsibilities with the unlimited use of power and assumed the role of the neighborhood bully, hampering and undermining the civil liberties of ethnic minorities and politically active individuals and groups. Liberal-minded members of the police commission, responding to sustained pressure from various civic organizations, devoted considerable attention to this disturbing situation and set down new and tough regulations which, at least on paper, emphasized the use of minimal force and guaranteed equitable and impartial law enforcement for all Angelinos regardless of their racial background or political persuasion. Tight controls and restrictions also existed in the gathering of intelligence information and kept the focus of police surveillance on the prevention of dangerous criminal activity. The painful experiences of innocent persons caught in gang sweeps and the homeless population, however, serve as a reminder that police power is always lurking around the corner and can come down hard upon unsuspecting residents, often with little regard for their constitutional rights and freedoms. Whether or not this state of affairs continues to be part and parcel of LAPD operations will greatly determine the future security and well-being of large numbers of the city's ethnic communities.

NOTES

1   Joseph G. Woods, "The Progressives and the Police: Urban Reform and the Professionalization of the Los Angeles Police," Ph.D. diss., University of California, Los Angeles, 1973, pp. 405-08.

2   Los Angeles Police Department, *Annual Report, 1949*, pp. 7, 9, 19; Woods, "Progressives and the Police," pp. 409-10.

3   Dean Jennings, "Portrait of a Police Chief," *Saturday Evening Post* 232 (7 May 1960): 87, 89.

4   James A. Gazell, "William H. Parker, Police Professionalization and the Public: An Assessment," *Journal of Police Science and Administration* 4 (Mar. 1976): 31-32; Woods, "Progressives and the Police," pp. 425-29, 434-35.

5   Los Angeles Police Department, *Annual Report, 1952*, p. 12; idem, *Annual Report, 1955*, p. 13.

6   Woods, "Progressives and the Police," p. 457; Gazell, "William H. Parker," p. 35.

7   George M. O'Connor, "The Negro and the Police in Los Angeles," M.A. thesis, University of Southern California, 1955, p. 136.

8   Jennings, "Police Chief," p. 89; Woods, "Progressives and the Police," pp. 437-38.

9   O'Connor, "The Negro and the Police," p. 135.

10 Los Angeles County Conference on Human Relations, Police Relations Committee, "Report to the Los Angeles Police Commission," 17 Mar. 1952, Edward Roybal Papers, Univ. of California, Los Angeles, box 29, pp. 2, 4-6.

11 O'Connor, "The Negro and the Police," pp. 126-27, 161-63.

12 William H. Parker, "The Police Role in Community Relations," address before the National Conference of Christians and Jews, East Lansing, MI, 19 May 1955, Roybal Papers, box 29, pp. 25-26.

13 Los Angeles *Sentinel*, 6, 20 June 1957.

14 Woods, "Progressives and the Police," p. 465. Charges, backed by evidence, of unequal enforcement of gambling laws were made by George A. Beavers, black director of the Los Angeles Housing Authority, at a hearing of the U.S. Commission on Civil Rights, Los Angeles, 1958. See Ed Cray, *The Big Blue Line: Police Power vs. Human Rights* (New York: Coward-McCann, 1962), 183.

15 Ed Cray, "The Police and Civil Rights," *Frontier* (May 1962): 10.

16 American Civil Liberties Union of Southern California, "A Proposed Ordinance to Create a Police Practices Review Board," 1 Mar. 1960, Roybal Papers, box 29, pp. 1-2.

17 Woods, "Progressives and the Police," p. 474; Edward M. Davis, "American Civil Liberties Union's Proposed Police Review Board," an address delivered to the Industrial Security Section, Los Angeles Chamber of Commerce, 27 Apr. 1960, Roybal Papers, box 29, pp. 2-3.

18 "Undermining the Police Force," *Los Angeles Times*, 19 July 1960.

19 John C. Bollens and Grant B. Geyer, *Yorty: Politics of a Constant Candidate* (Pacific Palisades, CA: Palisades Publishers, 1973), 122-23, 132-34; Woods, "Progressives and the Police," pp. 467-68.

20 "Special Muslim Report," Los Angeles Fire and Police Protective League, *News* 11 (May 1962):1-2; Cray, *The Big Blue Line*, pp. 130-31.

21 *Los Angeles Times*, 5, 11, 19 May, 12 June 1962.

22 U. S. Commission on Civil Rights, California Advisory Committee, *Police Minority Group Relations in Los Angeles and the San Francisco Bay Area* (Aug. 1963), 8-9; also see Hugh R. Manes, *A Report on Law Enforcement and the Negro Citizen* (Los Angeles, 1963), 9-31.

23 California Advisory Committee, *Police-Minority Group Relations*, pp. 13, 17-18. The police commission would not discuss with NAACP officials police mistreatment and ignored proposals for improving the LAPD's complaint procedures. Manes, *Report on Law Enforcement*, p. 49.

24 Eason Monroe, "Safeguarding Civil Liberties," Oral History Collection, University of California, Los Angeles, 1972, pp. 146-47; Paul Weeks, "Law Enforcement Hit by Negroes," *Los Angeles Times*, 25 June 1963.

25 Monroe, "Safeguarding Civil Liberties," pp. 147-49; Los Angeles Police Department, *Annual Report, 1963*, p. 7; Woods, "Progressives and the Police," pp. 455, 477.

26 *Los Angeles Times*, August 1, 21 Sept. 1963.

27 Paul Jacobs, *Prelude to Riot: A View of Urban America from the Bottom* (New York: Random House, 1966), 31, 101-02, 140-42; Robert Gottlieb and Irene Wolt, *Thinking Big: The Story of the Los Angeles Times, its Publishers, and their Influence on Southern California* (New York: Putnam, 1977), 376-77.

28 Spencer Crump, *Black Riot in Los Angeles: The Story of the Watts Tragedy* (Los Angeles: Trans-Anglo Books, 1966), 33-97.

29 Woods, "Progressives and the Police," pp. 485-87.

30 Governor's Commission on the Los Angeles Riots, *Violence in the City: An End or a Beginning?* (Los Angeles: State of California, 1965), 31-43, 49-56, 65-68; Robert M. Fogelson, *Violence as Protest: A Study of Riots and Ghettos* (New York: Anchor, 1971), 182-86, 192-94.

31 McCone Commission, *Report*, pp. 27-28, 30-37; Fogelson, *Violence as Protest*, pp. 187-88.

32 Woods, "Progressives and the Police," p. 491.

33 Ibid., pp. 492-93.

34 William W. Turner, *The Police Establishment* (New York: Putnam, 1968), 87, 101.

35 American Civil Liberties Union of Southern California, *Day of Protest, Night of Violence: The Century City Peace March* (Los Angeles: Sawyer Press, 1967), 2-

8, 12-14, 16-33; Harry Trimborn "Los Angeles Counts up Profits and Losses of President's Visit," *Los Angeles Times*, 25 June 1967.

36   Robert Conot, "The Superchief," Los Angeles *Times West Magazine*, June 9, 1968, pp. 14-15; Linda McVeigh Mathews, "Chief Reddin: New Style at the Top," *Atlantic* 223 (Mar. 1969): pp. 91-92.

37   Monroe, "Safeguarding Civil Liberties," pp. 155-57.

38   Philip S. Foner, ed., *The Black Panther Speaks* (New York: Lippincott, 1970), xv-xviii; Earl Anthony, *Picking up the Gun: A Report on the Black Panthers* (New York: Dial, 1970), 90-95. Anthony was a leader of the L.A. Black Panther organization .

39   Los Angeles Police Department, "The Chief's Message," 24 Apr. 1968; Mathews, "Chief Reddin," p. 92.

40   Anthony, *Picking up the Gun*, pp. 103, 130, 137; Phil Fradkin and Dial Torgerson, "Negro Leaders Urge Suspect in Police Shootout to Give Up," *Los Angeles Times*, 7 Aug. 1968.

41   Sylvia Guerrero, "The Political Development of the Mexican-American Community in Southern California, 1950-1978," M.A. thesis, California State University, Los Angeles, 1985, pp. 87-88; Rodolfo Acuña, *Occupied America: A History of Chicanos*, 3rd ed. (New York: Harper & Row, 1988), 337. LAPD Sergeant Robert J. Thoms admitted spying on the Brown Berets and other local ethnic organizations and recklessly accused many of their members of being involved in subversive and violent activity. U.S. Congress, Senate, Committee on the Judiciary, Subcommittee to Investigate the Administration of the Internal Security Act and other Internal Security Laws, "Extent of Subversion on the 'New Left'," testimony of Robert J. Thoms, *Hearings*, 91st Cong., 2nd sess., 20 Jan. 1970, pp. 1-44.

42   Guerrero, "Mexican American Community," pp. 93-111; Acuña, *Occupied America*, pp. 338-39. Upon appeal, the courts overturned the cases on the grounds that the charges were in violation of constitutional rights and liberties.

43   Rubén Salazar, *Stranger in One's Land* (Washington, DC: U.S. Civil Rights Commission , 1970), 40.

44   J. Gregory Payne and Scott C. Ratzan, *Tom Bradley: The Impossible Dream* (Santa Monica, CA: Roundtable, 1986), 99, 102-103, 108; Woods, "Progressives and the Police," pp. 504-05.

45   University of California, Los Angeles, Chancellor's Commission, *Violence at UCLA: May 5, 1970*, A Report by the Chancellor's Commission on the Events of May 5, 1970, pp. 1-12; Noel Greenwood, "Calm Returns to UCLA After Violent Eruption," *Los Angeles Times*, 7 May 1970.

46   Chancellor's Commission, *Violence at UCLA*, pp. 25-41.

47   Rodolfo F. Acuña, *A Community Under Siege: A Chronicle of Chicanos East of the Los Angeles River, 1945-1975* (Los Angeles: Chicano Studies Research Center Publications, Univ. of California, Los Angeles, 1975), 198, 200, 202.

48   Acuña, *A Community under Siege*, p. 202; idem, *Occupied America*, p. 346; Gottlieb and Wolt, *Thinking Big*, p. 425.

49   Acuña, *Occupied America*, pp. 346-50; also see Alejandro Morales, *Ando Sangrando-I am Bleeding: A Study of Mexican American Police Conflict* (La Puente, CA: Perspective Publications, 1972), 91-122.

50 Edward M. Davis, "Professional Police Principles," an address delivered before the Captains' School, July 1969, p. 8; idem, an address delivered to the annual conference of the International Association of Chiefs of Police, Atlantic City, 6 Oct. 1970, p. 3. Both speeches are in LAPD Library.

51 Gerald E. Caiden, *Police Revitalization* (Lexington, MA: Lexington Books, 1977), 277-79; Robert Rawitch, "Police Basic Car Plan—Review a Year Later," *Los Angeles Times*, 21 Feb. 1971.

52 Los Angeles Police Department, *Annual Report, 1973*, p. 21; idem, "Team Policing," 14 May 1974, pp. 1-3.

53 Caiden, *Police Revitalization*, pp. 284-85.

54 Jerry Belcher and David Rosenzweig, "Politics and the Police Department," *Los Angeles Times*, 18 Dec. 1977; Paul Hoffman and Robert Newman, "The Police Spying Settlement," *Los Angeles Lawyer* 7 (May 1984): 20.

55 Payne and Ratzan, *Tom Bradley*, pp. 127-31; Doug Shuit, "Bradley Names 140 to Commissions, Retains 21 of Yorty's Appointees," *Los Angeles Times*, 8 Aug. 1973.

56 Bill Hazlett, "Police Purge Nearly 2 Million Dossiers," *Los Angeles Times*, 11 Apr. 1975; Belcher and Rosenzweig, "Politics and the Police Department."

57 Narda Zacchino, "Intelligence Unit Rules Elude Police Panelists," *Los Angeles Times*, 28 Dece. 1975; "New Guidelines for Review of Police Intelligence Unit Okayed," ibid., 17 Dec. 1976; American Friends Service Committee, *The Police Threat to Political Liberty* (Philadelphia: American Friends Service Committee, 1979), 38.

58 Myrna Oliver, "Police Policy on Gun Use Being Revised," *Los Angeles Times*, 28 Aug. 1977; Dale Fetherling and Michael A. Levett, "Value of Life Must be Guide, Commission Says," ibid., 9 Sept. 1977; Dale Fetherling, "Police Board Upholds New Firearms Policy," ibid., 30 Sept. 1977.

59 "Gates Discusses Police Issues—Past, Present, Future," *Los Angeles Times*, 27 Mar. 1978.

60 "The Gulf is Still There," *Los Angeles Times*, August 13, 1978; Los Angeles Board of Police Commissioners, *The Report of the Board of Police Commissioners Concerning the Shooting of Eulia Love and the Use of Deadly Force: Part 4: Officer Involved Shootings*, 1980, pp. 48, 54-55.

61 *Los Angeles Times*, 20 Aug. 1978.

62 Los Angeles Board of Police Commissioners, *The Report of the Board of Police Commissioners Concerning the Shooting of Eulia Love and the Use of Deadly Force: Part 1: The Shooting of Eulia Love*, Oct. 1979, pp. 1-9.

63 Doug Shuit, "L.A. Deputy Chief Hits Love Slaying," *Los Angeles Times*, 25 Apr. 1979.

64 Doug Shuit and Penelope McMillan, "Police Board Cites Errors in Love Shooting," *Los Angeles Times*, 4 Oct. 1979.

65 Los Angeles Board of Police Commissioners, *The Report of the Board of Police Commissioners concerning the Shooting of Eulia Love and the Use of Deadly Force: Part 2: Investigation and Adjudication of Use of Force Incidents*, Oct. 1979, pp. 2, 5-6.

66 Los Angeles Board of Police Commissioners, *The Report of the Board of Police Commissioners concerning the Shooting of Eulia Love and the Use of Deadly*

Force: Part 3: Training and Community Relations, Jan. 1980, pp. 5-7, 13-14, 20, 26, 29-32.

67 "Help for the Police in a Tough Spot," *Los Angeles Times*, 10 Jan. 1980.

68 American Friends Service Committee, *Police Threat*, pp. 41-42.

69 Roxane Arnold and Joel Sappell, "Decree Leaves L.A. with Toughest Police-Spy Rules," *Los Angeles Times*, 23 Feb. 1984; Hoffman and Newman, "Police Spying Settlement," p. 22. The lawsuits are contained in *Coalition Against Police Abuse vs. Board of Police Commissioners*, No. C243458, Superior Court, County of Los Angeles, 1984.

70 Phil Kerby, "Disturbing Disorder in Police Intelligence Division," *Los Angeles Times*, 13 Jan. 1983; Joel Sappell, "Jay Paul," ibid., 30 Apr. 1984.

71 Los Angeles Board of Police Comissioners, Police Commission Subcommittee, "Reorganization of Anti-Terrorist Intelligence Function," 9 May 1983, pp. 1-3; Joel Sappell, "Police Intelligence Given to New Unit," Los Angeles *Times*, 10May 1983.

72 Arnold and Sappell, "Decree Leaves L.A. with Toughest Police Spy Rules"; Hoffman and Newman, "The Police Spying Settlement," pp. 23-24.

73 Kenneth Jost, "Opening a File on Police Intelligence," Los Angeles *Daily Journal*, 27 Feb. 1984.

74 Gene Blake, "Paul's Ex-Boss Says He Okayed Data Exchange," *Los Angeles Times*, 25 Feb. 1984; idem, "10-Day Penalty for Det. Paul," ibid., 3 May 1984; Andy Furillo, "Study Blames Gates, Top Aides for Spying Violations," *ibid.*, 18 Nov. 1984.

75 David Freed, "LAPD: Despite Gains, Race, Sex Bias Persist," *Los Angeles Times*, 28 Sept. 1986.

76 Ibid.

77 Frank Clifford and Penelope McMillan, "Raids Meant to Rid Skid Row of its Homeless Encampments," *Los Angeles Times*, 19 Feb. 1987; Penelope McMillan, "Sidewalk Encampment Sweeps Resume Amid Theatrical Atmosphere," ibid., 10 Mar. 1987.

78 Penelope McMillan, "L.A. Homeless on Skid Row to Face Arrest," *Los Angeles Times*, 29 May 1987; Penelope McMillan and George Ramos, "Homeless Fade Away as Police Move in for Arrests," ibid., 5 June 1987.

79 "Raids Clear Out 2 Camps of Homeless," *Los Angeles Times*, June 25, 1988; Michael Dear, "Sleeping on Sidewalk gets Rough When the City can Steal Your Blanket," ibid., 1 July 1988.

80 Eric Malnic and Mark Arax, "1,000 Officers Stage Assault Against Violent Youth Gangs," *Los Angeles Times*, 9 Apr. 1988; Robert Stewart and Paul Feldman, "Arrests top 850 as Anti-Gang Drive Continues," ibid., 10 Apr. 1988.

81 David Freed, "38 Police Officers Disciplined for L.A. Gang Raid," Los Angeles *Times*, 23 June 1989.

Chapter 7

IN SEARCH OF COMMUNITY: A COMPARATIVE ESSAY ON MEXICANS IN LOS ANGELES AND SAN ANTONIO

Carlos Navarro and *Rodolfo Acuña*

Since the Anglo-American conquest of Los Angeles, Mexicans have been systematically displaced and moved from one area to another. Numerous old barrios have disappeared before the onslaught of "economic development" which has ignored the needs and values of lower-income Mexican residents.[1] The result has been that no permanent Mexican community has been allowed to mature in Los Angeles County.

East Los Angeles, although often seen as being the heart of the Mexican community in the United States, did not become predominantly Mexican until after World War II. This important demographic and symbolic center for Mexican Americans is largely inhabited today by recent Mexican and Central American immigrants who know little of the traditions and historical struggles that Mexicans have experienced in Los Angeles.

Like Los Angeles, San Antonio has been the home of a very large and poor Mexican community. Since the middle 1970s, however, San Antonians have made, in contrast to Angelinos, significant political gains. This essay seeks to explain why Los Angeles' Latinos have failed to create the same sense of community that their counterparts have in San Antonio. For purposes of this exploratory essay we define community as an identification with a place by a social group which over time identifies its own leaders and builds local institutions, giving the group the potential for asserting political, economic, and cultural independence.[2]

In San Antonio, this greater sense of community has been a significant factor in allowing Mexicans to have a greater level of political influence than their Los Angeles counterparts. This essay reviews the historical and structural factors at work in the organizational and political development of the Mexican communities in these two important American cities.

Chicano activist-historian, Dr. Ernesto Galarza, often explained the failure of Mexicans to mature as a community by saying that a people on the move have never formed civilizations—institution building requires a rooting process. While Galarza spoke about rural migrants, the same principle applies to today's urban Chicanos. Communities are especially important to minorities with scarce economic resources since they give them an identity and a cultural presence. Time allows them to forge a group consciousness and common sense, or practicality, that is built by collective struggle. A stable location allows a rooting process, and the formation of a historical memory that permits community consciousness to develop. A sense of unity results and the community learns from its victories and defeats to deal with its crises.

Without a sense of community consciousness, residents are vulnerable to the whims of dominant groups that can, under the guise of urban renewal or urban redevelopment, displace them. The justification for this displacement is that blight is being eradicated. Former rural migrants are forced to become urban migrants because they are unable to afford homes or find employment in the newly redeveloped areas.

The thesis of this essay is that the lack of Mexican communities in Los Angeles partially explains their powerlessness. This lack of influence has inhibited the development of leaders and institutions, and frustrated the ability of Latinos to take advantage of developments like the Voting Rights Act. By contrast, Mexicans in San Antonio have made real political gains, after experiencing rigid institutionalized racism which is rooted in the "Texas War for Independence" from Mexico—memorialized in countless films and books and the battlecry of "Remember the Alamo!"

TALE OF TWO CITIES

Los Angeles is at the center of one of the world's largest metropolitan areas. Freeways connect the city's core with a massive network of expanding suburbs that have spread into the counties of Orange, Riverside, San Bernardino, and Ventura. East Los Angeles is a gateway into the civic center with the San Bernardino, Pomona, and Santa Ana freeways nearly converging at one point in the Boyle Heights community of the Eastside.

Geographic dispersion makes it difficult for Los Angeles to develop a sense of community. Los Angeles County is five times the size of San Antonio's Bexar County, while L.A. city is three times the size of San Antonio. Although the bulk of Latinos cluster in the greater Eastside and the numerous cities of the San Gabriel valley, Latinos are dispersed throughout most of the county's 87 cities and unincorporated areas. In contrast, Mexicans in Bexar County have lived on the Westside of San Antonio since 1836. Only until recently have middle-class Latinos begun to move to the more affluent and Anglo Northside.

Angelinos have had the difficult task of trying to organize a much larger population spread over a massive geographic area, while San Antonio's Mexicans are concentrated and significantly fewer in numbers. The dispersion of Los Angeles's Latinos has encouraged politicians to ignore them and exclude them from political representation.

While the Los Angeles Latino population is four times the size of San Antonio's Mexican community, San Antonio's Mexicans have always been a very significant proportion (in fact, nearly half the City's population for most of this century). Los Angeles Mexicans began the century with only five percent of the city's population. The 1980 Census indicated that Latinos were 27.6% of Los Angeles city and county, while Mexicans were 47% of San Antonio.[3] Being a proportionately smaller population, the Los Angeles Latino community has often found itself ignored by the corporate and governmental decision making bodies.

Vast demographic changes, resulting from the economic boom in Southern California during the World War II era, also created a much less rigid pattern of segregation in Los Angeles, allowing its Mexican middle class the option of moving out of the barrios. This group left for the suburbs where many joined the dominant Anglo culture.

In contrast, San Antonio's Mexican population has been historically concentrated on the Westside. The presence of a community for such a long period may help to explain why this city has been the birth place of important national Chicano organizations such as the Mexican American Legal Defense and Education Fund and the Southwest Voter Registration and Education Project. The largest and oldest national Chicano organizations—the League of United Latin American Citizens (LULAC) and the American G.I. Forum—originated in Texas. The interchange between these two Mexican communities has been extensive, but San Antonio leaders and organizations (LULAC, G.I. Forum, the Mexican American Youth Organization) have had a much greater impact on Los Angeles organizations and leaders than the converse. Currently San Antonian Mexicans enjoy considerably more political success than their Angeleno counterparts, particularly since electing in 1981 a Chicano Mayor, Henry Cisneros and having near control of the city council. It has the most successful grassroots organization in its Communities Organized for Public Service (COPS).

DEVELOPMENTS PRIOR TO WORLD WAR II

Within a few decades after the Mexican American War (1845-1848), the new Anglo ruling elite established Los Angeles as a frontier outpost of a world market system. By the late 1870s, with the entrance of the railroad and the arrival of massive numbers of Americans and Europeans, Los Angeles grew from a small pueblo of about 11,000 in 1880 to 50,000 in 1890. Only 2,231 Mexicans lived in Los Angeles by 1880 and, although L.A. expanded significantly in size, it was only 5,000 by 1900.[4] Mexicans grew proportionately smaller and became a submerged minority. The total Los Angeles population grew from 102,000 in 1900 to 1.2 million in 1930. As the Mexican presence and influence dramatically decreased, white Angelinos developed an attitude of indifference or apathy toward the founding minority community of the city.

In contrast, San Antonio Euroamericans could not afford to be indifferent to Mexicans. Historically it's political machine depended on the Mexican vote to keep it in power. In 1870, 2,309 of the total population of 12,000 were Mexicans. By 1900, the city grew to 53,321, with the Mexican population multiplying to 13,722. Thirty years later San Antonio numbered 231,542; the Mexicans constituted 82,373 people.[5] San Antonio Mexicans remained numerically larger than their counterparts in Los Angeles until the 1930s.

Throughout their Euroamerican experience, Los Angeles Mexican settlements have been uprooted. Sonoratown, situated next to the Plaza area, was the first Mexican community. Smaller isolated barrios existed in such dispersed areas such as San Fernando, San Pedro-Wilmington, Pasadena, and Watts. In the first thirty years of the 1900s, city leaders bulldozed Sonoratown to build government and commercial buildings, forcing Mexicans into the Eastside.[6] Mexicans moved into the crevices of Boyle Heights, living under bridges, in ravines, arroyos and on the side of Hills.[7] Simultaneously, a greater number moved into an unincorporated area known as Belevedere, which lay at the end of the Yellow Streetcar line, and just East of Boyle Heights.

San Antonio Mexicans have always lived on the Westside. And, while migrants used it as their winter home, many others resided permanently in the city. Its sizeable Mexican population encouraged the formation of a merchant and professional class to service the various community needs. The organization of the League of United Latin American Citizens in the late 1920s represented a natural evolution of an organic middle class organization, reflecting the growing number of second generation Mexican Americans who identified themselves as U.S. citizens.[8]

Los Angeles, a major national agricultural county until 1950, provided tens of thousands of seasonal and year-round agricultural jobs.[9] Mexicans' work alternated between farm labor and heavy construction. Mexicans often changed residences to meet the city's labor market needs. It was not until the 1930s that a permanent Eastside colony began.

As a result of the progressive reform movement of the first two decades of the century, local government officials derived their power through city-wide elections rather than ward elections. The creation of an at-large city council and at-large county supervisorial districts prevented the formation of a political machine, and it also destroyed any incentive to build strong neighborhood political organizations. Money and access to powerful local newspapers (such as the *Los Angeles Times*), rather than people, formed the basis of this structure. The dispersal of the Mexican population, and the fact that they were proportionately small enough to ignore, reinforced indifferent Euroamerican attitudes towards Mexicans. Adding to the Mexican dilemma was the problem that large numbers lived in the county's unicorporated areas where they had less potential for political participation than in the city.[10]

' The white populations of both cities differed. White Angelinos did not develop traditions based on anti-Mexican sentiments: the battles of the Alamo and San Jacinto have great significance to white Texans and are memorialized in many ways. Until recent times, Texans practiced the powerful Southern tradition of de jure segregation and violence against people of color that permeated all sectors of that society. White racism in L.A. was essentially Midwest urban in character and the overall record of institutional segregation and violence was not as pronounced in Los Angeles as it was in Texas.[11] Los Angeles had a racially and ethnically heterogeneous population, whereas in San Antonio Mexicans were the only significant minority community.

Los Angeles Mexicans had relatively more employment opportunities than San Antonians. In the 1930s, cottage industries thrived in San Antonio, while heavy industry had moved heavily into Los Angeles. New auto, rubber, and steel industries employed Euroamericans and relatively small numbers of Mexicans. Racism was common in the industrial trade union locals, but some Mexicans had the possibility of joining the unionized sector of the labor force. San Antonio never developed a strong industrial base, as its economy depended on tourism and military installations.

The Repatriation, or the massive Mexican deportation of the Great Depression, greatly disorganized the Mexican community throughout the United States. Some 50,000 to 100,000 were deported or left Los Angeles. The Euroamerican attitude towards the repatriation was callous disinterest. Local government officials cooperated with the immigration authorities because they felt it was just good business. It cost the city less money to ship Mexicans to the border than to feed them. The mass deportation disrupted the formation of a sense of place. It also removed a generation or two of future voters because a majority of the deported were U.S. citizens.[12] The Repatriation did not appear to have as devastating an effect on San Antonio.[13]

During the early 1940s, war and related industrial employment attracted thousands of Mexicans to the city of the Angels. Most newcomers settled in emerging communities such as Boyle Heights, Lincoln Heights and East Los Angeles where their arrival taxed existing facilities and housing. Boyle Heights was a polyglot community where, by 1950, Mexicans had become approximately one-half of the population.

THE POST-WORLD WAR II YEARS

By the end of World War II, definite patterns emerged. The San Antonio Chamber of Commerce advertised its abundance of cheap labor. San Antonio was, in fact, one of the poorest cities in the United States. Ironically, despite limited employment opportunities, homeowner-occupancy increased among Mexicans on the Westside.

Los Angeles, on the other hand, had become the West Coast's leading city and a world economic center. The Eastside barrios were adjacent to the city's powerful financial, commercial, and industrial centers. But, despite the fact that Angelinos had more economic options open to them, they were not able to attain home ownership to the same degree that their counterparts did in San Antonio. Those Mexicans who could afford to purchase housing did so in the predominantly Anglo suburbs, where it was relatively cheaper, newer and available. San Antonio Mexicans had less of an opportunity to buy outside the Westside.

During and after the war, many Los Angeles Mexicans were employed in heavy industry. Union jobs paid higher wages, allowing many Mexicanos the luxury of buying homes in the new suburban tracts. In San Antonio, Mexicans entered the civil service sector. They worked in local military installations where wages were lower than those in heavy industry, but in the long run were more stable.[14] Civil service employment was not effected to the same degree as industrial employment by the restructuring of industry that began soon after World War II.[15] Consequently, the Mexican middle class in San Antonio, an organic part of the Westside, could take political advantage of the legal changes effected by the civil rights struggles of the 1960s.

Freeways and new federal policies accelerated suburbanization in Los Angeles. Many of the Mexican middle class moved to new tract homes bordering the Eastside, or to the outlying suburbs of the San Gabriel Valley. Many returning veterans could afford to move because of higher paying jobs in heavy industry, in defense plants, and some even became professionals with the help of the G.I. bill.

Moreover, the housing boom in Los Angeles was in the suburbs. The Eastside itself was almost fully developed, surrounded by what was then white communities. Mexicans were forced to leapfrog to new housing tracts in Pico Rivera, La Puente, etc. In San Antonio, tracts for returning veterans could naturally flow west. Many whites fled the Eastside, expecting it to be redeveloped, but they held on to their property for speculative purposes.

In 1946, three-quarters of Boyle Heights' residential property was upzoned for multi-dwelling and commercial use. Few new arrivals, conseqently, could afford to become homeowners or renters in this area.

Federal land use policy further disorganized the Eastside. First, the 1949 Housing Act encouraged massive urban renewal programs under the guise of redeveloping blighted areas. Because of the Mexican community's proximity to the civic and commercial center, urban renewal programs had a greater effect on Los Angeles housing during the fifties and sixties than on San Antonio's. Chavez Ravine and Bunker Hill are monuments to the bulldozer mentality. Massive government funding further encouraged the development of land in and around the Civic Center. It rewarded the local government for clearing the land of houses and then selling the land below cost to developers. To protect their property investments, insurance companies and commercial enterprises such as Sears & Roebuck, which was situated at the southwest corner of the Eastside, lobbied for more extensive development programs. As a further incentives, local governments received millions of dollars in additional tax revenues for more intensively utilized land.[16]

Second, white flight was hastened by huge grants to states for highway building. It added incentive to the freeway construction and the development of suburban tracts. An estimated ten percent of Boyle Heights residents were displaced by freeways which sliced up the Eastside. Municipal government, in its development plans, deliberately and systematically ignored the human needs of the central city where the bulk of the poor people lived.

The 1950s were turbulent years for minorities. Mexican migration to Los Angeles County accelerated with its population climbing from some 400,000 to 600,000 Mexican Americans. The Alinskian Community Service Organization (CSO) was formed just after World War II.[17] The CSO, although dominated by lower-middle class Mexican Americans, strove to create a grassroots organization. It registered Chicanos to vote in unprecedented numbers, and played a key role in Edward R. Roybal's election to the Los Angeles City Council in 1949. The CSO still functions today, however, it operates at a much lower level than the '50s because many of its "young Turks" moved to suburbia.[18]

By 1959, Chicano professionals, business persons, teachers, trade unions and grassroots activists had formed the Mexican American Political Association (MAPA).[19] It reflected the increased political activity among Chicanos throughout the United States. Many Chicanos soon afterwards joined Víva Kennedy clubs which helped elect President John F. Kennedy. Most of these new organizations, while assuming to speak for the poor, were not totally barrio based. Increasingly much of the middle class leadership lived outside the impoverished and isolated barrios.

THE BREAKDOWN OF SOCIAL CONTROL

The 1960s, a decade of whirlwind change, was a time when the empowerment of minorities and the poor became, at least temporarily, part of the national debate. For Los Angeles Mexicans it meant changes in in-county migration, population growth, and employment. For San Antonio Mexicans, it was a time of broadened community participation in both the political and economic life of the city.

During the first half of the decade, the Mexican American civil rights movement echoed black civil rights rhetoric and demanded assimilation in a reasonable and patient way. By the late 1960s, however, Chicano youth were dominating public discussion with a militant rhetoric, again mirroring national and international trends.

By 1960, the L.A. Mexican American population, five times larger than that of San Antonio, comprised only nine percent of the Standard Metropolitan Statistical Area population. San Antonio Mexicans were 41 percent of that metropolitan area. Because Los Angeles had higher paying and diversified jobs, it attracted more national and international migration.

Greater mobility encouraged the continued migration of the middle class to the suburbs. With the relative fluidity of Mexican-Anglo social relationships in Los Angeles compared to San Antonio, there appeared to be higher rates of acculturation and assimilation in Los Angeles than San Antonio.[20] By the end of the decade, the barrios had become ports of entry for first generation, very low-income families as well as the home of the poorest sector of the established Mexican community. In 1960, only 45% of Los Angeles Mexicans had lived in the central barrio for 20 years or more versus 75% of the San Antonians.

In Los Angeles, the dispersed and rapidly increasing Mexican community challenged its leaders and organizations to effectively confront its major crises and problems. The constant movement of Chicanos out of East L.A. and other barrios found the community unable to deal with the rising crises. Every tension was a new experience. A lack of identification with place and an absence of institutions of social control partially explains why historically Los Angeles has been the scene of major turbulence during World War II and its aftermath. It was not by accident that the Sleepy Lagoon Case (1942), the Pachuco Riots (1943), the East Los Angeles Walkouts (1968), the Catolicos Por La Raza (1969), and the Chicano Moratorium (1970) all occurred in Los Angeles. On the surface, San Antonio would seem a more logical site for turbulence, with its more intense racism and poverty.[21]

It does not always follow that the poorest or the most oppressed are the first to revolt. Black urban rebellions in modern times have occurred in northern cities such as New York, Newark, and Detroit—not in the South where oppression was more overt. It could be argued that San Antonio's Mexican leadership and organizational structure acted as an institution of social control over its community. While Los Angeles barely forged a community, the structural restraints were greater in San Antonio. The Anglo authorities were more repressive and intolerant towards protest. They had a greater ability to isolate and punish identifiable troublemakers or radicals.

The Catholic Church was also more influential among Mexicans in San Antonio. Since the beginning of the 1940s, the San Antonio Catholic hierarchy had spoken out in defense of the Mexican community encouraging, or instance, trade unionism.[22] Cardinal James Francis McIntyre of Los Angeles catered exclusively to the middle class Irish and German Catholic elite. Politically and economically, he could afford to ignore the large, poor Mexican population.

A lack of presence within the political structure made L.A. Mexicans restless. In 1962, city Councilman Edward R. Roybal was elected to the Congress after having served the Eastside since 1949. As a councilman, Roybal had courageously championed the rights of Mexicans and other poor folk. His election to Congress left a local political vacuum.

Westside Democrats formed a coalition with blacks and ignored the issue of fair representation for Los Angeles's Mexican community. Led by liberal Democrat Rosalind Wyman, council members refused to name a Mexican American to replace Roybal, and instead appointed Gilbert Lindsay, a black, to complete Roybal's term. They also reapportioned the district to favor Lindsay's incumbency by increasing the number of black voters and, in 1963, Lindsay easily won the general election. Because of this political betrayal, Mexicans would remain without representation on the Los Angeles City Council for almost a quarter of a century, until 1985. The reapportionment made possible the election of two more blacks (Tom Bradley and Billy Mills) to the Council. The favoritism of the white establishment of black over brown, and the blatant exploitation of the Mexican vote by the Democratic party encouraged a black-brown rivalry during the "War on Poverty", and increased the competition that exists to this day.

Angelinos were unprepared for the tumult of the sixties. A lack of political organization and experience prevented Mexicans from taking advantage of social changes made possible during this period. It was impossible to plan a long-range consistent strategy since there was a continuous turnover in leadership and organizations. Economic and political objectives were sacrificed for more superficial cultural goals.

Mexican Americans were not able to plan a political agenda nor capture popular support comparable to blacks. In fairness to the Mexican community, there were many variables which explain the greater sophistication and access that blacks had in the political system. One major factor was that blacks were truly a national minority, and there was a significant black population in every major U.S. city. The Democratic party was sensitive to this and this explains why President Lyndon Johnson's "War on Poverty" has been seen as an effort to maintain the loyalty of the black political elite. Mexicans had no counterparts to the Black colleges and professional schools as only recently has there been enough Mexican intellectuals nation-wide capable of having an impact on their community and the larger society.

By the second half of the 1960s, internal political cleavages appeared within the Mexican community. Young Latinos challenged groups such as LULAC, G.I. Forum, and the Political Association of Spanish Speaking Organizations (PASSO). Like the Black movement, many Chicanos became angry and their tactics were more strident as the decade progressed. Unlike the black experience, an effective internal organizational network to negotiate substantial social change did not exist. LULAC and the GI Forum were ineffective cliques, when compared to the web of black ministers and professionals extending through the black communities. Moreover, the established Mexican leadership had little or no influence on the younger activists within the Mexican community.

During the mid-1960s, César Chávez emerged as a nationally recognized, but largely symbolic, civil rights leader. The farmworkers' struggle, however, did not attempt to set up an organizational structure which could formulate programs for urban Chicanos. The value of "La Causa" was the raising of the Chicanos' social consciousness and giving Mexican issues legitimacy in the national civil rights forum.

Most social programs in Los Angeles during that decade were outer developed—emphasizing awareness rather than organization building. The War on Poverty, as well as municipal, county and state programs, influenced Chicano youth. As early as 1963, the Los Angeles County Human Relations Commission sponsored a group called the Mexican American Educators. It was formed in Los Angeles to discuss, among other issues, the dropout problem among Chicano youth. The poverty programs created an awareness of the needed goals but they did not develop networks and procedures for achieving those goals.

The War on Poverty changed the attitude of many minorities. Some Mexicans believed the rhetoric of "power to the people!" and, for the first time, many questioned civic authorities. Yet the inability of Mexicanos to achieve even proportional equity with blacks shattered the illusion that the War on Poverty was designed to aid them, and it created new tensions. The black population in the Alamo city was never large enough to threaten the Mexican community for resources. The existence of a white liberal-black coalition in Los Angeles meant that Mexicans were outsiders to the political process and thus under serviced.

The Vietnam War, meanwhile, broke down the moral authority of the state. For many activists, especially the youth, mass demonstrations legitimized a cult of dissent, and grassroots activists for a time became the legitimate spokepersons for the community. As the Black movement gained momentum, cultural nationalism increased in Mexican American barrios throughout the United States. Cultural nationalism, however, varied region by region and state by state. Cultural nationalism was more of a feeling—a spontaneous outburst than an intellectual commitment to structural change. It was more fragile in Los Angeles where the issue of cultural identity was not firmly grounded in historical experiences and conciousness.

By the end of the decade, Mexican students on college and university campuses formed a critical mass, and they asserted their presence. By 1967, they met at Loyola University at Los Angeles and formed the United Mexican American Students (UMAS) organization. In Texas, the formation of the Mexican American Youth Organization (MAYO) had been underway for three years. Youth participation in Los Angeles was spontaneous, and it lasted from 1968-1971. Students literally entered with a bang: 20,000 Mexican school children walked out of five Eastside high schools in 1968, and, for a time, they occupied valuable political space within the movement.

Chicano youth leaders as a group did not affect Los Angeles politics after 1971 to the same degree as former MAYO members did in San Antonio. After 1971, Los Angeles Chicano youth leader's hegemony slipped dramatically and by the mid-1970s they ceased to be a significant force. In San Antonio, during the 1970s most youth activists were incorporated into city organizations and many became movers and shakers in the political process. The political presence of the community increased. The heavy concentration of Mexican voters and the close residential proximity between the lower and middle income families served to form a community of interest.

The L.A. barrios continued as ports of entry for massive numbers of Mexican and Central American immigrants. Although the size and distribution of the community grew at an incredible rate, Latinos in Los Angeles appeared to be as powerless as ever.

By 1968, the flow of undocumented workers reached high levels. United States policy had encouraged the flow of immigrants from Mexico. A backlash developed because of what Euroamericans perceived as a threat to their hegemony. Bert Corona, a veteran activist, anticipating the wave of anti-alien hysteria which occurred in the 1970s and 1980s and formed Centro de Acción Social Autonoma-Hermandad General de Trabajadores (CASA-HGT) to organize the undocumented workers. Corona predicted that nativism would resurface after the Viet Nam War, and the foreign born would suffer a new and more vigorous form of discrimination. Meanwhile, the war persisted, causing a high number of Mexican casualties.

On Christmas 1969, off-duty sheriff deputies arrested Chicano protestors in front of the basilica of St. Basil's Catholic Church which was located in an exclusive area of Los Angeles. Essentially, they protested the indifference of the Catholic Church to the plight of the Mexican American. Significantly, this action did not occur in San Antonio where, for all of its defects, the Catholic Church was part of the community building process.

In 1970, demonstrations against the Viet Nam War increased. On 29 August, some 30,000 Mexican Americans from throughout the United States marched against the war in the National Chicano Moratorium. The Los Angeles Police Department and the Los Angeles Sheriff's Department brutally suppressed this march and rally and those that followed. After this effort, California Mexicans attempted to duplicate the success of the Texas La Raza Unida Party (RUP), and formed a California RUP. The RUP did not enjoy any political success in Los Angeles and by 1974 it had died.[23] In contrast, the Texas RUP for a time challenged the power structure, winning some local elections, and playing the role of a spoiler in state office races.

While political splintering occurred in Texas, it was not as prevalent as in California. The established San Antonio Chicano communities also allowed Mexicans to form a "them and us" mentality. Lastly, youth leaders, although considered strident by established Texas Mexican leaders, were more accepted as a legitimate part of the community than they were in Los Angeles.

THE RISE OF THE HISPANIC

With the landslide reelection of Richard M. Nixon in 1972, the activist era ended. In 1973, the Viet Nam War was concluded and this signaled the return to traditional American domestic concerns. The elimination of poverty ceased to be a part of public policy and its apparatus was purposefully dismantled. Nixon also developed the strategy of Republicanizing Latinos; he ignored the needs of the poor and concentrated on catering to the self-interest of middle-class Chicanos. Nixon perpetuated the myth that the success of the masses depended on a prosperous middle class.

While Latinos in the 1960s took the initiative in controlling their own symbols and cultural identity, in the 1970s that role was assumed by the federal government and the private sector. They packaged all Latinos into an artificial coalition labelled HISPANICS. The corporate world and the two major political parties recognized the potential in the bourgeoning Spanish speaking population of cities like Los Angeles, Chicago, Miami and New York. The Hispanicization of U.S. Latinos by Washington D.C. and the corporate world allowed the existing divergent forces within the Mexican community in Los Angeles to be pulled even farther apart.[24]

Suburban middle class, educated, and acculturated Mexican Americans could call themselves Hispanics, allowing them to distance themselves socially from their lower income immigrant and inner city counterparts.[25] For many Chicano activists, the "rise of the Hispanic" era harkens back to an earlier time, where successful Mexicans would identify themselves as Spanish. Mexican restaurant owners in Southern California, so as not to offend Anglo customers, would call their cuisine "Spanish food."

The 1970s and 1980s saw the resurgence of nativism among the majority society. The Immigration and Naturalization Service, the media, and certain racist politicians pushed a deliberate campaign to blame the undocumented worker for the downturn in the economy.[26] The once peaceful Mexican worker became a criminal, an "illegal alien" who was a welfare leech and out to steal jobs from real Americans. This freed society from the sense of guilt it had fleetingly displayed in the previous decade. To the credit of Chicano organizations, they fought the repressive legislation until 1986 when liberals and conservatives in Congress joined to pass the Simpson-Rodino Law.

The campaign against Simpson—Rodino demonstrated the weakness of community structures within the Mexican barrios. Politicians were not afraid of the consequences for they knew that they controlled the historical memory of Chicanos. The elite by the 1970s had learned how to effectively undermine the progress minorities had been making in the 1960s in developing their identity and culture. The elite did, however, fear the weakening of control, a breakdown of law and order, as well as any challenge to their hegemony. The result was an intense Americanization campaign in education and the media with the sole purpose of integrating the Latino and black middle classes and dividing them from the masses of the poor—which further disorganized the formation of organic communities. Los Angeles was more susceptible than San Antonio; in the case of the latter nationalism served as a brake to integration and the complete erasure of the community's historical memory.

The arrival of large numbers of Mexican nationals after the mid-1960s also caused a severe housing shortage in the already overcrowded barrios of Los Angeles. The more affluent left the community, but Chicano baby boomers came of age, putting additional demands on the already limited housing.   Inflated house values contributed to the upward rent spiral. And the presence of large numbers of undocumented Central Americans and Mexicans who could note vote reinforced a "not counting Mexicans" attitude historically held by Euroamerican society.[27]

By the mid-1970s, San Antonio Mexicans embarked on a series of political sucessess. Communities Organized for Public Service, an Alinskian organization, formed under the sponsorship of the Catholic Church, began to challenge the control of municipal government. Through the enforcement of the federal Voting Rights Act, the city ended the practice of the at-large elections to the city council. This allowed the elected of a near majority of Hispanics to the San Antonio City Council in 1977; in contrast, at the same time Los Angeles Mexicans remained unrepresented in the City Council or on the Board of Supervisors.

Much of San Antonio's lower middle-class Mexican leadership came from the civil service sector. In the 1960s, San Antonio housed Brooks, Kelly, Lackland, and Randolph Air Force Bases and Fort Sam Houston. Kelly alone employed 21,000 workers, 17 percent of the city's workforce, ranking as the city's largest employer. By the 1980s over 50 percent of the workers at Kelly were Mexican American. In contrast, the number of Angelinos entering municipal, state and federal employment until the 1970s was quite small.[28]

As discussed earlier, salaries were much higher in heavy industries than in the public sector. However, by the 1980s, heavy industry had been nearly wiped out in Los Angeles by a restructuring that saw plants either closing or moving out of the area. Civil service proved more stable, with wages becoming competitive with the private sector during the 1960s and 1970s. San Antonio's Mexicans acquired enough surplus to buy their own homes before inflation and the high interest rates of the 1970s made ownership almost impossible.[29]

Having a strong sense of community is a necessary condition for community empowerment, but it is not sufficient. A community lacking the economic and political resources and political direction may be misled and manipulated by various political forces, including leadership originally emanating from that community base. Recently, Martin Sánchez Jankowski suggested that the existence of a strong community has in many ways allowed ideological control of Mexicans in San Antonio:

> The political structure of San Antonio was closed to Chicanos until very recently. At the time of the initial phase of this study, 1977, there was only one Chicano on the city council, a remarkable statistic given the fact that the city was over 50 percent Chicano. In 1984 there were four Chicanos on the city council and a Chicano mayor; however, this does not signal a changing of the guard in terms of political power. The Anglo-American community controls much of the economic activity in San Antonio primarily through the power of the banks, and as a result it controls a great deal of local government activity.[30]

The Euroamerican economic and political elites on the Northside, which have until recently exercised unquestioned hegemony, will continue to develop strategies to neutralize leaders and organizations from the Westside. Thomas A. Baylis shed light on this changing composition and behavior of San Antonio's elite which raises important issues about those who would seek fundmental change in local politics. According to Baylis, the ruling class in San Antonio, as elsewhere, is conservative and unwilling to relinquish political control. At the present, the Alamo city's politics are going through a transition. The elite now seeks out alliances with Southside voters, comprised principally of poorer Euroamericans, in an attempt to reassert its political control although in a less obvious manner than in the past.[31]

Although the Mexican community in San Antonio does not have self-determination, a community structure exists in San Antonio that facilitates organization and a sense of unity. The use of Spanish among 3rd and 4th generation Mexican Americans is still common. That the extended family is more intact in San Antonio is evidence of the cohesiveness of a family support network. A recent study shows that 92 percent of San Antonio youth surveyed knew their god parents in contrast to 52 percent in Los Angeles.[32] In a recent three generation study of Mexican American religious behavior in San Antonio, Markides and Cole found that "the family remains an important vehicle through which religious behavior and attitudes are transmitted from generation to generation." and that San Antonio "has a large and fairly stable Mexican American population...."[33]

The authors visits to San Antonio revealed that community activists as well as the common folk knew their elected officials and these officials' families. Former mayor Henry Cisneros was born and raised in the city's Westside. His grandparents came to San Antonio during the Mexican Revolution; they were from the political exiled upper middle class. His maternal grandfather was a leader in the city during the 1920s and 1930s.

Negatively, Cisneros also had excellent relations with conservative Republicans and reactionary businessmen such as billionaire Ross Perot. Cisneros was the darling of conservatives because he preaches a gospel of "trickle down economics"; according to him, the way Chicanos could make it was to become middle class. At the same time, he promoted a free enterprise zone where industry could get tax credits and pay workers $3.35 an hour. The existence of a strong cultural nationalism among San Antonians and the media hype obscured Cisneros's class interests and how they clashed with the poor Mexican.

The concentration of Mexicans in the Westside, and the presence of a stable community encouraged the growth of Communities Organized for Public Service and made possible an effective voter registration program which resulted in Cisneros' election. White voters voted for him because the election of a Mexican mayor was inevitable, and Cisneros was the most acceptable. That Cisneros was a product of the Westside also made it possible for San Antonio's elite to impose him on the people who forget that he was first elected on the elite-dominated Good Government League's slate.

It will help to clarify some important differences between the Mexican communities in Los Angeles and San Antonio by analyzing the two most important grass roots organizations that have developed in the 1970s and 1980s: Los Angeles's United Neighborhoods Organization (UNO), and San Antonio's Communities Organized for Public Services (COPS). COPS began in 1973 with Ernie Cortés, a native San Antonian, setting up a network based on local parishes and with financial support from sources in the Catholic Church and some Protestant churchmen.[34]

In 1976, Cortés was invited to Los Angeles's Eastside to organize UNO, which was also supported by a network of Catholic parishes and some Protestant church leaders. Both COPS and UNO use the local parish as a basic organizing unit. However, critical differences exist in the background, composition, and development of COPS and UNO.

The Eastside did not have the benefit of a native son or daughter who could build a viable network of grass-roots organizations. The Eastside had few college graduates with the training, networks, and commitment necessary to develop a mass-based community organization. Cortés, therefore, had to rely more heavily on the parish network, training many priests and nuns to take leadership roles. Some community leaders, such as former UNO President Lydia López, lived outside the target area and were essentially from middle class backgrounds.

The Mexican communities of COPS and UNO also differed. In San Antonio, Cortés used the existing networks which resulted from the Parish Advisory Councils of San Antonio. Los Angeles, with its very conservative and authoritarian Catholic Church hierarchy, offered no real parallel. Los Angeles' Mexican parishes were limited by the lack of effective organized units to channel concerns to the Los Angeles Church; a structural flaw that was not accidental.

Father Edmundo Rodríguez, an important resource for Cortés, helped to garner support in the Eastside. Relatively fewer Mexican American priests worked in Los Angeles. Unfortunately, some of these Latino priests reflected conservative, sometimes even reactionary, attitudes of the Los Angeles Archdiocese's chancery.[35]

Another important difference between the parishes in San Antonio and Los Angeles was that all of San Antonio's COPS parishes were within the boundaries of the city. This obviously makes it easier to form a united front against one governmental entity. At least half of UNO's parished are outside L.A. city boundaries, in unincorporated Los Angeles County. A greater proportion of UNO members are recent arrivals and are less likely to be homeowner/occupants, less likely to be citizens and voters, and more likely to move outside the area within the next five to ten years. All these factors seriously weaken the community's possible political impact. There is a strong possibility that the Eastside might not exist as a lower income haven for predominantly Mexican residents in the next twenty years as it becomes redeveloped for Los Angeles' more affluent residents.[36]

Comparing the attitudes of high school seniors in Los Angeles, San Antonio and Albuquerque, Chicano sociologist Martin Sánchez Jankowski underscores the differences between L.A. and the Alamo city, stating that conditions in Los Angeles

> ...have acted to create a more integrated social structure, but the consequence has been that there are few social attachments to objects and/or people and places. The vast majority of middle-class relationships one would find in other social settings (in fact, in other cities) are not extensive in Los Angeles. Those primary groups with which people could and would identify, such as ethnic organizations, do exist in Los Angeles per se...[but] they are weak....[37]

Los Angeles's middle class Mexican Americans have not been able or willing to establish the networks that one would find in other Latino urban areas. While groups such as LULAC or the G.I. Forum function in a few areas of L.A., they do not enjoy the popularity and or tradition that they do in San Antonio, where membership is often a family affair.

The cultural ties of the middle class in Los Angeles are diluted as a result of living in predominantly Anglo or integrated neighborhoods. Los Angeles's illusion of tolerance seduces Chicanos, as their desire to be accepted by Euroamericans causes the middle class to become alienated from the Mexican community. Chicano's acceptance of Los Angeles' mass culture has facilitated a psuedo-integration, with the poor left to shift for themselves. The legacy of residential segregation, meanwhile, resulted in a unified the San Antonio Mexican community.

Politically, while San Antonio Mexicans remained alienated from the political process during the sixties and early seventies, the ruling elite had to recognize the voting power of Mexicans by endorsing token or safe Mexicans for the City Council. In contrast, from 1962 until 1985, Latinos remained voiceless in the L.A. city Council. That year Eastsiders elected Assemblyman Richard Alatorre in the 14th Councilmanic District (CD).

Latinos, who represented about twenty-eight percent of Los Angeles City in 1980, had six percent (or one fifteenth) of the representation on the city Council in 1985. But even in the election of Alatorre, Chicanos paid a price. Alatorre won election to the 14th CD when the white incumbent, Arthur Snyder, retired during his term of office and endorsed Alatorre. Many doubt whether anyone could have beaten Snyder, for although personal and political scandals made him seemingly vulnerable, he had continued to win reelection in the face of recall efforts and united fronts against him. Snyder had a substantial campaign war chest largely financed by powerful L.A. developers. He adroitly took credit for all government projects in his community by having a very high profile throughout the 14th Councilmanic District. He spread the patronage well and developed a successful electoral machine by never allowing any of his Chicano aides to forge a political base. Snyder adapted himself for his own political survival in an overwhelmingly Latino district. He not only ignored indigenous grass roots groups that sought influence but skillfully prevented them from gaining access to power and influence in Los Angeles city government.

UNO was unable to shake Snyder's base because it did not have a large and cohesive voting bloc: thus it was ineffective in challenging his hegemony. This is an important difference between UNO and COPS. COPS not only challenged the city's ruling elite early in its career, but it has also consistently criticized Mayor Cisneros.[38] COPS has had a major effect on important municipal and educational electoral campaigns; therefore, it was able to have considerable leverage on important policy issues affecting the Westside community.[39]

UNO has never had that type of leverage. Issues have not emanated from the grassroots; nor have they taken on the moral outrage of the "burning bush." Often UNO's middle class leaders mechanically apply Alinskian theory and shy away from community issues such as the fight to prevent the building of a state prison in downtown L.A. or the Archdiocese's attempt to close an inner city Latino Catholic boy's high school. UNO chose to define those problems as unwinnable.

The last important difference between UNO and COPS is the heterogeneity of the Latino community in Los Angeles compared to San Antonio. Los Angeles' Latinos can no longer be described as being solely of Mexican origin. Because of a U.S. interventionist foreign policy in Central America, the last decade has witnessed a flood of Salvadoran and Guatemalan political refugees entering Los Angeles. Although they were not accurately counted in the 1980 census, current data suggest that almost 350,000 Salvadorans currently reside in the county. With over 60,000 Guatemalans, and other Latin American immigrants, this reconfiguration of the Los Angeles Latino community has delayed the formation of cohesive organizational units. This massive influx of new immigrants has hampered the development of a common historical memory or identity. The pressure on available housing in the barrios and the physical deterioration of these neighborhoods has accelerated the moving out of those leaders and families who would have the resources to become active in grass-roots community organizations like UNO.

Politically, this has meant that the population of the barrios cannot support the cost of electing their own representatives. Alatorre, a powerful kingpin in Eastside politics, spent over $300,000 for his election to the city council although there was no serious challenge to his candidacy. In major metropolitan areas like Los Angeles, the population size of a council district is approximately 198,000. This forces the candidates to rely on very costly professional campaign organizations with computerized, specially targetted mailings. In a smaller city like San Antonio, the councilmatic districts population size is approximately 79,000—less than half the size of Los Angeles' districts.

In the smaller San Antonio council districts, well-organized grass roots organizations can have a greater effect on who gets elected, but also, more importantly, on what policies politicians pursue. According to contemporary observers, organizations like COPS have been able to effect the votes of representatives of predominantly Mexican American and Black districts, especially in the allocation of crucial neighborhood improvement projects. Joseph D. Sekul describes the situation:

> It [COPS] has evolved into a force to be reckoned with in city politics. In the years since its founding tens of millions of dollars have flowed into its communities, most of it in accord with COPS' priorities. Numerous government policies that threatened the vitality of its neighborhoods have been checked....Finally, COPS has taken a giant step toward raising the quality of life in older neighborhoods, some of which may now become places where people can stay if they choose, rather than leave because they must.[40]

Predictably, there is not a single Latino organization in Los Angeles' Eastside with a plan to preserve the residential integrity of that area.

The size of the districts, along with the enormous cost of campaigning, limit electoral office to the very affluent or those who are connected to a political machine. Alatorre heads the so-called Eastside political machine. An alliance with Assembly Speaker Willie Brown helped him to raise the large sums of money needed to get elected and to promote those who he has selected to run for office. This has enabled Alatorre to deliver powerful support on behalf of "brown capitalists" such as The East Los Angeles Community Union (TELACU), a redevelopment corporation.

Alatorre, a man of uncanny political skill, has learned to master the political game. His rule, however, has not gone unchallenged. Gloria Molina broke with Alatorre and Eastside State Senator Torres in 1982 when they attempted to pressure her not to run for the assembly. They claimed that a woman could not win, that she was not tough enough, and that she could not raise sufficient funds. Molina, supported by feminist and independents, defeated Alatorre's candidate, Richard Polanco.[41]

When elected to the Council in 1985, Alatorre tried to name Polanco to succeed him in his old Assembly district by intimidating potential challengers with his money and organization.

Assemblywoman Molina supported another candidate in the Democratic primary, Mike Hernández, who challenged but failed to defeat the machine—and Polanco. A U.S. Justice Department suit brought in 1982 charged that: "The Los Angeles City Council has demonstrated over the last two decades that it is unwilling to include the public interest of the city's Hispanic population in apportionment of Council Districts."[42] The case was settled in 1985, when after a great deal of manipulation and political negotiation, the council created another Latino councilmatic district.

As expected, Alatorre attempted to impose his candidate, Los Angeles Unified School Board member Larry Gónzalez (a former aide to Senator Art Torres), on the people of the first councilmanic district. Again Molina challenged the machine and ran against the Alatorre-Torres nominee with both the candidates spending in excess of $200,000. Molina's victory in February 1987, left a vacant assembly seat which was to be captured by Lucille Allard Roybal, Congressman Edward Roybal's daughter.

The candidacy of Lucille Allard Roybal clearly underscores the lack of an Eastside community structure. When she decided to run for Molina's old assembly seat, Allard had the support of Molina, the Alatorre-Torres machine, and of course her father, the venerable Congressman Edward R. Roybal, sometimes known as "Mister East Los Angeles." She immediately announced she would raise between $100,000 to $150,000, discouraging many qualified candidates from running. Her strongest asset was that she was the daughter of Congressman Roybal.

Critics of her candidacy stated that Allard had not been involved in local community organizations or local politics. As expected, she won the election by a two to one margin. The question here is not Allard's competency for she is developing into a capable and independent elected official. The question is whether the Eastside has the structure to elect its own organic community leaders. In San Antonio, the election of a candidate to local office who had not shared a Westside work experience would be difficult. In Los Angeles, the concept of place is not as strong; Angelinos are urban migrants who have great difficulty rooting an identity with a place. Finally, it should be reemphasized that, at any level of government, the Angeleno Latino community plays only a very small role in

selecting its leaders. The process begins only after a candidate lines
up the money and establishes her or his own candidacy.
Community organizations such as UNO or a network of Democratic
clubs have not play a role in naming candidates; indeed, UNO has
been mute. As for the Mexican American Political Association, it is
essentially a "paper organization" which is not able to deliver
campaign workers or financial resources to support particular
candidates. The lack of an internal community political network
creates a vacuum in which there is no check on politicians such as
Alatorre who respond more to well-financed interest groups such as
TELACU than to ordinary community constituents.   In San
Antonio, Cisneros, for all his popularity, could not openly ignore
COPS.

CONCLUSION

Given the history and political structure of Los Angeles, what
does the future hold for the Latino community? From present
trends there is every reason to believe that the fragmentation and
dilution of power of the Latino community will continue. The high
spatial mobility, the continuing influx of poor undocumented
workers from crisis-ridden Mexico and Central America, and the
seemingly endless campaign contributions from developers are all
powerful factors that undermine the development of a community
which might influence the public policy agenda.

The Eastside is trapped in a "Catch-22" situation. Its lack of
financial resources prevent it from effecting local politicians and
public policies. Those same politicians and policies actively
undermine the ability of low income barrio residents to protect and
promote their community interests. The ability to raise enormous
sums of money is the primary determinant of political leadership.
Politicians from poverty areas such as the Eastside must obtain
campaign funds from interests outside their formal constituencies.
The interests of the benefactors of local Latino politicians often
clash with the interests of poor barrio dwellers. Although the
people of the Eastside vehemently reject the construction of still
another prison in or adjacent to their community, the political

agenda of powerful Assembly Speaker Brown clearly conflicts with the wishes of Eastsiders.

It is likely that in highly desired areas such as the Eastside, which is adjacent to the Los Angeles Civic Center, the pressures for redevelopment or what has been called by activists, "Mexican Removal," will be increased. It is predictable that with skyrocketing of land values in Los Angeles, barrio dwellers will be replaced by white, Asian, black, and brown professionals. Trends indicate that the affluent and educated will be the only ones who hare able to pay the high cost of living close to the civic and corporate center of this powerful metropolitan region.

The extremely high property values and a continuing demographic explosion in Southern California make it almost a certainty that the percentage of Latinos owning their own homes will decline in the older Mexican communities of Los Angeles. Presently, only 21% of Boyle Heights (L.A. city) and 36% of unicorporated East Los Angeles are homeowner occupants. Rising housing costs and rents will further displace the Eastside residents. The deteriorating housing, schools, and streets of the area will result in the increased flight of middle and working class Latinos from the barrios of the Eastside. The outcome will be a community populated increasingly by impoverished temporary residents with little stake in the community or hope for the future. This might put into motion conditions for repeating the large-scale racial violence witnessed in the urban riots of the 1960s.

The San Antonio experience differs from the Los Angeles experience. Approximately 65% of the Mexican community own their own homes. Most bought them at a time when prices and interests rates were low. Consequently, they will remain in or near the Westside, and will not be very affected by the spiralling housing costs which have negatively affected potential Latino home buyers. A community consciousness, for better or for worse, does exist. San Antonio Mexicans preserve a common historical memory along with a strong sense of place to a much higher degree than exists in Los Angeles.

The presence of a community has allowed COPS to develop, flourish, and maintain itself as a significant player in the public policy arena of San Antonio. The Anglo Northside, over the past decades, has reaped enormous benefits from city policies while the rest of the city has languished. COPS can take credit for slowing down the almost unilateral favoritism in San Antonio politics toward the Northside. This social process in which demographic growth and a favored pattern of local government resource allocation in the mostly suburban Anglo areas is part of the structure of our capitalist political economy. COPS has not overturned the political economy, but the Northside business elite must now contend with people of the barrio. Revolutionaries might disdain COPS' reformist politics, but the alternative is Los Angeles' community, which is virtually excluded from the major policy decisions. It demonstrates that there is a clear relationship between political influence and the physical survival of the community. San Antonio's Mexican community may lose a battle here or there but it has a greater likelihood to survive and fight future battles. Realities in Los Angeles suggest that the barrios with their potentially rich resources, and their memories may not be around in future generations to fight another day.

The existence of a community in San Antonio means that it will be more difficult to erase its cherished values and institutions. Although it is a much smaller community in size and distribution compared to Los Angeles, it is quite correct for Professor Arreola to refer to San Antonio as "The Mexican American Cultural Capital."[43] In Los Angeles, the lack of a community increases its vulnerability to interests like developers who are not concerned whether a community's way of life is destroyed. There is also no check on brown politicians who combine with brown developers to profit from the destruction of community.

Areas like the Eastside might not exist in twenty years. If the neighborhoods in which Mexicans have flourished are to survive, then there must be a continual rebuilding of this community's consciousness, skills, and networks. The likelihood of meeting this very difficult challenge, under the conditions and trends that exist in Los Angeles, is not great. Yet, there is a great moral and political responsibility for those Latinos who have the education, training, and resources to help grass roots leaders and organizations who thus far have singularly carried the fight to confront this challenge.

NOTES

1   Antonio Ríos-Bustamante and Pedro Castillo, *An Illustrated History of Mexican Los Angeles: 1781-1981*, (Los Angeles: Chicano Studies Research Center, UCLA, 1986); Rodolfo F. Acuna, *A Community Under Siege: A Chronicle of Chicanos East of the Los Angeles River, 1945-1975* (Los Angeles: Chicano Studies Research Center, UCLA, 1984).

2   Ernesto Galarza, "Mexicans in the Southwest: A Culture Process," in Edward H. Spicer and Raymond H. Thompson, eds., *Plural Society in the Southwest* (New York: Weatherhead Foundation, 1972), 266; Ithiel de Sola Pool, ibid.

3   Albert Camarillo, *Chicanos in California: A History of Mexican Americans in California*, (San Francisco: Boyd & Fraser, 1984), 34; Carey Davis, Carl Haub, and Jo Ann Willette, "U.S. Hispanics: Changing the Face of America," in Norman R. Yettman, *Majority and Minority: The Dynamics of Race and Ethnicity in American Life* 4th Ed. (Newton, MA: Allyn & Bacon , 1985), 469.

4   Albert Camarillo, *Chicanos in a Changing Society: From Mexican Pueblos to American Barrios in Santa Barbara and Southern California, 1848-1930* (Cambridge: Harvard University Press, 1979), 116, 200; Also see Richard Griswold Del Castillo, *The Los Angeles Barrio, 1850-1890: A Social History* (Berkeley: University of California Press, 1979), 35; Ricardo Romo, *East Los Angeles: A History of a Barrio* (Austin: University of Texas Press, 1983), ch. 1.

5   See Richard García, "The Making of the Mexican American Mind, San Antonio, Texas, 1929-1941. A Social and Intellectual History," Ph.D. diss., University of California, Irvine, 1980.

6   See Pedro Castillo, "The Making of a Mexican Barrio: Los Angeles, 1890-1920," Ph.D. diss., University of California, Santa Barbara, 1979.

7   See Guadalupe Compean, "Where Only the Weeds Grow: An Environmental Study of Mexican Housing in Boyle Heights, 1910-1941," unpublished paper, School of Architecture and Urban Planning, UCLA, 1984.

8   See Rodolfo Acuña, *Occupied America: A History of Chicanos*, 3rd Ed. (New York: Harper & Row, 1987); Garcia, op. cit.; Larry Dickens, "The Political Role of Mexican Americans in San Antonio, Texas," Ph.D. diss., Texas Tech University, 1969.

9   See Carey McWilliams, *Factories in the Field: The Story of Migrant Labor* (Santa Barbara: Peregrine, 1971).

10 Robin Fitzgerald Scott, "The Mexican American in the Los Angeles Area, 1920-1950: From Acquiescence to Activity," Ph.D. diss., University of Southern California, 1971.

11 Leo Grebler, Joan W. Moore, Ralph C. Guzmán, *The Mexican-American People: The Nation's Second Largest Minority* (New York: Free Press, 1970), 301. See Romo, *East Los Angeles*, p. 11, for a critique.

12 Abraham Hoffman, *Unwanted Mexican Americans in the Great Depression: Repatriation Pressures, 1929-1939* (Tucson: University of Arizona Press, 1976).

13   On repatriation of the 1930s see, R. Reynolds McKay, "Texas Mexican Repatriation During the Great Depression," Ph.D. diss., University of Oklahoma, 1982.

14   Wages are based on a national norm, whereas the private sector jobs depend on the ability of workers to organize. Because Texas is an Open Shop state, it has been near impossible to build strong unions there, consequently, wages remained low.

15   Tucker Gibson, "Mayoralty Politics in San Antonio, 1950-1979," in David R. Johnson, et al, eds, *The Politics of San Antonio* (Lincoln: University of Nebraska Press, 1983), 116-226.

16   See Acuña, *Community Under Siege*, ch. 3.

17   Saul Alinsky (1909-1972), who founded the Industrial Areas Foundation to train community leaders, organized neighborhood residents around the principle of self-interest. He worked with poor whites, blacks, and Chicanos. CSO was an IAF project headed by Fred Ross who trained organizers, the most prominent of whom was César Chávez.

18   CSO has been kept together as an organization through the efforts of Tony Ríos. Ríos is controversial and some former members attribute some of the problems of the organization to his personality. However, he has stayed with CSO—through thick and thin. In recent years Ernie Cortes of San Antonio, Texas, has started IAF projects in Texas and California. The most important of these being Communities Organized for Public Service (COPS-San Antonio) and United Neighborhoods Organization (UNO-Los Angeles).

19   See Acuña, *Occupied America*, ch. 9; and Acuña, *Community Under Siege*, ch. 4.

20   See Grebler et al, *The Mexican American People*, pp. 378-399, 420-439.

21   "Thorns on the Yellow Rose of Texas," *New Republic* (19 Apr. 1969): 19.

22   Sr. Frances Jerome Woods, *Mexican Ethnic Leadership in San Antonio, Texas* (Washington, DC: Catholic University Press, 1941), 92-96.

23   See Acuña, *Occupied America*, chs. 9, 10; and Acuña, *Community Under Siege*, chs. 7, 8.

24   See Acuña, *Occupied America*, ch. 11.

25   Grebler et al, *The Mexican American People.*, pp. 378-399, 420-439.

26   See Acuña, *Occupied America*, chs. 10, 11.

27   This presence of large numbers of undocumented workers and their families has sparked a debate over whether they should be counted in the Census and for reapportionment. Fortunately, the U.S. Constitution refers to persons and not citizens.

28   Blacks have done much better in government employment. They make up some 30% of Los Angeles county's workforce while comprising only 12% of the population. In contrast, Mexicans make up over 30% of the population and only 18%of the workforce. Some leaders in the Black community argue that undocumented people should not be counted for affirmative action and government employment.

29   Acuña, *Occupied America*, chs. 9-11.

30   Martin Sánchez Jankowski, *City Bound: Urban Life and Attitudes Among Chicano Youth* (Albuquerque: University of New Mexico Press, 1986), 13.

31   Thomas A. Baylis, "Leadership Change in Contemporary San Antonio," in Johnson et al, *The Politics of San Antonio,* pp. 95-113.

32   Sánchez Jankowski, *City Bound*, p. 35.

33   Kyriakos S. Markides and Thomas Cole, "Change and Continuity in Mexican American Religious Behavior," in Rodolfo O. De La Garza, et al, *The Mexican American Experience: An Interdisciplinary Anthology* (Austin: University of Texas Press, 1985), 409.

34   Joseph D. Sekul, "Communities Organized for Public Service: Citizen Power and Public Policy in San Antonio," in Johnson et al, *The Politics of San Antonio,* pp. 175-192.

35   Carlos Navarro was active in the Sacred Heart parish chapter of UNO in 1979-1980. The Monsignor, who was Mexican American and pastor of that parish, indicated to Navarro that he was opposed to Alinsky's method of community organization. At no time was he supportive of, or cooperative with, the UNO chapter. The parish in which Navarro was raised, Santa Teresita, is located immediately north of Boyle Heights, and is one of the poorest Chicano parishes in the city. It's pastor was also Mexican American and he refused to allow an UNO chapter to be organized because of his loyalty to the conservative city Councilman, Art Snyder, who represented the area.

36   As segregation has decreased in San Antonio, more affluent Latinos have begun to move out, and areas in the Westside are becoming ports of entry for undocumented Latinos. This is forcing COPS to make organizational adjustments.

37   Sánchez Jankowski, *City Bound*, p. 18.

38   Despite the negative publicity Cisneros has had concerning his marital situation, he has retained surprisingly support and popularity among the Mexican community, not only in Texas but in California. At a January 1989 conference of the California Associate for Bilingual Educators, he received a standing ovation before he even began speaking.

39   Sekul, in Johnson, *The Politics of San Antonio*, pp. 175-192.

40   Ibid, p. 190.

41   Assembly Speaker Brown sought to punish Molina for supporting Mike Hernández against Polanco. Assembly Speaker Brown appointed Polanco to the site committee selecting a state prison in Los Angeles. During the campaign Polanco promised Eastsiders he would oppose a downtown prison; but in revenge and an effort to repay Brown, Polanco voted for the bill designating the downtown prison to go to the full assembly where it was approved. Polanco's betrayal mobilized the Mothers of East Los Angeles, who were able to organize a rally of 3,000 at the proposed site to demonstrate their objection. This show of strength for a time stalemated the approval of the downtown site; however, President Pro Tem David Roberti of the State Senate reversed himself and the downtown site was approved. Under Brown's protection, Polanco has become a broker in the Assembly, raising the question whether the Eastside Machine is actually a viable, independent machine such as the Waxman-Berman

machine on the Westside, or a mere satellite of other more powerful politicians who have no real link to the Eastside.

42   Acuña, *Occupied America*, p. 425.

43   Daniel C. Arreola, "The Mexican American Cultural Capital," *The Geographical Review* 77 (Jan. 1987): 17-34.

POSTSCRIPT

LOS ANGELES: TOWARD THE 21ST CENTURY

H. ERIC SCHOCKMAN

From the social history discussed in the previous chapters, Los Angeles stands at a crossroads, poised to master its destiny or be devoured by it. Considerable human resources will be needed to over-come past structural and cultural barriers. In short, will Los Angeles be the "City of the Future" or an entity personifying the "Broken Dreams of the Past"?

As Norman M. Klein's essay indicates, Los Angeles was established by 1900 as a New Jerusalem, a City on the Hill for the Midwest tourist. Through boosterism, it remained "a city of the future," and of the past, a mini-Manifest Destiny, with many dreams that camouflaged a social history that must be addressed today. Conditions have changed, yet the prevailing ethos remains strong. Two dreams, "progress" and "urban renewal," have become buzz-words for providing new buffer-zones between the "haves" and "have nots" in Los Angeles. The sacrifice of historic buildings, particularly the redevelopment of the Bunker Hill area, serves as a capping testimonial to the dominant white ethos that has and still does drive public policy decisions.

This leaves some haunting questions. With the changing demographics of the Asian and Latin American population in this region, is the dominant ethos still the correct pattern to emulate for the future? Will we degenerate further into autonomous isolated communities signalling the onset of a process of "balkanization" into a hellish "Blade Runner" society? Will the new polyculturalistic society bring a new ethos for public policies of the future? The uniting thread among these questions and the essays in this work is the development of governance and power that must emerge in the 21st Century. In particular, bureaucratic gridlock and infrastructural decline need to be retuned to produce more realistic public policies for the greater good.

One of the more interesting governance battles today pertains to the City Council's attempt to seize and harness the Community Redevelopment Agency (CRA). The CRA, some critics would allege, has been a Frankensteinish creation, developing Los Angeles in its own image (or at least the image Mayor Bradley wants). As Klein's essay highlights, this turf battle will have significant impact on the future development of what he terms the "multi-tropolis".

Also threatening the multi-tropolis and its static governance is the inevitable growth in population. And even more significant that the population explosion itself is the shift in ethnic composition. Hispanics, who made up 14 percent of Southern California's population will reach approximately 40 percent, while non-Hispanic whites will decline from about 75 percent to 40 percent by the year 2010.

For years, Hispanics and other minorities have been locked out of the local representational system, or played-off against one another to obtain control of a Council seat. "Papacito" Edward Roybal was elected to the Ninth Councilmanic District. When he went on to Congress in 1962, a major feud between the governing elite broke out. The Chicano candidate, a cousin of Roybal who was a loyal Mayor Yorty staffer, lost to the consensus candidate that the City Council united behind—Gilbert Lindsay, a black former field deputy to Supervisor Kenneth Hahn. Two years later, when the Supreme Court's reapportionment ruling was implemented, Councilman Lindsay got the major chunk of the downtown area, including a high proportion of newly arrived Hispanic immigrants. Once the downtown corporate donors knew where Lindsay stood vis`a vis redevelopment, a steady stream of campaign contributions to Lindsay's reelection committee has prevented a successful challenger be they Hispanic, Asian or Anglo. Ironically, the only other "high propensity" Hispanic area was the Fourteenth Councilmatic District, ruled by an Anglo (Irish-Catholic), Arthur Snyder who survived mostly due to the lack of a cohesive political opposition.

In 1985, the Department of Justice, the Los Angeles Chapter of the National Association for the Advancement of Colored People (NAACP) and the Mexican American Legal Defense and Education Fund (MALDEF), filed a lawsuit against the City of Los Angeles charging that the 1982 reapportionment of Councilmatic Districts intentionally fractured Hispanic communities and diluted the Hispanic vote, a direct violation of the Voting Rights Act of 1965. In the early 1980s the Hispanic population of the city was approximately one-third of the entire population, yet only one Hispanic, Edward Roybal, served on the City Council in this century.

The City initially decided to fight the lawsuit, but eventually it was settled out of court, due mostly to a weak legal defense and the unfortunate death of Councilman Howard Finn from the North Valley.   Before Finn's departure, the Council was poised to sacrifice the only Asian-American ever elected to the Council—Michael Woo—by having him run in the same district against a veteran Anglo incumbent, John Ferraro.   The result, like deus ex machina, was the creation of second "Hispanic dominant" district (the First District) which was eventually captured by Gloria Molina. The Fourteenth Council District was won by Richard Alatorre in a 1986 special election when Arthur Snyder finally decided to retire.

The control over who governs is not just limited to the City of Los Angeles. The County of Los Angeles (which is larger than 42 states of the Union), is currently fighting a 1988 lawsuit by the Department of Justice (DOJ) and MALDEF. The lawsuit contends that the County Reapportionment Plan designating five Supervisorial Districts (each with approximately 1.7 million individuals), violated the Voting Rights Act by splitting the highest propensity of Hispanic voters found in the eastern and central portions of the County into three different Supervisorial Districts. Thus on the face of the matter, it appears that the County has managed to structurally deny minority representation on the County Board of Supervisors since its founding in 1852. In this context, the thesis of the Navarro and Acuna essay that the lack of Mexican communities in Los Angeles partially explains their powerlessness has great relevance to the pragmatic realities occurring today in the county. Their "Tale of Two Cities", a comparison of Mexicans in Los Angeles and San Antonio, demonstrates that the break up of organic communities does have a linkage to the lessening of political empowerment.

Recent developments however centering on the County suit may spell a forbidding future for the continued all-white, male governance club. Joining with the DOJ and MALDEF are two new partners to the suit—the NAACP and the Asian-Pacific American Legal Center.

This action signifies more than just symbolic solidarity. Those who redraw the reapportionment lines can impact the composition of the future Board. It is with this empowerment that policy decisions affecting public health, welfare, disease control, criminal justice, planning, and redevelopment, can better reflect the changing political landscape. As Donald and Nadine Hata's essay argues, Asians will not permit themselves anymore to be misperceived as the "model minority" to "suffer silently", with uncomplaining Horatio Alger tenacity. This community knows only too well the impact of historically being an "indispensable scapegoat" sacrificed to the mania of urban renewal, redevelopment, and gentrification. Gloria Miranda's discussion in her essay of the Social Darwinist's desire to destroy and level old Sonoratown and Plaza district barrios is very similar to the Hata's account of the sacrifice of old Chinatown and Little Tokyo to the bulldozer mentality of urban planners.

The same Sisyphean struggle against racism and minority community development are present in Lonnie G. Bunch's essay as well. The "Golden Era" for Afro-American's in Los Angeles all comes to a crashing conclusion as the racial lines harden by the 1930s as personified by the arrogance and disregard by local governance.

Equally disturbing is the fact that institutional patterns designed to conform to the dominant motif of governing have factored out democratic reform elements to make local officials and agencies less accountable to the majority of the citizens. The heads of police, water and power, airport, and harbor have been the true chiefs of bureaucratic Los Angeles. The great icon of William Mulholland, who brought water to the City from 233 miles away through the Owens River Aqueduct, and helped create a revenue-generating Department of Water and Power (DWP) is presently personified by a strong general manager. A Commission does sit as a "citizen adjunct" to DWP, but many would allege is just a rubber-stamp for issues ranging from water hike increases to water quality and conservation. This situation is more than just technocrats controlling a part-time citizen Commission. It is enraptured in the great mystique of "water"—its civilizing influence to the City—as well as the political message it has telecasted: "Those who control water control development and the future".

Another department and its general manager also have a unique position in the City's structure—i.e. the Los Angeles Police Department (LAPD) and the Chief of Police. Some critics have alleged that the Los Angeles Police Commission was established as "window dressing" given the historical domination of the policies that the Chiefs of Police have followed in the political evolution of the City. For example, Richard Whitehall's essay poses an interesting question: Why hadn't organized crime and mob activity taken hold in Los Angeles as elsewhere? He argues that in Los Angeles the police didn't fight crime—they protected it by controlling and directing vice and gambling activities. According to Whitehall, even before the mob could come in, the government was corrupted to serve a certain set of special interests thus allowing law enforcement to selectively enforce the municipal law and permitting the police department to fulfill the mob function of organizing crime. He also vividly describes competition among gangsters, particularly in the film industry.

Perhaps Martin J. Schiesl's essay is even more to the point in exposing the unique development of the LAPD and the continuous, but largely unsuccessful, struggle to place it under citizen and legislative control. Schiesl sees a "highly partisan system of policing which, while serving well the interests of white residents, caused considerable discomfort and hardship for the city's racial minorities." As "civilian review boards" have been cast aside and "Red-baited" as Communist fronts, much conflict has arisen over questions of police accountability, citizen control and the preservation of basic civil liberties. Schiesl's analysis views the LAPD as traditionally having little tolerance for political activism and organized dissent, especially from militant minority sectors. He concludes that strong-will general managers (the Chiefs of Police), have set their own course of law enforcement in Los Angeles, outside the domain of checks-and-balances and ultimate citizen accountability.

Today, Los Angeles is a dangerously divided, highly segregated city. Nothing seems to reflect this more than the drug sub-economy, and the problematical, and, as Schiesl shows, discriminatory way that it is handled by the LAPD.

Where are we heading in the governance of Los Angeles by the year 2000? A "City for the Future", as envisioned by the final report of the "Los Angeles 2000 Committee", attempts to provide a plan for the future and begin a dialogue amongst the disparate elements of the region. To its credit, the final report recognizes that Los Angeles is rapidly becoming a bimodal society—divided along ethnic, racial and economic lines. A full decade before the year 2000 social scientists and other scholars are observing a widening disparity between the affluent and the poor—be it in term of the quality of life issues, education or employment. The minority populations, who will soon be the majority population, have been by-passed in the massive economic boom created in Los Angeles. This is demonstrated by two different economies of scale. There has been a movement out of the technical/craft occupations into lower-paying sales and clerical jobs. Indeed, there is strong support to the claim that this "ethnic division of labor" supports a hierarchical economic structure, and that the bottom-tier is unable to adjust to the rapidly changing sectors of high-tech manufacturing, finance, tourism, telecommunications and health care.

Also to its credit, the 2000 Committee calls for a Growth Management Agency and an Environmental Quality Agency to end the municipal "balkanization" that frustrates regional solutions and a common zeal. Regional problems such as traffic, air pollution, solid waste disposal, do not lend themselves to solutions within neat micro-geographic boundaries.

Perhaps the boldest agenda recommendation is the call for a Governmental Restructuring Commission to address head-on the anachronisms of the current governance structures. This radical move, comparative to the call for a Constitutional Convention, is an attempt to increase accountability of elected officials and redefined the relationship between governmental entities and their resource allocation.

This is definitely a step in the right direction. What is interesting to note, however, is that both the City and the Southern California metropolitan area have reached a kind of critical mass. The momentum for radical restructuring behind the 2000 Committee's report is being driven by the systemic problems in the *ecosystem* and not especially in the *political* system. The discussion to date has focused on HOV lanes, job-housing balance and emission reduction. The authors of these essays have made a strong, historically grounded, case that we now need to shift the focus of this discussion and reorient ourselves to a new public ethos that is profoundly inclusive of all ethnic groups and social classes. The public policy ramifications must also proceed on a dual track, but without the political will and the opening of the governance structure, we shall never master our destiny and the future.

CONTRIBUTORS

Co-editor **Norman M. Klein** is a member of the Department of Critical Studies at California Institute of the Arts, where he specializes in the history of mass culture and the media. In addition to essays on Los Angeles, he has written on the social history of televison, cinema, the fine arts, and consumerism. He has also served as a consultant for public television, co-edited *Twentieth Century Art Theory* (1990) and is completing a history of the animated cartoon.

Co-editor **Martin J. Schiesl** is Professor of History at California State University, Los Angeles. He is the author of *The Politics of Efficiency: Municipal Administration and Reform in America, 1880-1920* (1977). He has written articles and book chapters on politics, government, and economic development in the Los Angeles region during the 20th century. His latest essay is on the Irvine Company and suburbanization and appears in *Postsuburban California: The Transformation of Orange County Since World War II* (1990), edited by Rob Kling, Spencer Olin and Mark Poster. He also has served as a consultant for public television on a series dealing with the history of Los Angeles.

Rodolfo Acuña is Professor of Chicano Studies at California State University, Northridge. He is the author of *A Community Under Siege: A Chronicle of Chicanos East of the Los Angeles River, 1945-1975* (1984) and *Occupied America: A History of Chicanos*, 3rd ed. (1988). He wrote a column for the Los Angeles *Herald Examiner* and is co-chair of the Labor Community Strategy Center.

Lonnie G. Bunch III is a Curator at the National Museum of American History of the Smithsonian Institution. Formerly the founding curator of the California Afro-American Museum in Los Angeles, he has written *Black Angelenos: The Afro-American in Los Angeles, 1950-1930* (1988), *Vision Toward Tomorrow: Black Life in the East Bay* (1989) and numerous articles pertaining to the history of African Americans.

Donald Teruo Hata is Professor of History at California State University, Dominguez Hills. He was an inmate of the U.S. War Relocation Authority relocation camp at Gilas Rivers, Arizona. He has served on the Gardena City Council and has been vice-president of the California Historical Society. He has published *"Undesirables:" Early Immigrants nd the Anti-Japanese Movement in San Francisco, 1892-1893. Prelude to Exclusion* (1978). Additionally, Donald and Nadine Hata jointly have published numerous essays and *Japanese Americas and World War II* (1974)

Nadine Ishitani Hata is Dean of Behavioral and Social Sciences and Professor of History at El Camino College. She has served as vice-chair of the California Advisory Committee to the U.S. Commission on Civil Rights and as chair of the California State Historical Commission.

Gloria E. Miranda is chair of the American Cultures Department at Los Angeles Valley College and Professor of Chicano Studies. She is a trustee of the California Historical Society and has served as a consultant on a number of local projects on Los Angeles history. She has published several essays on the early California family and social patterns.

Carlos Navarro is acting Associate Dean of the School of Humanities and Professor of Chicano Studies at California State University, Northridge. Over the past twenty years he has been active as a researcher and activist in the fields of education and politics. He takes take great pride in his involvement with the United Neighborhoods Organization (UNO), Californios for Fair Representation, and the National Association for Chicano Studies.

H. Eric Schockman is Director of the Edmund G. "Pat" Brown Institute of Public Affairs, California State University, Los Angeles, and is an Adjunct Professor of Political Science at both CSULA and the University of Southern California. He has been a legislative analyst for the California state legislature and the Los Angeles city council. A frequent contributor to the Los Angeles *Times*, the *California Journal* and several scholarly journals, he also has edited*The Perfecting of Los Angeles: Ethics Reform On the Municipal Level* (1989).

English-born, **Richard Whitehall** worked as a film editor in British films before coming to the United States. For the past eighteen years he has taught film history at the California Institute of the Arts. He has published widely in British and American film journals and wrote a pioneering essay on the American gangster film that was published in the Winter (1964) issue of *Films and Filming*.

INDEX